THE MURDER
OF THE ROSENBERGS

BY STANLEY YALKOWSKY

THE
MURDER
OF
THE
ROSENBERGS

ACKNOWLEDGMENT

My gratitude is wholeheartedly extended to Aaron Katz, director of the National Committee to Reopen the Rosenberg Case. It was Katz who convinced me that the United States government's primary motive in its determination to convict Julius and Ethel Rosenberg was to destroy the Communist Party in America.

Katz supplied the perspective that made understandable the unconstitutional laws and irrational cruelty that governed during those troubled times. The passage of the Smith and McCarran Acts, the ascendancy to power of Joseph McCarthy and Pat McCarran, and finally—the most decisive act of them all—the murder of Julius and Ethel Rosenberg, indeed virtually eliminated the Communist Party in America.

PRELIMINARY STATEMENT

The author has been criticized for having reached conclusions concerning the loyalties of certain individuals without sufficient supporting evidence. The author's claim that Jacob Golos, today an obscure individual, was a spy for the United States Government rather than for the Soviet Union as he was purported to be is disturbing to Communist's and liberals who had been so frequently disappointed by those they trusted. To think that Golos, who held such an important position in liberal circles, being the main travel agent for the securing of passage in the 1930's for young men and women willing to give their lives to fight fascism in Spain, was all the while, as the author claims, turning over to the Director of the FBI, J. Edgar Hoover, the information he collected is heartbreaking and not believable or bearable to many, especially when the author himself admits that although he may have found the evidence against Golos convincing and his theory of a Golos - Gold - Bentley - Hoover connection compelling, it did not necessarily lead to the inescapable conclusion that Golos was an undercover agent for the FBI.

CONTENTS

PREFACE

It was a week-end night in 1951 when a misguided group of youths, the author among them, decided to visit a Bronx Social Club, which was a meeting place for liberals. The group, thinking they were acting out of patriotism and fighting Communism, waited for the members to leave, and when they did, assaulted several of them.

The police were summoned. They viewed the scene of mayhem, smiled, winked at the group, and then left, ignoring the protests of the victims who demanded that arrests be made.

In the Federal Courts in downtown Manhattan, Judge Irving Kaufman and the prosecutors, Irving Saypol and Roy Cohn, were using slander, false evidence, and suborning perjury in order to murder an innocent liberal-minded couple, while almost an entire nation smiled and winked at what they were doing.

HARRY GOLD

KLAUS FUCHS

In reviewing one of America's blackest moments—the prosecution, conviction, and execution of Julius and Ethel Rosenberg for spying for the Soviet Union—examination almost necessarily begins with the British physicist Klaus Fuchs. Late in January 1950 Fuchs, on his own initiative, confessed to British authorities that while he was working in the United States in the 1940s he had given the secrets of the atomic bomb to the Russians.

Fuchs, a brilliant scientist and expatriot from Nazi Germany, was arrested on February 2, 1950. He went to trial March 1 and was convicted. It was Fuchs's arrest and conviction that led to the arrest of Harry Gold, to the arrest of David Greenglass, and finally to the arrests of Julius and Ethel Rosenberg.

The officially presented facts were that Klaus Fuchs, while working at Los Alamos, New Mexico, in 1945, passed to Harry Gold, an American industrial chemist, the secrets of the atom bomb. Gold also at the time received atom bomb secrets from David Greenglass, an enlisted man in the U.S. Army who was also working at Los Alamos; and then passed the secrets to Anatoli Yakovlev, a member of the Russian Consulate in New York, who forwarded them to the Soviet Union. Greenglass's brother-in-law Julius Rosenberg, an electrical engineer in New York, and his wife Ethel were the masterminds of the spy operation.

These facts, however, on inspection, evaporate. The evidence indicates that Gold never met Fuchs or Greenglass, that Gold was never in New Mexico, particularly at the times he claimed he received the A-bomb data. What is more, the Russian Yakovlev, variously described as blond with blue eyes by one FBI informant, and dark with black eyes by another, was reported to have been in France by yet another FBI informant at a time when Gold said that he was giving him the atom secrets.

Other facts accepted at the time were that Harry Gold and Elizabeth Bentley were espionage agents working for the Soviet Union who later turned against the Communists; Gold after his arrest in 1950, and Bentley on her own volition in 1945.

But these facts of yesterday are not the facts of today. The internal evidence contained in the FBI files points out that Gold and Bentley were part of an unsavory group of misfits and informers who had been working for the Bureau all along.

At the time, Gold's acceptance of a thirty-year sentence was regarded as proof that he was a spy, on the theory that only a guilty man would have

2

consented to such a long term. This point was so convincing to the Rosenberg lawyers that they did not even question his credentials and credibility. Today we simply do not know whether something in Gold's bizarre personality led him to agree to spend thirty years in prison, or whether the FBI had some hold over him that was powerful enough to compel his assent.

Bentley's evidence also was generally accepted in her many court appearances. FBI Director Hoover himself claimed that her testimony had proved to be honest in every case. Actually, her testimony turned out to be dishonest in almost every instance.

If a fact is defined as an occurrence not subject to dispute, the study of the murder of the Rosenbergs begins now, and everything is in dispute.

From the time of Fuchs's apprehension until mid-May 1950 it is unclear what the FBI actually uncovered. All we do know is that during this period, the FBI's concentration was on someone named Joseph Regenstreich, the man Fuchs identified as Raymond. But on May 9, 1950, J. Edgar Hoover ordered an all-out search for Harry Gold, who might be this Raymond. And on May 22 Gold confessed that he was indeed Raymond. Yet two days before this confession, Fuchs was unable to identify Gold as Raymond from any of the photographs presented to him by the FBI agent visiting him in England.

On May 22 after Gold insisted that he was the American to whom Fuchs had given A-bomb secrets, motion pictures of Gold were rushed to Fuchs. This time Fuchs, recognizing what was wanted, said, "I cannot be absolutely positive, but I think it is very likely him." Finally on May 24, after viewing still more photographs and motion pictures of Gold, Fuchs announced, "Yes, that is my American contact."

But years later when Marshall Perlin, a lawyer representing the two sons of Julius and Ethel Rosenberg, visited Klaus Fuchs and asked him if he had ever identified Harry Gold as his contact, Perlin said that Fuchs answered, "No, he never identified Gold as the courier, either to the FBI, British Intelligence or to his attorney." Perlin explained how Fuchs was set upon by an FBI agent who told him, "For God's sake, say he is the man. Gold insists he is," and that Fuchs, wishing to please, in substance responded, "Alright, if he wants to be that person, I'll say he is that person."

There were other problems confronting the FBI in building a case against Gold. J. Edgar Hoover, in an article, "The Crime of the Century," for the May 1951 edition of *Reader's Digest*, conceded that Fuchs described his contact as "forty to forty-five years of age, possibly five feet ten inches tall, broad build." Harry Gold was delicate, frail, about five feet, four inches tall, and thirty-four years old. Furthermore, Fuchs's sister Kristal Heineman, who supposedly also saw Raymond, gave the same description that Fuchs had. Obviously it did not fit Harry Gold.

Nevertheless when the FBI learned that Regenstreich could not have visited the Heineman home at any of the times that Fuchs was there, having been elsewhere at the time, the need to substitute someone else—like Harry Gold—became essential to the U.S. government's case. With that objective in mind, Hoover wrote, "Our starting place was Cambridge because Fuchs had admitted meeting the agent there, and because it was the home of Fuchs's sister, Kristal Heineman."

KRISTAL AND ROBERT HEINEMAN

Kristal Fuchs Heineman was born in Germany on July 22, 1914. She entered the United States in October 1938 and married Robert Bloch Heineman. They had three children, all born in Cambridge, Massachusetts. According to evidence in the FBI files Robert Heineman was a Communist who had turned informer for the U.S. government.

Throughout this book the reader will find references to informers and possible informers. While the term is opprobrious and most people believe that the existence of an informer is rare, the realities of life dispute this assumption. Having a chance to review the FBI files, thousands on thousands of pages, an investigator loses naiveté. Informers are everywhere; friends, best friends, even brothers turn against those they are supposed to love in order to save themselves.

Kristal Heineman, her husband, their three children, and a man named Konstantin Lafazanos all were present when the visitor whom Klaus Fuchs knew as Raymond arrived at the Heineman home. Yet none of them were asked to identify Harry Gold as that visitor. Kristal Heineman in particular was rejected as a witness by the FBI because they considered her mentally incompetent. An FBI report stamp-dated February 5, 1950, when she was a patient at Westboro State Hospital in Massachusetts, read:

> *It is noted that she is receiving treatment because her mental illness had caused confusion in her mind as to time, persons, and places.*

To stress the seriousness of Kristal Heineman's

5

mental state, the report continued—

> Mrs. Heineman recited the following:
> Approximately 3 weeks before Klaus Fuchs's visit in Cambridge in Feb. 1945, a chemist rang her doorbell and asked if Klaus had arrived. He introduced himself as a chemist who had worked with Klaus and she is under the impression that he worked at Los Alamos. Questioning revealed that there was no basis in fact now known to her for this assumption....
> Sometime in the following few months, this same unidentified chemist again stopped at her home and made inquiry as to whether her brother would visit her in the near future... She has a dim recollection that her husband may have met this man as he left the house with a brief introduction.
> Mrs. Heineman described the unidentified chemist as follows: about 40 years of age; height, 5'8" to 8 1/2"; build, stocky; weight, possibly 180 lbs.; hair, very dark brown, thin and not curly...
> Mrs. Heineman indicated that she might recall the name of the unidentified chemist if it was spoken to her. There also exists the possibility that she might recognize him from a photograph.

Actually, Kristal Heineman's responses to the FBI queries were balanced and forthright; it was just that she disappointed the agents, who appraised her as someone not likely to alter her testimony to suit their plans.

On February 14, agents interviewed her again at Westboro State Hospital. At this interview she said very little that differed from earlier interviews, except that she mentioned another witness who might have been present at the time: a man named Konstantin Lafazanos.

KRISTAL AND ROBERT HEINEMAN

Nothing in the FBI reports indicated that there were disturbances in Kristal Heineman's thinking. Whatever her emotional problems, they did not affect her ability to give a coherent description of the visits to her home by an unidentified chemist. Nonetheless, the slanders against her and the other witness she named, Konstantin Lafazanos, began and accelerated. An FBI teletype reported that she was

> completely hallucinated and undergoing shock treatments, impossible to interview her currently according to medical authorities, testimony of no value in view of condition. Lafazanos is considered unreliable by Boston [agents] who have talked to him. Has medical records as psychoneurotic and is believed likely to be "publicity hound."

Another FBI memo, dated March 3, read:

> On the late afternoon of March 2, 1950 Dr. Rollins K. Hadley, director of the Westboro State Hospital, advised Special Agents John J. O'Lalor and Preston S. Gordon that Dr. Samuel Holt, who is in charge of Kristal Heineman's treatment, had made a suggestion that Kristal be given a dose of Amitol, a truth serum.

The Philadelphia office of the FBI was not willing to go that far. They opposed the suggestion, saying:

> This office was in no way responsible for the decision to conduct such treatment, nor will any agent be present or participate in this phase of medical treatment.

The FBI's position concerning the Heinemans had a great deal of mystery about it. There was much afoot, and complete answers will probably never be obtained.

7

Those lucky and thankful researchers who had the opportunity to read the FBI files that finally reached the Columbia University library sometime in 1989, more than ten years after they were initially released by the government, found them invaluable. The insights they offered on life itself were well worth the months required to read them.

The FBI files were probably released because the FBI wanted them released. Certainly they kept much from view. But if the Bureau wanted to, it could have concealed a great deal more. It was time to have the work of Director J. Edgar Hoover reappraised and the malodorous stench of his administration removed. The FBI left enough information in those files to expose Hoover for what he was.

On May 22, 1950, according to an FBI memo, Agent August Belmont was expecting Kristal Heineman to come to Philadelphia to identify Gold. That appointment was quietly canceled. She would never be given the opportunity to see Harry Gold face to face; not when the FBI knew that she would not identify him as the chemist who had visited her Cambridge home.

Other examples of the government's investigative methods surfaced. The Heinemans were involved in a divorce struggle, and Robert Heineman's lawyer was a former FBI agent, James F. Mahan. Informers characteristically hired former FBI agents and former U.S. Attorneys to represent them in court. Elizabeth Bentley chose U.S. Attorney Thomas Donegan for her lawyer. David Greenglass, his wife Ruth, and Max Elitcher, another self-confessed spy, were represented by former U.S. Attorney O. John Rogge. A Boston FBI memo dated May 29, 1951, read:

Former Special Agent and now Attorney James F. Mahan advised Special Agent Preston S. Gordon, of this division, on May 29, 1951, of the following.

In late April 1951, Mr. Mahan filed a petition for a divorce...on behalf of Robert Heineman. The grounds for the divorce are adultery and the correspondent named is Konstantin Lafazanos, of Lowell, Massachusetts...

The court has been requested to appoint a guardian to act for Mrs. Heineman, who remains an inmate at the Westboro State Hospital for the mentally ill.

A memo dated two days later said:

On the afternoon of May 31, 1951 Konstantin Lafazanos...appeared at the office of this Division and advised SA Richard W. Dow of the following:

Lafazanos declared that he has been subpoenaed as a witness in the divorce action now being instituted by Robert Heineman against his wife...Lafazanos said he intended "to prove" these three items:

(1) That Robert Heineman was a member of the Communist Party.

(2) That Robert Heineman was a ▪

(3) That he, Lafazanos, was the ▪

Lafazanos then commented that the interviewing Agent might well note that he had lost considerable weight since the last time the Agents had interviewed him in connection with the Fuchs and Gold case. Here again Lafazanos stated, "My loss in weight is the result of the psychological warfare being waged upon me by SA Gordon and SA Dow..."

It is noted that the attorney representing Heineman has previously advised that he intends to avoid publicity in connection with his client's domestic problems. It can be noted

9

however, that Lafazanos will undoubtedly attract newpaper attention if he makes the allegations he declares above.

What were the allegations Lafazanos made that were so worrisome to the FBI? That Robert Heineman was a government informer? He was; a February 1951 FBI report said: "This review reflects that during 1950 Robert Heineman has been carried as a temporary informant in several reports emanating from the Boston office." The date when he began working for the FBI was not given.

But the most glaring unanswered question is why the government did not use Heineman to identify Harry Gold, especially when Gold had already said that he met him and would assuredly not contradict his identification?

J. Edgar Hoover was building a case that he described as the "crime of the century," but he was not presenting the available witnesses who could identify Harry Gold as Klaus Fuchs's contact. There was a good reason for the FBI's decision: Robert Heineman, as well as Kristal Heineman and Konstantin Lafazanos, had already been tested with the FBI's first suspect, Joseph Regenstreich. At that time, the FBI very much wanted Regenstreich identified as the mysterious Raymond. Yet try as the FBI might, they could not persuade any of the three to identify Regenstreich, even though Fuchs had done so. They were truthful witnesses and not pliable. This was good enough reason for Hoover to not use them. Fuchs, on the other hand, demonstrated his ability to identify the suspect of the FBI's choice; he identified Harry Gold. By FBI standards, Fuchs could be counted upon; the Heinemans and Lafazanos could not. It was essential that

10

they not be permitted to testify.

Since Hoover couldn't use these three witnesses, no one else would be able to. Just in case the defense ever got hold of them, they would be so tarnished or so afraid of government retaliation as to be of no use to anyone. Kristal Heineman had to be presented as incurably insane; Konstantin Lafazanos would be given similar treatment. He had a big mouth; FBI harassment would close it. He lost a lot of weight because of FBI intimidation; he would lose a lot more if he continued to diplay an independent spirit. Lafazanos received clear messages as to what was in store for him if he did anything to upset the government's objectives. Only Robert Heineman would be treated politely and simply told to stay away from the case.

Although the government had concluded that Kristal Heineman could be expected to remain in an institution for the rest of her life, once Gold had testified in court that he knew Klaus Fuchs, she quickly recovered. Soon after she was released from the hospital, and after divorcing Robert Heineman, married a man named Albert Holzer on October 8, 1954.

MUTUAL IDENTIFICATIONS

When Harry Gold was arrested in America some six months after Klaus Fuchs confessed, it was because the U.S. authorities decided that Gold would be Raymond. The evidence in the FBI files is compelling that Hoover and the inner circle of agents working with him always knew that Gold had never visited the Heinemans and never met Fuchs. The Bureau had others like Gold working with them; strange men and women who were ready to admit to all sorts of crimes, crimes they had not committed. The government's case rested on aberrant personalities like Harry Gold and Klaus Fuchs.

The United States was embroiled in a bitter political war with the Soviet Union. Communism was perceived as a threat to the nation. To many officials in our government, it seemed essential for a Communist spy ring to be discovered in order to prove to all Americans that the country was in grave danger.

The existence of a spy ring, especially since Russia now possessed the atomic bomb, would confirm the nation's need to rid itself of Communists and Communist sympathizers. With a Communist atomic bomb threatening from the outside and a Communist internal revolution threatening from the inside, the government officials who were direcly involved made a pragmatic, visceral decision. A hoax conspiracy was formulated—a spy ring engaged in passing atomic secrets to the Russians was invented. Julius and Ethel Rosenberg would be the leaders of this ring, and the nation would become a giant lynch mob. The Rosenbergs would die, for history had to move in this way.

Fuchs pleaded guilty: to what, no one really knows. His statement of guilt was an unsupported conclusion. William Skardon, the British police official who investigated him, testified: "Until Fuchs confessed there was no evidence with which the Crown could have gone to court against him." The British authorities were reluctant prosecutors of Fuchs. They saw him for what he was: a disturbed man carrying a psychological burden, who may very well have been guilty of nothing.

On May 23, 1950, Harry Gold was named as a conspirator. It looked as if Fuchs had led to Gold. But that was not the case; Gold had been interrogated by FBI agents before they went to London to question Fuchs. Gold confessed on May 22, the day before Fuchs was persuaded to identify him.

Once the U.S. government had Harry Gold's confession, the FBI called their London-based investigators to tell them that "efforts should be made to reconcile discrepancies in statements of Fuchs and Gold." As a result, the discrepancies were carefully reconciled. For instance, Fuchs's signed confession of May 26 repudiated a statement he made three days earlier claiming that he had met Raymond at "the end of June" 1945. In the new statement he simply changed his testimony, saying "June" rather than "the end of June," so as to have his latest statement conform with Gold's claim that they met in New Mexico on June 2, 1945. But June 1945 was not mentioned at all in the original charges brought against Fuchs, nor was a visit by anyone to him in New Mexico mentioned.

Changes in Fuchs and Gold's statements multiplied. Fuchs originally said that he met his contact once in

New York City. Gold, in his May 22 statement, said he remembered three meetings with Fuchs in New York City. By the time of Gold's July 10 statement, he remembered at least five meetings with Fuchs, and recalled: "The relationship between Klaus Fuchs and me was that of two firm friends."

Once the FBI had a way of connecting Klaus Fuchs with Harry Gold, the next step was for them to connect Gold with another contact: the as yet unidentified young soldier whom Gold later identified as David Greenglass, the brother-in-law of Julius Rosenberg.

Everything about the meetings between Gold and Fuchs and Gold and Greenglass was contrived. Gold first stated that he had met Fuchs in Santa Fe in September 1945. Later he also insisted that he met David Greenglass in Albuquerque the same month. Gold's insistence upon September 1945 could have destroyed the case from the start, since Greenglass was not in Albuquerque in September; he was on furlough in New York City. The meetings had to be in June—making it necessary for the FBI to add a few words to Gold's statements. Still, with all the FBI's machinations, too many statements were already in the files that mentioned only the September meeting, not a June meeting. For example, a May 23 FBI memo read, "The Philadelphia Division advised that Gold had admitted contacting Fuchs at Santa Fe, New Mexico in September 1945. Gold also admitted that he stopped at the Hilton Hotel in Albuquerque in September of 1945." Not June, and still no mention of the soldier's name.

On June 2 Special Agent Edward Scheidt noted for the first time that David Greenglass might be the unidentified soldier named by Gold. On June 3 FBI agents visited Gold in the Tombs, the New York City prison he was in, and the next day Gold identified Greenglass from a number of photographs as the one who most resembled the man he had met in Albuquerque. On June 5 Gold's identification of Greenglass still was not certain. It was not until June 15 that Harry Gold at last made a positive identification of David Greenglass as the soldier he had visited in Albuquerque. The same process that had enabled Gold to identify Fuchs now enabled Gold to identify Greenglass—Greenglass's willingness to be identified.

Just as Klaus Fuchs and Harry Gold's testimonies were reconciled, Harry Gold and David Greenglass's testimonies had to be reconciled. These adjustments in testimony were made by the government with a feeling of righteousness. To destroy an enemy who was perceived as a threat to national security, it was considered entirely proper to falsify evidence.

Reliable evidence was never submitted to explain what led the FBI to Gold. Fuchs was in British custody for six months, voluntarily providing information of every kind in his effort to convince everyone of his guilt. In that time he never once mentioned having been visited by Gold in Santa Fe.

We were asked to believe that Klaus Fuchs failed to include in his confession the most important element of his crime: delivery of the secret of the atomic bomb to Raymond, who was now Harry Gold, in Santa Fe. And we were not expected to find it odd that in so many months of providing voluntary confessions, Fuchs forgot about what had happened in Santa Fe.

The jurors at the Rosenberg trial never learned that there was considerable doubt about Gold's meeting with Fuchs in Santa Fe in September 1945, or ever, for that matter. Thus they were not given the opportunity to make the deduction that if the Gold-Fuchs meeting did not occur, the Gold-Greenglass meeting in Albuquerque probably did not occur.

The government's need for a Klaus Fuchs and a Harry Gold was so great that these master spies had to be created. Fuchs and Gold were ever willing. Gold even referred once to a mystical bond that existed between him and Klaus Fuchs. Indeed, it does seem that two men who were willing to pretend to have done what they did, and plead guilty to what they did not do, were mystically connected on some level.

In his one public statement before sentencing, Fuchs said, "I have committed certain crimes...I expect sentence. I have also committed some other crimes, which are not crimes in the eyes of the law...and when I asked my counsel to put certain facts before you—I did it in order to atone for those other crimes." Thus Fuchs as much as admitted that he was confessing to something he did not do in order to punish himself for some unrevealed thing he did do.

Fuchs and Gold's willingness to make mutual accusations and admissions was guided by one principle—that each of them demonstrate this willingness to the other's satisfaction. Each refused to identify the other until it was proved to his satisfaction that the other had entered into this pact. Once they recognized that they mutually agreed to be accused and identified by one another, they quickly did so.

Though rare, bizarre actions of this kind are not unknown in human experience. Jack Ruby killed Lee Harvey Oswald so that, as Ruby claimed, the wife of the assassinated president would be spared the ordeal of attending the suspected assassin Oswald's trial. One must delve much deeper to determine the true motives for such conduct.

But Gold, while willing to accept a thirty-year prison term, was not willing to plead guilty to the charge that he passed atomic bomb secrets to the Russians "with intent—to the injury of the United States." As a result of his protests, the prosecution dropped the phrase. For the government to have acceded to such a request by a purported spy was further evidence of the United States Government's long and curious relationship with Harry Gold.

In its final wording Gold's indictment charged that he collected information from Klaus Fuchs and delivered it to persons designated as John and Sam. The indictment was returned under the wartime Espionage Act, making Gold's crime punishable by death or thirty years' imprisonment.

But by not requiring Gold to plead guilty to "injuring" the United States, the government omitted an essential element of the crime he was charged with. It was as if he had pleaded guilty to unlawfully possessing a loaded gun, after the prosecution had acknowledged that the gun contained no bullets. The deletion of the word "intent" from the statutory charge allowed Gold to plead guilty to the lesser crime, when the judge would punish him as if he pleaded guilty to the greater crime. A new charge was thus created for the first time, by judicial and prosecutorial fiat. The charge was not part of the Federal Criminal Code. It was manufactured by the Government and the prosecution. The new crime included mutually incompetent, vague, and incongruent specifications. The impermissible admixture would in its new form be the basis for the indictment of the Rosenbergs and Sobell.

Only days after Gold's arrest, his brother told a reporter, "One thing is certain. We want nothing to do with a lawyer with the slightest Red tinge." John D. M. Hamilton, a former Republican national chairman, and August B. Ballard were the attorneys appointed by the court to represent Harry Gold.

On December 9, 1950, five months after his indictment, Gold was sentenced to thirty years' imprisonment for conveying American atom bomb secrets to the Russians during World War II. The sentence was the maximum penalty short of death. Before it was imposed, Hamilton, after conferring with Gold, announced that there would be no petition for a reduction of sentence. This was Gold's decision, he said.

"Mr. Gold," asked Judge McGranery, "do you have anything to say?"

> *Yes, Your Honor, [replied Gold.] I will be very brief...*
>
> *First, nothing has served to bring me to realization of the terrible mistakes as this one fact, the appointment by this court of Mr. Hamilton and Mr. Ballard as my counsel. These men have worked incredibly hard and faithfully in my behalf and in the face of severe personal criticism and even invective, and they have done this not for the reason that they condone my crime, but because they believed that, as a basic part of our law, that I was entitled to the best legal representation available.*
>
> *Second, I am fully aware that I have received the most scupulously fair trial and treatment that could be desired, and this has been not only in this court, but has been the case with the FBI, with the other agencies of the Justice Department, and with the authorities at various prisons where I have been lodged, both here and in New York.*
>
> *Most certainly, that could never have happened in the Soviet Union...*
>
> *Third, the most tormenting of all this concerns the fact that those who mean so much to me have been the worst besmirched*

by my deeds. I refer here to this country, to my family and friends, to my former classmates at Xavier University, and to the Jesuits there, and to the people at the heart station of the Philadelphia General Hospital.

The judge then imposed the sentence, stating that it had been determined "after long and deliberate application of the principles to the facts."

Gold's praise of his lawyers, who offered no defense in his behalf, coupled with his patriotic comments and unmistakable happiness in receiving his sentence, could hardly be called a normal response. Who was Harry Gold, and what were his true motives?

HARRY GOLD AND FRIENDS

Harry Gold was born on December 12, 1910, in Berne, Switzerland, to Mr. and Mrs. Samuel Golodnitsky of Kiev, Russia. Four years after his birth the family moved to the United States.

In 1930, a year after graduating from high school, Gold began his career as a chemist at the Pennsylvania Sugar Company in Philadelphia. He would work there for sixteen years until 1946, when the company sold its buildings. His employment at Penn Sugar was interrupted only by a layoff in 1932 because of the Depression and by several leaves of absence to attend various colleges, including Xavier University in Cincinnati. He graduated from this institution with honors in 1940 at the age of thirty.

Information obtained about Gold's job, which apparently gave him leeway to travel about the country almost at will, is difficult to understand. One plausible explanation is that his employment was a cover fcr his espionage work for a covert arm of the United States government.

The description of Harry Gold that was leaked to the press portrayed him as a gullible pawn of the Communists. At the time of his arrest in 1950, he was employed as a senior biochemist on a federally financed heart research project at Philadelphia General Hospital. "Gold was extremely conscientious and hard-working," said Dr. Daniel W. Lewis, a research fellow in cardiology at the hospital. "He frequently put in more time on his job than he was called on to do."

"You wouldn't really take a second look at him,"

said Dr. Pascal F. Lucchesi, superintendent and medical director of the institution. "He's only about five feet four inches tall, has stooped shoulders and always seemed to mind his own business."

Other releases said that in college Gold tutored fellow students without pay, even going to their homes to save them carfare and travel time. At a local hospital he donated excessive amounts of blood, offered himself as a subject in dangerous scientific experiments, and did long hours of volunteer work with an intensity that left his colleagues with a lasting memory of him. His lawyer John Hamilton described him as "the most selfless person I have met in my entire life."

The press carried stories, never substantiated, of Harry Gold's willingness to loan money to anyone who was in need, even people he had never met. More than that, if someone asked for a loan when he did not have the money, he would borrow it himself at usurious rates so he could make the loan. Harry Gold was described as a naive man who had been duped, like many other kind-hearted Americans, into advancing the cause of Communism, which they would soon learn was the greatest evil threatening mankind. J. Edgar Hoover wrote of Gold:

> *In promoting the Red cause, he had been almost morbidly self-sacrificial. Denying himself luxuries, spending hard-earned mon y, wasting vacation periods, making long trip ...he gave everything he had, including his honor...Although too late he had come at last to see that Communism had robbed him of the conscience of a free American.*

In reality, Gold was very different from the man portrayed in the press. As mentioned, the information available in the FBI files suggests that he was part of a select group of informers whom the FBI recruited, voluntarily or involuntarily, to search out Americans who were inclined to give industrial information to the Soviet Union, gather their names for future reference, check the material received from them first to appraise its value, and then either keep the material or alter it in such a way that the Soviet Union could not benefit from it. Beside Gold, the group included Morrell Dougherty, Elizabeth Bentley, Jacob Golos, Thomas Black, and Ferdinand Heller, as well as several others.

Thomas Black and Ferdinand Heller had been doing business for years with the Amtorg Trading Corporation, the company representing the Soviet Union in the United States. In 1934 Black visited Amtorg to inquire about seeking employment in Russia and he was introduced to one Paul Petersen. According to both Black and Gold, Peterson was a Soviet agent who became Gold's first contact.

The FBI had no difficulty in having Petersen identified as a Soviet agent, since people like Harry Gold, Thomas Black, and Elizabeth Bentley were so accommodating in identifying suspects. To protect themselves from mistakes, they would at first use phrases such as, "It looks like him," or "It could be him." The FBI would then check to see if that person was elsewhere when the crime or incriminating act was committed. If he was, the identification would be discarded and a new suspect presented. Aside from suspects who were dead, or who had left the country, the best suspects were those who were willing to confess to crimes they did not commit.

This identification procedure, however, was not always accomplished without embarrassing errors.

According to an FBI report dated April 1952, both Black and Gold identified a photo of one John Henry De Graaf as the person they knew under the name of Paul Petersen. Both furnished signed statements to that effect. A June 3, 1952, FBI report stated:

> *As of May 1952 Thomas L. Black and Harry Gold had positively identified Johnny De Graaf as their Soviet espionage superior from 1935 - 1938 and the subject of instant case.*

But a serious problem arose. John De Graaf, who was not expected to be heard from, surfaced unexpectedly in Montreal and vehemently denied that he was Paul Petersen.

Black and Gold, who claimed to have known Petersen, took several months to revoke their identification of De Graaf as their contact Petersen, though they were confronted with him face to face. This was astonishing conduct. They were claiming that a total stranger was the same man that they had known for some fifteen years. Black, in finally withdrawing his identification, still "hesitated to say so definitely." Gold, after "considerable thought...believed De Graaf was not Petersen." If De Graaf had not appeared or if he had been dead, like others who could not defend themselves from the FBI's identification system, he would have remained in our history books as the Soviet agent Paul Petersen. Worse, had De Graaf not had an alibi for his whereabouts, he might have been indicted.

Gold stated that Black introduced him to Petersen in the latter part of 1935. They met in the vicinity of Pennsylvania Station in New York, and Black then left the two men together. Gold said that Petersen told him never to see Black again but that over the years he frequently met Black in violation of these instructions.

Since Black was an apparent homosexual and Gold lived with Black after Gold's mother passed away, there is an inference that Black and Gold were lovers. Jacob Fass was another close friend of Black's who was a homosexual. Ferdinand Heller, though he was married, was also a close friend of Black's who may have been a homosexual.

The homosexual implications surrounding Harry Gold are not mentioned to defame him, but because being a homosexual during those times was as dangerous as being a Communist. Homosexuality had to be kept secret, and it may be one of the reasons that men like Gold and Black could be controlled by organizations such as the FBI. The threat of exposure to their family or employers was terrifying.

An FBI report dated October 24, 1950, said, "Gold steadfastly denies any act of homosexuality or of ever having been involved in anything of the sort." Morrell Dougherty, Gold's good friend, backed up Gold's denials, claiming that the allegation that Gold was a homosexual was laughable. What else could a friend of so many years say?

Harry Gold's relationship with Thomas Black was so close that when it came to proving that he was in Albuquerque in 1945, he relied on Black to support his claims. Gold said he told Black that he was the person to whom Klaus Fuchs gave the information on atomic energy. Gold was confident that Black would support his story.

But on May 31, when Black was first interviewed by the FBI, he stated that he never had any reason to doubt Gold's loyalty to the United States, and that he did not know of any trip made by Gold to Albuquerque. Black's statement made him eligible for indictment. As we shall see, however, the government never had any intention of charging him with perjury, since once Black was certain of what was wanted, he quickly made his testimony conform to Gold's. Two weeks later on June 15, his statement to the FBI read:

> *In the early part of February 1950 after the arrest of Fuchs, Harry Gold...told me that he had been Fuchs's American contact...I know this because he telephoned me from a hotel in Albuquerque...In retrospect I very deeply regret that I did not at that time come forward with the information which would have aided in Harry's apprehension.*

These were very odd people, whose minds are almost beyond understanding. Black's comments about his group were protective of them in every way. Black stated to the FBI:

> *Dougherty is in no way involved in this thing, I'm sure, and the reason I'm sure is that he is very anti-Soviet and he's as good a Catholic as comes...*
> *I met Dougherty through Harry and Harry never said anything about him except that he was very religious and anti-Soviet and of course, I knew that after talking with him for five minutes...*
> *At the present time Heller stands precisely where I stand. I believe that this is by far the best country in the world for anybody to live in...*

It was time, however, for the group to draw away from Harry Gold. They had to appear to repudiate him. Even Morrell Dougherty, who was so close to Gold that they were referred to as the "Golddust twins," was forced to sever their relationship. An FBI memo which contained notes of interviews with Dougherty quoted him as saying, "I had been a friend of Gold's through working with him at the Penn Sugar but after what he had done to this country to his friends and family, I felt that my friendship obligation had ended..." Not likely; Gold and Dougherty had both been engaged in criminal conduct of all sorts for years, espionage being only one of their many illegal enterprises. Indeed, Gold, when interviewed by an FBI agent on October 24, 1950, admitted that he and Dougherty regularly stole as much as ten gallons a week of alcohol from Penn Sugar and then sold it to employees for $5 or $6 per gallon.

It is likely that Gold's enrollment at Xavier University in Cincinnati was for the purposes of initiation into the government's group of informers. His stay at Xavier was filled with discrepancies. The uninformed FBI agents investigating his comings and goings, unaware of his actual involvement, found a plethora of inconsistencies and unverifiable data. For instance, while Gold was attending Xavier, he claimed he worked at the Moorneier Brothers Dairy Company for one year and ten months. An FBI agent noted that the proprietor of the dairy found no records to indicate that Gold worked for the company and also "does not recall Gold, which he claims he would if employed one year ten months." There were other discrepancies. The same agent noted that "Gold furnished an address, 19 Glendale Street, Cincinnati, during the summer of 1936. There is no number 19 on Glendale Street."

There were many other puzzling questions about Gold. When the FBI visited him in May of 1950, he requested that they wait several days to search his home. They complied—a strange performance by an agency investigating the passing of atomic secrets to a foreign power. After all, if the FBI were truly worried about Gold and considered him a spy, they would certainly have been concerned about the information in his house. One day, much less a week, would have given Gold or the relatives he lived with ample time to destroy the evidence.

It seems likely that a covert unit of the government was preparing Gold and themselves for what was to be his partial uncovering. Apparently the agents who first apprehended Gold were sincerely shocked when they were instructed by their superiors to give Gold the time he needed to shape up his cellar before they finally arrested him. It is this writer's thesis that Gold's undercover role was a secret so carefully guarded that it was kept from the ranks of the FBI and known only to a select few.

The FBI interviews of Morrell Dougherty were so superficial that it is fair to surmise that the interviewer knew Dougherty's secret status. An FBI report dated June 27, 1950, containing Special Agent Albert L. Pierce's notes on one of these exchanges appeared to avoid all questions that would have established Dougherty's glue-like relationship with Harry Gold. In the same way, Dougherty's friendships with Thomas Black and Ferdinand Heller were not areas the government wished to have explored. The FBI had enough difficulty explaining the documents they found among Gold's effects in the basement of his Philadelphia home. His notes describing his contacts and their views on Communism sounded as if they had been written for the FBI rather than the Russians. The federal agents who searched the basement, especially the agents who were unaware of Harry Gold's many secrets, must have been even more confused by the vast amount of scientific blueprints and secret data that Gold had kept, instead of sending it to the Soviet Union like a real Communist spy.

Gold's contacts with the Amtorg Trading Company occasionally allowed him to forward information to the Russians, who thereby received data that was either worthless or incorrect. Indeed, the Soviet Union frequently received useless information from major U.S. corporations who were pretending to be helpful. The process of providing a country that was our ally at the time with data that sabotaged its industrial growth was described by Gold at the trial of Abraham Brothman. Thomas Black also explained this process to FBI interviewers. Black claimed that he lied to his Soviet superiors about the nature of the work he had done, and that the written reports he gave them on such subjects as sorbose and the production of penicillin were wholly fabricated and in some instances "set out processes which were impractical." Black's inhumanity was spectacular. He provided the Russians, who were so respectful of the Americans, with sabotaged medical information that could have led to the deaths of many Russian citizens.

The secret notes found in Harry Gold's basement did not sound like the writings of a Communist. Here is a sample:

> *I have been unable to locate the man I heard speaking in favor of Trotskyism at an acquaintance's home about a year ago. Have been trying to locate several people I formerly knew who may be able to introduce me to a member of that organization but I had not had the time to follow this up as well as I want to.*

These jottings, written in the form of a diary,

indicated that Gold was investigating Communists rather than working for them. The style resembled a typical FBI report on suspected Communists or Communist sympathizers. An FBI memo dated June 23, 1950, concluded that the notes were fictitious; under the circumstances the Bureau had no other choice.

Looking through Gold's address book, the FBI found the name of a woman, Vera Kane, whom they interviewed on June 17, 1950. Their report said:

> *During the period of the depression from 1932 to 1935, she had an apartment at 325 West 11th Street which she used as a sort of continuous open house for her Bohemian friends. She gave out some 27 keys to the place, and always had a meal ready for any of her friends who had a key and who might be hungry...sometimes over weekends when a lot of the group would stop in at the place, they would sometimes stay overnight in groups of six or more.*

Thomas Black, in discussing Vera Kane, told the FBI in June 1950 that he

> *did not know for certain that Vera Kane was aware of Harry Gold's espionage activities, but he suspected that she was aware because between 1937 and 1944 Vera Kane on a number of occasions told Thomas Black that Harry Gold was not one for Heller and Black to associate with and that it was very dangerous for them to associate with him.*

Kane apparently did not realize that Black and Heller were working for the government as well.

Black also told the FBI that he and Heller had had a falling out because of Heller's jealousy over a woman Black had lived with in New York. The woman was Vera Kane, and Black told the story to contradict any impression that he was a homosexual. He was deeply concerned with preventing his sexual preferences from being publicly exposed. Heller supported Black by confirming his story in every way he could, even to the point of remembering the date of the incident of heterosexual jealousy: November 7, 1934.

Jacob Fass was another member of the Heller-Black-Gold group. The background information on Fass supplied by the FBI files was that he was rejected for military service because of homosexuality. Fass said he was introduced to Gold by Black in 1945. His signed statement to the FBI, dated July 17, 1950, gave this account:

> I made the acquaintance of Thomas L. Black when we were both employed at the National Oil Products Co. in Harrison, N.J. in 1938...He confided in me that he had once been engaged in collecting technical information for the Soviet Union...He was quite dramatic about these revelations, and told me that he was the only man in the United States to have been awarded the Order of Lenin, though the medal was not delivered to him...
>
> He had told me previously that...when he decided to cease his activities for the Soviet Union...2 agents tried to forcibly remove him from the country and drove him to the Canadian border, in Michigan, if I remember correctly. He escaped...Thereafter he had lived in constant fear of his life...
>
> From my intimate knowledge of Tom Black...to the best of my knowledge he engaged in no political activity of any sort...
>
> As for the reason why Tom did not turn Gold in, he told me that he could not do it, because he considered Gold a friend...Perhaps on further reflections he would have recognized the other aspect of the man, and taken action. But Gold was arrested before he could come to any decision.

Unmistakably evident in FBI documents such as this were the loyalty, friendship, and support Black, Heller, Gold, and Fass gave one another. But this loyalty and friendship was not shared with other fringe members of the group, as the following FBI note referring to Dr. Joseph Skilton, dated July 13, 1950, demonstrates:

> *Black advised the interviewing agents that Fred Heller had told him the previous day that Dr. Joseph Skilton committed suicide on Friday, July 7...*
> *Black had learned from Heller that Skilton had come to the conclusion that Black's purpose in giving him some air-conditioning equipment for his office was to provide an excuse for Black to use the office as a meeting place for espionge activities...*
> *It appeared from Black's story that Skilton considered himself the victim of a plot concocted by Black and Heller.*

Black, Heller, Gold, and Fass's extended circle of friends and acquaintances was a bizarre group with a complex social structure. Blackmail and extortion were an integral part of their lives. Another FBI memo, dated June 14, 1950, tells us a little more about them. In it Dorothy Wiswell, the ex-wife of Ferdinand Heller, stated that

> *she first met Ferdinand Heller in 1937 and started going with him socially. They were married in 1943 and subsequently divorced around 1945...*
> *Between 1937 and 1945 at the time of her divorce, she estimated that she and Heller would drive to Newark, N.J. to see Black approximately once a month. There were times when Heller would visit Black without the presence of Miss Wiswell...*
> *She described Black as being a "screwball."*

For example, she stated, Black had a pet black crow which had the run of his apartment. He also had some type of animal which she could not recall which Black kept in the bathtub. This animal lived in the bathtub...Black, according to her, did not drink and she never saw him in the company of women.

Thomas Black and Harry Gold, though they were odd men, were extremely useful witnesses. Their bizarre personalities and the ease with which they provided false statements made them invaluable to the U.S. government.

ALFRED DEAN SLACK

Many innocent people would suffer as a result of Harry Gold's testimony. Alfred Dean Slack was one of them. Slack was charged with espionage for having sold industrial information to Gold from 1940 to 1944, while Slack worked at Eastman Kodak.

In mid-June 1950, highly regarded news services described Slack as an atom bomb spy connected with Klaus Fuchs. Slack was universally condemned.

On September 1, 1950, Slack, relying on his counsel's advice that he had no other choice, pleaded guilty. On September 22, he was given a sentence he never dreamed he would receive—a fifteen-year term. When he attempted to withdraw the guilty plea, his request was rejected. Yet Slack did absolutely nothing wrong. Every bit of information he gave to Gold could be found in the public library.

The circumstances of Slack's arrest, guilty plea, and sentence were distressing. After being arrested and held on $100,000 bail, which he could not possibly raise, he was held incommunicado for about a week, then given solitary confinement, and finally placed on a "suicide watch." Meanwhile he was constantly interrogated by the FBI. After three weeks of this, Slack was permitted for the first time to tell his assigned counsel that he was innocent and had never even heard of Klaus Fuchs.

In arguing his right to withdraw his plea of guilty, Slack said that from the day of his arrest until the day he pleaded guilty, he was constantly questioned by the FBI. He argued that one of his lawyers, Kyle King, saw him only twice, once at his initial arrest and again on the day of his sentencing; and that his other lawyer, Ray Jenkins, refused to see him, even though he had written to Jenkins requesting a meeting.

Slack maintained that Jenkins had not properly represented him. Slack explained that he had asked Jenkins to check certain scientific archives which would prove that the information he gave Gold was taken from the public library in Cincinnati. Slack said that Jenkins ignored his requests.

In the meantime the only messages Slack received from Jenkins were delivered to him by the very FBI agents who were interrogating him. These messages, which Jenkins admitted sending, repeatedly cautioned Slack to cooperate with the FBI. Jenkins, who would later join Senator Joseph McCarthy in hunting Communists, was actually aiding the FBI while representing Slack.

The next time Slack saw Jenkins was in September, the day after his indictment. At that time Slack was told by the U.S. Attorney that if he pleaded guilty he would be sentenced to ten years in prison, but would serve only about three years. Slack said that Jenkins explained to him that because of the "public hysteria" there was no choice but for him to plead guilty.

Judge Robert Taylor found no merit in Slack's arguments. The judge even added an additional five years to Slack's sentence, over the prosecutor's request that Slack be given ten years. Judge Taylor explained his decision by saying, "Mr. Slack contends...that the information he gave did not violate the law. Now if he had known at that time that it did not violate the law then he would not have entered a plea of guilty." Judge Taylor was arguing that even if Slack was not guilty of anything, once he pleaded guilty, it meant that he considered himself guilty, and that was enough to make him guilty whether he was or not.

Once Gold's testimony was deemed essential to the prosecution of accused Communists, nothing could be allowed to remain that could detract from his authenticity as a legitimate Soviet agent. Slack had been accused by Gold; Slack had to be found guilty.

PRELUDE TO TRIAL

According to the FBI, Harry Gold first came to their attention in May 1947, while they were investigating Abraham Brothman, an enterprising chemical engineer who was head of his own company. Brothman was suspected of having dealings with an industrial spy ring led by the notorious Russian agent Jacob Golos and his assistant Elizabeth Bentley. One result of the investigation was that Brothman and Gold were compelled to testify before a grand jury that same year. Neither was indicted then.

But in 1950, with the arrest of Julius and Ethel Rosenberg, Abraham Brothman had to be arrested as well. His and Gold's 1947 testimony before the grand jury, if allowed to remain uncontradicted, could establish that Bentley, Gold, and Golos knew each other at a time when it was essential that it be established that they had not met.

Once Harry Gold was chosen to be a government witness against Julius and Ethel Rosenberg, major changes in his 1947 testimony were absolutely necessary. So although Gold had sworn that he had met Golos, he now swore he never did. Gold recanted all his testimony given to the FBI and the grand jury in 1947.

Somehow, based on Gold's recantation, we were to believe that he was telling the truth about Golos in 1950. We had to conclude that just about everything he told the FBI and the grand jury in 1947—statements such as that he was introduced to Golos by a man named Carter Hoodless, an executive of Pennsylvania Sugar Company, and even his identification of a photo of Golos supplied to him by the FBI—was all fabricated testimony, instigated and manufactured by Abraham Brothman, who persuaded him to lie to the grand jury. Gold, we were to assume, was no longer a liar. He had lied in the past when he was a Soviet agent, but now, as a government witness, his testimony was to be considered beyond reproach. "The real circumstances under which Gold and Brothman met in 1941," according to the prosecutor, Irving Saypol, in 1950, were that Gold was introduced to Brothman by a Russian, Mr. Semanov, alias "Sam."

What was remarkable about this new "real circumstances" testimony was that it was manufactured in a way that could not be disputed. Almost every witness who could shed any light on the events was dead or unavailable. Jacob Golos was dead—he died on November 25, 1943; Carter Hoodless was dead—he died on July 2, 1942; and Sam Semenov had returned to Russia.

Abraham Brothman and Miriam Moskowitz, his friend and business partner, would be charged with an assortment of crimes relating to espionage and perjury in connection with Brothman's statement that Gold knew Bentley and Golos. At the trial Elizabeth Bentley and Harry Gold would be the chief witnesses for the prosecution, Irving Saypol and Roy Cohn the prosecutors, and Irving Kaufman the judge, just as in the Rosenberg trial that would later follow.

Judge Kaufman's credentials were formidable. At the age of twenty he graduated from Fordham Law School, first in his class and the youngest graduate in the school's history. Soon afterwards he was appointed a special assistant to the U.S. Attorney. In 1940 at the age of thirty he entered private practice with a friend, Gregory K. Noonan. Kaufman did extremely well. He was politically astute and found himself a confidential coordinator of federal patronage. At a young age he had the power to choose prospective appointees for the U.S. Attorney's office and even had influence in appointing judges.

Judge Kaufman, who was only forty years old when he presided over the Brothman trial, was carefully chosen by the government. His reputation as an anti-Communist had already been established during his tenure as an assistant U.S. Attorney. He was so obviously and vehemently pro-government that the Administration was concerned only that his overly zealous rulings against accused Communists could result in reversals in the appellate courts.

The government's proposed case against Brothman and Moskowitz was not without internal opposition. Not only did agents of the FBI find the charges unsupportable; so too did members of the U.S. Attorney's office. An FBI teletype from New York City, dated July 19, 1950, gave Assistant U.S. Attorney Thomas Donegan's appraisal of the contemplated indictment:

> *Donegan does not feel he can prove Brothman perjured himself before [the] forty-seven grand jury since at time of testimony Brothman might have felt he actually met Gold through Golos.*

Donegan was not objecting on technical grounds; he was saying that the government had no case and that Brothman had done nothing to warrant prosecution. Yet abruptly and unexpectedly on July 28, 1950, the Administration decided to indict Brothman and Moskowitz. An FBI memo read:

> *Saypol does feel that it is possible to prosecute Brothman for obstruction of*

justice...US Attorney Saypol is calling US Attorney Gleeson in Philadelphia to arrange for Harry Gold to come before the Federal Grand Jury in the Southern District of New York on Saturday, July 29 in order that the Grand Jury can consider this before the Statute of Limitations runs.

Just hours before it would have been too late to bring charges against Brothman and Moskowitz, Saypol had them indicted by a hastily assembled grand jury. Then he arranged for bench warrants against them and had them both arrested that same day, July 29, 1950. There was so much antagonism toward Brothman after his arrest that even though he had the $25,000 bail, a bondsman would not write the bond, fearing that it would be considered unpatriotic.

The crux of Saypol and the government's case was that Brothman had persuaded Gold to falsely claim that Gold had been referred to him by Jacob Golos and Elizabeth Bentley.

From the start the FBI was confused over what position to take on whether or not Bentley knew Gold. Bentley was equally unsure about what to say. To complicate the issue, as late as May 25, 1950, Gold was still maintaining that he knew Golos, making it axiomatic that he also knew Bentley, especially since he had already told the Grand Jury in 1947 that he did.

Although the newspapers reported that Bentley and Gold knew each other, for the time being Bentley remained vague and noncommittal. She would await further instructions from the government before she decided whether or not she knew him.

A larger question is why the FBI did not ask Gold about having told the 1947 grand jury that he knew

Bentley if he really didn't. This was not a minor discrepancy that the grand jury and the prosecutor could have ignored at the time. Although Golos was dead and could not contradict Gold, Bentley was alive and a witness for the government.

Jacob Golos's status and the government's treatment of him were equally peculiar. While Golos had been under investigation from, at the very least, late 1938 until his death on November 25, 1943, the FBI files contained scarcely a word about the man they considered one of the most important Soviet espionage agents working in the United States. As for Bentley, who had worked for Golos during that period, the FBI made it appear that she first became known to them in late 1945, two years after Golos died.

It was not until June 6, 1950, that Harry Gold agreed to change his story about Golos. Gold now said that he never knew Golos and explained that the only reason he said he did at first was that Brothman had made him invent the story. Gold also said he had never met Bentley. So Bentley could now confidently state that she had never met Gold. Irving Saypol was ready to petition for his indictments.

The charges against Abraham Brothman were obstruction of justice and perjury. They were based on the government's claim that Brothman and Moskowitz had persuaded Harry Gold to tell a fictitious story to the grand jury in 1947, "to throw the Grand Jury off the track."

THE BROTHMAN-MOSKOWITZ TRIAL

OPENING STATEMENTS

The trial of the United States of America versus Abraham Brothman and Miriam Moskowitz began on November 8, 1950. Irving Saypol, the government prosecutor, addressed the court:

The Indictment which is before the Court charges what concededly is the gravest of offenses—obstruction of justice...affecting the very stability of government, a witness was induced corruptly by these defendants to give false testimony, both the defendant Brothman and the witness did so, resulting in a diversion of the attention of the jury to a false track with a consequent delay of more than three years before the investigative processes of the Government were put back in the right direction...

Saypol expanded upon his comments, until what he was saying was nothing more than an anti-Communist speech. Saypol continued:

The world-wide quest for Communist totalitarian domination under foreign inspiration and direction is a movement to bring about by any available means and by force if necessary, the overthrow of all existing governments of all countries, including the United States.

That the designation of this movement in any country as a political party is merely a false front of respectability behind which lurks a conspiratorial force devoted to violence and coercion ready to strike down the freedom preserving means by which the people of the United States govern themselves...

Saypol was expounding the prevalent fear of the day. Communism and Marxist-Leninist teachings were considered democracy's most serious threat. In the time of the Roman Empire it was Christianity. Ideas disruptive to the entrenched authorities have always been met with crushing force—including laws created to deny civil rights.

In 1940 the Smith Act was passed, proscribing penalties for the teaching and advocacy of the overthrow of the government by force and violence. The law was mainly directed at Communists.

But the violence which the Smith Act sought to curb and which Saypol referred to in his opening statement did not come from the American Communist Party. Whatever violence that did occur was directed at them.

The Smith Act was not invoked very much in the

early 1940s. The world was at war and Communist Russia was America's ally against fascist Germany. But once the war ended in 1945, the anti-Communist drive was renewed with vigor. The FBI under Director J. Edgar Hoover, the McCarran Committee led by Senator Pat McCarran, and the House Committee on Un-American Activities became the leading warriors in the battle to destroy Communism in America.

In June 1947, several high-ranking members of a group known as the Joint Anti-Fascist Refugee Committee, who were suspected Communists, were charged with contempt of Congress and convicted of refusing to give the Un-American Committee the names of their contributors. They received sentences of up to six months in jail.

In December 1947, ten motion picture executives and artists, later known as the Hollywood Ten, were indicted and eventually convicted and sentenced for refusing to tell the Un-American Committee their beliefs or to list their friends and affiliations. For this, the group of suspected Communists were given terms of up to one year in prison.

Since numerous additional arrests had not destroyed the Communist Party, the government decided that greater force was required. A new weapon was added: the blacklist. During 1947-1948 Attorney General Tom Clark, whom Irving Saypol and Irving Kaufman had formerly worked for, arbitrarily listed 160 organizations as "subversive". To qualify a group had to do little more than advocate equality for blacks, or higher wages for laborers.

The government's drive intensified. On July 20, 1948, twelve leaders of the Communist Party in America were indicted for violating the Smith Act. They were charged in essence with thinking freely, speaking freely, and assembling together. None of the twelve were charged with a specific act, there were no specific acts. Instead they were accused of "conspiring to teach and advocate" the violent overthrow of the Government. The basis of the Government's case was extracts taken from the *Communist Manifesto* and other Communist literature. Philosophical remarks of Communist theoreticians were quoted out of context by government prosecutors in order to persuade the public that the non-violent American Communist Party was actually bent on the violent overthrow of the United States Government.

As in most of the trials against Communists the government usually had an informer who, in exchange for liberal treatment and other rewards, turned against his former friends and associates. For the Smith Act trial, Louis Budenz, the former editor of the Communist newspaper, *The Daily Worker*, was the government's star witness. Budenz testified that the Communist Party only pretended to defend democracy and that they used "Aesopian language." In other words, Budenz claimed that when Communists said they wanted peace, they really wanted "war." This was the kind of evidence presented by the government.

On the other hand, the Party showed that far from advocating violence, their program was directed toward improving conditions for the workers, toward racial equality, and toward peace. The Party also presented evidence that they were not dominated or controlled by Moscow or any other government. Little that could be said mattered. On October 14, 1949, the jury found all the defendants guilty. Judge Harold R. Medina sentenced all but one of them to terms of five years in jail. (Their lawyers also were given six-month jail terms, having been found in contempt of court.)

Appeals all the way to the Supreme Court did not help; the Court declared the Smith Act constitutional and upheld the convictions.

Communists and their sympathizers were on the run. Six-month sentences, then one-year sentences, and now five-year sentences were being given to people whose beliefs did not meet the approval of those in power in America. It was becoming more and more costly to be a Communist, but still, Communists were unwilling to give up their right to believe as they did.

The persecutions intensified with an additional law enacted on September 23, 1950, the McCarran Act. This law declared that Communism was an international conspiracy and all Communists were foreign agents. The law also required all Communists and all officers of "Communist Front" organization to register with the Subversive Activist Control Board.

Once registered, however, the registrants were immediately subject to prosecution under the Smith Act. The Smith Act and McCarran Acts, taken together, made Communist Party membership a crime; made those who were not members but had similar beliefs subject to prosecution; and made them all the equivalent of agents of a foreign power. Going even further, the McCarran Act provided that in case of war or insurrection, concentration camps would be established to incarcerate people whom the authorities decided were "subversives," with no need for trials

The destruction of the Communist Party in America was a program undertaken in earnest. The Brothman-Moskowitz trial was one more step toward the Government's objective.

After completing his reading from a congressional report, Saypol stated:

As your Honor may see from the indictment, the clerk's notes indicate that this indictment was found on July 29, 1950, on the very eve of the running of the statute of limitations...

Here Saypol made the first of his many false statements to the court. The indictment was filed late—on July 31, 1950. The clerk of the Court's records was altered, as shown in the accompanying exhibit, to indicate July 29, 1950.

C 133/106

U. S. DISTRICT COURT

THE UNITED STATES OF AMERICA

vs.

ABRAHAM BROTHMAN and MIRIAM MOSKOWITZ,

Defendants

INDICTMENT

Conspiracy to defraud government; influencing a witness (Title 18, U.S.C., Section 55 (1946 Edition), Title 18, U.S.C., Section 241 (1946 Edition)).

IRVING H. SAYPOL
United States Attorney

TRUE BILL

M'FILMED

FILED
U.S. DISTRICT COURT
JUL 1950
S. D. OF N. Y.

July 29-1950
3 Pm
Indictment Orders Sealed, a bench warrants orders as to each Defr.
Shugar
3:30 PM Indictment Ordered open
Suga

JUL 31 1950
Both defendants arraigned.
Pleading adjourned. Ht 8/2/5
Bail $25,000 for each. Defts
Defts to submit to fingerprint
the usual requirements that
be necessary for identification
a condition of bail.
T. Hay

AUG -2 1950
Both defendants plead not gu
motions to be made by 9-1-50
Motion to reduce bail as to bo
motion denied.
T. Hay

47

Saypol sought to have Brothman and Moskowitz put in jail immediately at the start of the trial. William Kleinman, counsel for the defense, protested.

Mr. Kleinman: But there is no reason why your Honor should even feel that it is necessary for the orderly process of this case to commit them. There is $25,000 bail for each defendant.

Judge Kaufman: We have a policy in this court, regardless of what type case it is, that it is wise upon the commencement of a trial to remand defendants...Aside from any application by the Government, purely on the motion of the Court itself, I would remand the defendants.

Mr. Kleinman: But the case has not yet started. Won't you wait until the case starts?

Judge Kaufman: This case has started...

On Friday, November 10, Judge Kaufman set out the legal basis for the trial:

There are two laws involved in this case. One of them...states in part, and I will read only that part which is relevant to this case that, whoever corruptly or by threats or force or by any threatening letter or communication shall endeavor to influence, intimidate or impede any party or witness in any court of the United States, or who corruptly or by threats or force or by any threatening letter or communication shall influence, obstruct or impede or endeavor to influence, obstruct or impede the due administration of justice therein, is guilty of a crime...

Another section of the Criminal Code states that it is a crime if two or more persons conspire to violate

48

the statute that I have just read to you, and if one or more of such persons does any act to effect the objects of the conspiracy...

For the prosecution Saypol stated to the jury on November 13:

This is not a contest between opposing lawyers. This is a trial of issues arising out of charges that the defendants deliberately, corruptly, sabotaged an investigation conducted by a grand jury of this court so that it was misled and misdirected, and thrown off its proper course and thereby the true administration of justice was defeated. I am fully confident of your verdict that these defendants are guilty after you shall have heard the evidence...

For the defense Kleinman told the jurors:

It is our contention that there was no corrupt agreement between Brothman and Gold to have their testimony conform; indeed, I think we shall be able to show to your satisfaction that in salient points their testimony did not conform, that there was no agreement—there was no corrupt agreement, to impede the investigation then being conducted by the grand jury...

Kleinman then addressed Judge Kaufman:

Your Honor, I move for the exclusion of all witnesses during the trial and during the taking of testimony.
Mr. Saypol: That is acceptable except the usual formula, that agents of the Federal Bureau of Investigation may remain.

Judge Kaufman ruled in favor of Saypol. Thus, for no acceptable reason, FBI agents, who were witnesses like anyone else, subject to the same rules governing all witnesses, were permitted to remain in court, and hence could make sure that their testimony was consistent.

Irving Saypol then called Donald E. Shannon to the witness stand.

FBI AGENT DONALD SHANNON

Mr. Saypol: What is your occupation, please, Mr. Shannon?

A. Special Agent, Federal Bureau of Investigation...

Mr. Saypol: Now, Mr. Shannon, on May 29, 1947, were you engaged in your official duties as a Special Agent in the Federal Bureau of Investigation?

A. That is correct, I was...

Mr. Saypol: Will you tell us where you were?

A. I was out at the offices of A. Brothman Associates, in the Chatham-Phoenix Building in Long Island City, 41st Avenue...

Mr. Saypol: At about what time did you arrive at those offices, Mr. Shannon?

*A. At about 11:15*A.M. in the morning.

Mr. Saypol: Were you alone?

A. No, I was accompanied by Special Agent Francis D. O'Brien...We waited at the office, and approximately half an hour later Mr. Brothman came into the office. We introduced ourselves to him. We exhibited our credentials...and at the very outset of the interview, we exhibited to him a photograph...

Mr. Saypol: That is a photograph of Jacob Golos?

A. We asked him to look at the photograph and to advise us, to tell us, if he knew the party whose picture we had shown him.

Mr. Saypol: What did he say or do?

A. He looked at the photograph a short time...He turned the photograph back to us and he said, "no, I don't know that man." We asked him to look again, to look carefully at the photograph. He did. He turned it back and he said, "No, I don't know that man."

We then asked him if he ever heard of a man by

the name of Jacob Golos. He said the name meant nothing to him. At that point we showed him another photograph...

Mr. Saypol: Did Brothman examine the photograph?

A. Yes, he looked at the photograph. We asked him if he knew the party whose picture we had shown to him at this time. He said yes, he did know the party...

He then told us he did know the party whose picture we had first shown to him. I asked him who he was. He said he couldn't remember the name, but he knew the party...I then asked him why he had told us in the first place that he didn't know this party. He stated that he thought when we showed him the picture and we said we were investigating a violation of the United States and that espionage was involved, that this party perhaps had some connection with a Russian spy ring and that for that reason he didn't want to be involved...He said when we showed him the other photograph of Elizabeth Bentley that he realized then that perhaps we knew the story, and at that time he told us he did know both people...

Mr. Saypol: Did you have any further conversation in the course of your interview about his connection with Elizabeth Bentley and with Golos, whose picture he had identified, but whose name he was still unable to furnish?

A. Yes, we asked him how he met this party Golos...He stated that this party Golos had come into his office sometime in 1938 or 1939 and that he advised him, Brothman, that he had some connections with the Russian Government and that he thought that perhaps he could get some business for Brothman with the Russian Government...

He stated that subsequently after this meeting with

Golos, also in 1938 or 1939, Helen, [the name by which Brothman knew Elizabeth Bentley,] whose picture he identified, came to his office and advised him that she represented Golos. He stated that he turned over blueprints in his office to this party Helen...

We then asked him if anybody else ever came up to his office and represented Golos or Helen and to whom he might have turned over blueprints. He said, yes, there was another party that came after Helen had stopped seeing him. He identified this person as a Harry Gold. We asked him where Harry Gold was at that time when we were interviewing him...

He stated Harry Gold was employed as a chemist by him, by A. Brothman Associates, and that he was presently in the laboratory in Long Island City...

We asked him when Harry Gold came to his office. To the best of his knowledge, he said, it was around 1940, subsequent to the time that Helen had come up to the office...He stated that in the course of his coming to the office, he turned over blueprints to him...

Brothman told the FBI that he gave blueprints to Harry Gold after he had given blueprints to Jacob Golos and Elizabeth Bentley. He supplied the FBI agents with Harry Gold's name and where he could be located. If the FBI were looking for spies, Brothman told them who they might possibly be. He candidly explained why he was at first reluctant to identify Golos and why he then corrected himself almost immediately.

FBI agent Shannon asked Brothman to sign a statement that summarized the interview, which Brothman did. Special Agent Francis D. O'Brien was with Shannon at the time. The statement, dated May

29, 1947, was read to the court.

The questioning resumed. This time Roy Cohn, the precocious assistant prosecutor, whose life and career were associated with infamy and scandal, appeared for the government.

Mr. Cohn: In the course of your interview, Mr. Shannon, did you have any conversation with Brothman concerning any affiliation at any time by Brothman with the Communist Party?...

Mr. Kleinman: I object to that. I submit it is irrelevant and immaterial and not within the issues of this indictment.

Mr. Cohn: Your Honor, the Government submits that affiliation with the Communist Party on the part of both defendants in this case is the motive for the crime here charged and on the basis of the well-established law concerning our right to prove motive, with the Court's permission, I intend to offer testimony along those lines.

Mr. Kleinman: I say it is too inflammatory, too prejudicial. It is not relevant to this issue.

Judge Kaufman: Your objection is overruled...

Mr. Cohn: Did you question Brothman concerning any affiliation he ever had with the Communist Party?

A. Yes, we did.

Mr. Cohn: What did he say to you?

A. We asked Mr. Brothman if he was a member of the Communist Party at that time.

Mr. Cohn: What did he say?

A. He said he wasn't. We asked him if he belonged at any time to the Communist Party or any organizations similar to the Communist Party. He stated that he did belong sometime in the early 30s to the Young Communist League while he was, I believe, a student at Columbia University...

Mr. Cohn: Now, did you do anything else in the course of your official duties on that day, May 29, 1947?

A. Yes, we went out to the laboratory of Abe Brothman, to the address he gave us out in Elmhurst...

Mr. Cohn: Now, what happened after this man...came forward and told you that he was Harry Gold?

A. Agent O'Brien and myself exhibited our credentials to him and told him that we were Special Agents of the Federal Bureau of Investigation; that we were conducting an official investigation and desired to speak with him...

The prosecution spared no effort to make it appear that the FBI never heard of Harry Gold until he was called to their attention on May 29, 1947, by Abraham Brothman. Every means was utilized to conceal Gold's relationship with the FBI. But isn't it odd that only two months after Gold began working fulltime for Brothman in mid 1946, and a year before the FBI agents met Brothman for the first time, they were able to covertly enter Brothman's office? An FBI report dated July 27, 1946 and signed by Special Agent Francis D. O'Brien, the same FBI agent who, along with Special Agent Donald Shannon, visited Harry Gold read:

> *Since the inception of this case, a technical surveillance has been maintained on Brothman at his place of business...*
> *It is believed that an examination of the material in Brothman's office will determine exactly what type of work he is doing and for whom he is doing it. A confidential source is available at the premises at 114 East 32*

55

Street, and this source has been previously developed and used by Agents of this office.

Abraham Brothman had been under constant surveillance by the FBI since November 1945. He was watched at work and at home. His mail was read since 1945. His telephones were tapped since 1946. How could Agents O'Brien and Shannon not have known of the Gold's existence until May 1947? After all, Gold visited and spoke to Brothman frequently in 1945 and on a daily basis from mid-1946 when he began working for him.

Although the FBI made extreme efforts to pretend that Harry Gold was unknown to them, the trail of evidence is there. Again and again, it leads directly to Gold; the FBI agents had to know him.

Agent Shannon continued:

At the outset of the interview [with Gold], we exhibited to him a photograph of Jacob Golos.

Mr. Cohn: The same photograph you displayed to Brothman?

A. The same photograph of Jacob Golos we had shown to Brothman that morning. He looked at the photograph for several seconds, maybe sixty seconds, maybe one hundred seconds, and said, yes, he could recognize that photograph. It wasn't too clear but he was able to recognize it, and I asked him who it was.

He said, "That is John Golish or Gulish."

I asked him where he met this person, and he said he met him sometime in 1940...at a meeting of the American Chemical Society in Philadelphia...Gulish or Golish, gave him a telephone number at which he could contact Abe Brothman in New York City...and about two weeks later, he said, he put a phone call through to Brothman in New York City and made arrangements to meet Brothman.

He said that the meeting took place some time after this telephone call which, to the best of his recollection, was in November of 1940...he said that on this occasion...Brothman turned over some blueprints to him...

Gold's statement summarizing this interview was read to the court, and Brothman's attorney, William Kleinman, then cross-examined Special Agent Shannon.

Mr. Kleinman: Mr. Shannon...In May, 1947, when you showed the picture of this Golos to Mr. Brothman, did you know whether he was alive or dead?

A. I did.

Mr. Kleinman: What was he?

A. He was dead.

Mr. Kleinman: When you showed the picture of Elizabeth Bentley, who was recognized by Mr. Brothman as Helen, you knew something about her, didn't you?

A. I did.

Mr. Kleinman: She had been under investigation, had she not?

A. I didn't know that she was under investigation.

Mr. Kleinman: You know that this man Golos had been under investigation? Just yes or no.

A. I really didn't know whether he was under investigation...

Mr. Kleinman: Now, at the time that you first saw Mr. Brothman, can you tell us whether or not Miss Elizabeth Bentley had made any statements to the FBI or given any evidence to any agency of the Government?

Mr. Saypol: That is objected to as improper cross and is irrelevant...
Judge Kaufman: I will sustain that objection...

John Foley, another government prosecutor, then questioned Mrs. Adelaide E. Lowe, the secretary to the grand jury that heard Brothman and Gold's testimony in July 1947.

1947 GRAND JURY

Mr. Foley: Mrs. Lowe, were you a member of the Federal Grand Jury that was convened on June 17, 1947?

A. I was...

Mr. Foley: And would you tell us on what date Mr. Brothman testified before the grand jury?

A. Mr. Brothman testified before us on the 22nd day of July, 1947...

Mr. Foley: Mrs. Lowe, did a Mr. Gold, Harry Gold, testify before the grand jury?

A. He did.

Mr. Foley: On what date did he testify?

A. Harry Gold testified before us on the 31st day of July, 1947...

Mr. Foley: Mrs. Lowe, what was the grand jury concerned with or directing its efforts towards at the time when Mr. Brothman and Mr. Gold testified before the grand jury?

A. We were investigating acts of espionage...

Mr. Kleinman: I have no questions of Mrs. Lowe.

Judge Kaufman: Very well. You are excused.

Saypol began to read the 1947 grand jury minutes.

Abraham Brothman, called as a witness, having first been duly sworn by the foreman, testified as follows...

Q. Mr. Brothman, you were interviewed May 29, 1947, by Special Agents of the Federal Bureau of Investigation; is that correct?

A. Yes.

Q. And did you furnish those Special Agents Shannon and O'Brien with a signed statement?

A. Yes...

Q. I show you Grand Jury Exhibit No. 6, and ask you...Is that the photograph that was exhibited to you by Special Agents of the Federal Bureau of Investigation?

A. Yes.

Q. And you identified him as the man that contacted you?

A. That's right.

Q. And that is Jacob Golos?

A. Yes.

Q. Now, can you tell the grand jury about what date you first met him?

A. Well, as I have recollected the thing, I believe it was about the early part of 1940, the very early part of 1940...

Q. What commission did he say he was attached to and from which he had been dismissed at the time that you met him?

A. As I recall, he said he was attached to the government purchasing commission.

Q. Which government?

A. The Russian Government Purchasing Commission...

Q. How did you happen to employ Gold?

A. Gold had been working for the Penn Sugar Company...When he could no longer work there...I offered him a job in my place because I thought he was a very good man, and he has worked out to be such...

Q. But your original contact with Gold was through Golos and Helen?

A. That's how I originally met him...

This statement made by Brothman that he met Gold through Golos and Bentley was the crux of the government's charges that Brothman committed perjury and obstructed justice.

Mr. Saypol: I desire now, your Honor, to read the testimony of Harry Gold, a co-conspirator, before the same grand jury...

Mr. Kleinman: Do I understand, Mr. Saypol, that

you are about to read Harry Gold's testimony?
  Mr. Saypol: That is right...

Saypol then read the grand jury minutes containing Gold's 1947 testimony.

> *Harry Gold, called as a witness, having first been duly sworn by the foreman, testified as follows:...*
> *Q. I show you a picture, Grand Jury Exhibit 6, and I ask you if you recognize the person appearing on that photograph?*
> *A. Yes, I do.*
> *Q. Under what name did you know this individual?*
> *A. I knew this man under the name John Golush...I was introduced to Golos by Carter Hoodless...*
> *Q. Did he mention that he had connections with a foreign country?*
> *A. No, he didn't.*

Gold said Golos never mentioned any connection with the Russians. Brothman said Gold had connection with the Russians. Gold's testimony often contradicted Brothman's in ways that drew suspicion to Gold rather than Brothman. The reading of Gold's testimony before the grand jury continued:

> *Q. All right, go ahead. Then you met Brothman?*
> *A. Then I met Brothman...*
> *Q. When you talked with Brothman, did you tell him who you were?*
> *A. Yes, I told him who I was.*
> *Q. What did you say to him?*
> *A. I told him that I had met Mr. Golos and that Mr. Golos had wanted me to come up to go over these various processes...*
> *Q. How long have you been employed by Mr. Brothman now?*

A. I have been employed by Mr. Brothman since May of 1946...

Q. Do you hold any office in his corporation?

A. I am the Chief Chemist, and I am due to be made a partner in the firm shortly.

Q. Are you a member of the Communist Party?

A. No.

Q. Do you consciously belong to any Communist-front organizations?

A. I wouldn't know what a Communist-front organization is. No, I would never belong to anything like that.

Q. You are not married?

A. I am single...

Q. You said on the first two trips Brothman gave you some material to turn over to Golos.

A. That's right.

Q. You did not turn that material over to Mr. Golos?

A. No; I never saw him again...

Q. You took those blueprints back to Philadelphia?

A. That's right...

Mr. Donegan: Did Mr. Brothman tell you the questions he was asked before the grand jury and what his answers were?

The Witness: No. He just told me that they would go into my background, my training and so forth, and that they would go into any connection that I had with John Golos...

The reading of Brothman and Gold's 1947 testimony to the grand jury seemed innocent enough. How could Brothman's lawyers know that Thomas J. Donegan, the U.S. attorney who questioned them, was personally involved with another government witness called before that same grand jury—Elizabeth Bentley?

But in 1950, after Irving Saypol decided to prosecute Brothman and Moskowitz and advised his staff that Elizabeth Bentley would be one of his witnesses, he admitted he had learned that one of his assistants, Thomas J. Donegan, had known Elizabeth Bentley for years and had represented her in a civil action back in 1947. Saypol conceded that this fact, if known to the defense, could embarrass the government. But the FBI noted that nevertheless, "Saypol seemed to be determined that Mr. Donegan take part" in the scheduled trial. The dishonest and malevolent participation of the U.S. Attorney's Office was evident throughout their connection with the case.

The civil suit in which Thomas Donegan, although he was an assistant U.S. Attorney, privately represented Elizabeth Bentley was against U.S. Service and Shipping Corporation. This was a company that Bentley had once run, which was being investigated for Communist-inspired activities. Bentley, who was serving as a government witness in 1947, sued for back pay. According to an FBI memo, she threatened that "she would probably be of no further use to the Government unless this matter was resolved promptly and to her satisfaction." The case was settled on June 5, 1947, to Bentley's satisfaction. In the years that followed, Bentley demanded and often received cash payments from the FBI and U.S. government for her testimony. While several of the FBI agents refused to be intimidated by her and, as we shall see later, recommended that she not be paid for her testimony, finding her unreliable and mentally unbalanced as well, U.S. Attorneys Irving Saypol, Roy Cohn, and Thomas Donegan catered to her whims.

After Harry Gold's grand jury testimony of July 31, 1947, had been read in its entirety, Elizabeth Bentley was called to the stand.

ELIZABETH BENTLEY

Elizabeth T. Bentley, called as a witness on behalf of the Government, being first duly sworn, testified as follows:

Mr. Saypol: Were you ever a member of the Communist Party?

A. Yes, I was.

Mr. Saypol: When did you join the Communist Party?

A. About the middle of March, 1935...

Mr. Saypol: Will you tell us the circumstances under which you met Mr. Brothman first, and when?

A. Yes, in the spring of 1940, after a conversation with Mr. Golos, I met Mr. Brothman at a Chinese restaurant which is on 53rd Street...We had a meal there and after that we had a long discussion.

Mr. Saypol: Before you had the meal, was there an introduction all around?

A. Yes, Mr. Golos introduced Mr. Brothman as Abe Brothman, and he introduced me as Helen.

Mr. Saypol: Now go on and tell us, the introductions having been effected, the dinner having been had, what was the conversation amongst the three of you?

A. Mr. Golos explained to Mr. Brothman that it would be rather difficult for him in the future to see him each week or each two weeks, and that therefore I would take his place in order to bring him directives from the Communist Party, to collect his Communist Party dues and to collect any material that he had to be relayed to Mr. Golos...

Mr. Saypol: In respect to the payment of dues to

which you have testified, did Mr. Brothman pay Communist Party dues to you?

Mr. Kleinman: I object to this, if your Honor please, as not relevant to the issues and as incompetent and immaterial.

Judge Kaufman: I overrule you on that. I thought yesterday I made my position clear, that on the question of motive, they will be relevant...

A. Yes, Mr. Brothman did pay Communist Party dues to me.

Mr. Saypol: How long did these meetings continue from the time of the first meeting in the spring of 1940?

A. Until the early fall of 1941...

Mr. Saypol: Remember if you will the end period of your meetings with Mr. Brothman. Can you recall any particular matters which were discussed between you?

A. Yes, there were a number of matters discussed between us. Perhaps the most important was that Mr. Brothman was dissatisfied with dealing with Mr. Golos and myself. He felt that neither of us were engineers or had any technical background, and that we did not understand his explanations as to the blueprints. He began to ask if we couldn't put him in touch with an engineer with whom he could talk them over...

Mr. Saypol: Thereafter, did you have anything to say to Mr. Brothman about that?

A. Yes, not too long after that I told Mr. Brothman that it had been decided that he would be turned over to a new contact. He objected...I then asked Mr. Brothman to give me the license number of his car so that that license number could be turned over via Mr. Golos to the new contact. Mr. Brothman objected again. He said he did not understand why he had to meet people via that odd way, why couldn't I or Mr. Golos do the introducing? I explained to him again that this was a decision of the Communist Party and he must abide by it. He ended by agreeing, and I wrote down his license number which I passed on to Mr. Golos...

Mr. Saypol: Did you know the person who was to be the new contact?

A. No...

Mr. Saypol: Did you ever know a man named Harry Gold?

A. No.

Mr. Saypol: Around this period of time that you have described, in 1940 and 1941, had you ever heard of the name Harry Gold?

A. No, I had never heard of Harry Gold...

Mr. Kleinman: Did you testify before a Congressional Committee in July of 1948?

A. I think it was the last day of July that I started testifying. I am not entirely certain whether it was the 1st of August or the 31st of July...

Mr. Kleinman: When did you first testify before a grand jury?

A. In June 1947...

Mr. Kleinman: At that time, in June of 1947, were you asked questions concerning Harry Gold?

Mr. Saypol: That is objected to, if the Court please. That is within the confines of the grand jury, and I do not think counsel has a right to go into that...

Saypol's interjection at this point demonstrated his knowing participation in a fraudulent indictment. Saypol had introduced portions of the grand jury minutes to support his indictments, which hinged to a substantial degree on Bentley's claim that she did not know Harry Gold. Whether or not she testified before the 1947 grand jury that she knew Gold was of critical importance. Had she said she did, the indictments of Brothman and Moskowitz would almost certainly have been dismissed. Saypol's choice to withhold Bentley's grand jury testimony concerning her connection with Gold demonstrated a fraudulent intent that was endorsed by Judge Kaufman.

Judge Kaufman: I do not quite see the relevancy.

Mr. Kleinman: Do you want me to make it clear?...She has denied here on direct examination that she knew Harry Gold or that she ever saw him. I want to find out if there is any conflict between the position she took in 1947 and the one which she is stating now. I think that I would have a right...

Mr. Saypol: I do not think it is at all material...

Mr. Kleinman: I want to find out if she testified about Brothman on any of those occasions and, if so, if there is any inconsistency between her testimony before the grand jury and her testimony in this court...

A. Your Honor, I can't answer that by yes or no...I can only tell you that I don't remember...

Mr. Kleinman: But sometime in 1950, did you testify before a Federal grand jury in this building?

A. Yes, I did.

Mr. Kleinman: At that time, were you asked questions concerning one Harry Gold?

A. I think I was; I can't recall.

Mr. Kleinman: Well, at that time, the name Harry Gold did have some significance to you, did it not?

A. Well, very vaguely, Mr. Kleinman...

Mr. Kleinman: You mean it was not reported in the

newspaper that a man had been arrested for spy activities in May of this year?

A. Very vaguely; I paid little attention to it...

But an FBI memo dated March 9, 1950, conclusively disputed Bentley's testimony. The memo confirmed that Bentley, who was a confidential informant identified by the FBI as Gregory, knew Gold and knew about his relationship with Golos. Prepared by Special Agent John R. Murphy, Jr., the memo stated: "Gold, according to confidential informant Gregory, acted on behalf of Jacob Golos, known Soviet agent now deceased, in 1940 and 1941, in picking up blueprints from Abraham Brothman."

The memo showed that Bentley knew Gold all along, and it provided confirmation of the Golos-Gold connection. It also established that Elizabeth Bentley, while working under her alias, confidential informant Gregory, told the FBI that Gold acted in behalf of Golos. It proved that Bentley, who claimed that she never knew Harry Gold, was the government's primary source for determining that Gold acted in behalf of Golos. It proved that Bentley committed perjury during the Brothman-Moskowitz trial when she testified in November 1950 that she never met Gold and only vaguely heard of him, when months before in March of the same year she provided the FBI with extensive material concerning Gold's relationship with Jacob Golos, the very relationship that Brothman was charged with having falsely described.

ELIZABETH BENTLEY

Identity of Source	Date of Activity And/or Description of Information	Date Received	Agent to whom Furnished	File Number where Located
Confidential Informant Gregory	1940,1941,1946			

THE FOLLOWING INFORMATION IS NOT TO BE DISSEMINATED TO ANY
OUTSIDE AGENCY WITHOUT THE AUTHORIZATION OF SECT. b
AND IS NOT TO BE MADE A PART OF ANY CORRESPONDENCE IN ANY
OTHER FILE WITHOUT AUTHORIZATION OF SECT. b

The following excerpts were taken from NY rpt.
3/9/50 of SA J.R. Murphy, Jr.:

"HARRY GOLD

"GOLD was born December 12, 1910, in Switzerland.

"Employment

"In February, 1946, he began work for A. Brothman
and Associates, 85-03 57th Avenue, Elmhurst. During unknown
periods, GOLD worked for the Holbrook Manufacturing Company,
Jersey City, and the Moormeir Dairy Company, Cincinnati.

"GOLD, according to Confidential Informant Gregory,
acted on behalf of JACOB GOLOS, known Soviet Agent now deceased,
in 1940 and 1941 in picking up blue prints from ABRAHAM BROTHMAN.
GOLD admits he did this in 1940 and 1941, making trips to
Philadelphia and New York to see BROTHMAN for this purpose.
GOLD stated that it was on GOLOS' instruction that he, GOLD,
evaluated these blue prints before turning them over to GOLOS.
It is GOLD'S contention, however, that GOLOS showed no interest
in these blue prints."

NY rpt. SA John R. Murphy, Jr
3/9/50, entitled: EMIL JULIUS
KLAUS FUCHS, was
ESP-R
65-15136-394, p73,74

69

The FBI kept this document of critical importance away from Abraham Brothman and Miriam Moskowitz. Hence they were prevented from proving they were framed and establishing their innocence.

The cross-examination of Elizabeth Bentley continued.

Mr. Kleinman: Did you go along to introduce this new contact to Mr. Brothman?

A. No.

Mr. Kleinman: Do you know if Mr. Golos went along to introduce this new contact to Mr. Brothman?

A. Mr. Golos told me he didn't.

Mr. Kleinman: You never saw that contact, did you?

A. No.

Mr. Kleinman: You never asked who he was?

A. No...

Mr. Kleinman: Did you not say in your testimony before the committee that, after Golos's death, you met a great many Russians, and that was the thing that decided you that you did not want to be a Communist?

A. I don't know what I said in the testimony. I can tell you exactly how many Russians I met since Mr. Golos's death...

Mr. Kleinman: Were they, in fact, Russians?

A. That I don't know. One was definitely Russian. One I think was Lithuanian. The other, I don't know...

Mr. Kleinman: And because of the conduct of these Soviet agents, you decided not to remain a Communist?

A. That is correct. Since one of them was the head of the Russian secret police in this country, it was a foregone conclusion that his behavior represent-

ed the sentiments of the rest of them...

Mr. Kleinman: As soon as you quit, did you go to the FBI?

A. No, it took me some months to make up my mind what I should do...

Mr. Kleinman: Did you tell the grand jury all that you have testified to here concerning Brothman, just yes or no.

A. Are you referring to the first grand jury, the second or the third, Mr. Kleinman?

Mr. Kleinman: Well, please help me out. I do not know. How about the first one? Let us take it that way. Did you tell them—

A. I can't recall whether I was asked questions about Mr. Brothman...

Mr. Kleinman: How about the second grand jury?

A. I can't recall either of those two grand juries asking me about Mr. Brothman. They may well have, but I don't recall...

Mr. Kleinman: Search your memory, please. I would like to find out whether you were asked anything about Brothman by that grand jury or before that grand jury.

A. I am sorry, Mr. Kleinman, I don't remember. I was asked about too many people.

Mr. Kleinman: Can you tell us whether or not you testified concerning Brothman before the 1947 grand jury?

A. No, I cannot tell you...

Mr. Kleinman: I make the request to make available to me, or to have your Honor read in order to determine whether the minutes should be made available to me, the grand jury testimony of Miss Bentley in 1947 and in 1950.

Judge Kaufman: On what ground?

Mr. Kleinman: On the ground that there may be matters there which are inconsistent with her present testimony, and which should be made available to me for the purpose of cross-examination.

Judge Kaufman: That may be present in every case that is tried here. You have to make some showing before me, as I understand the rule, that there is something inconsistent.

Mr. Kleinman: Well, with a witness who denies any recollection of what she said, there never can be an occasion for showing any inconsistency, but I think it is the duty of the Court, and I respectfully urge it...

Judge Kaufman: There is an obligation on the Court to read these minutes when there has been something that has occurred during the course of the case or during the course of the testimony of a particular witness to indicate that before the grand jury the witness said something which was inconsistent with what the witness is testifying to today...And to ask this Court to sit down and go through that testimony and for this Court in effect to be your counsel and determine wherein she was inconsistent with her present testimony, I do not think that is an obligation which should be...

Kaufman prevented Brothman's lawyer from being able to show Bentley's inconsistent statements. Merely by saying she did not "recall" what she had previously said, her testimony, with Judge Kaufman's help, was unimpeachable. Judge Kaufman would not allow Kleinman to view the testimony she previously provided to grand juries. Kaufman's ruling in effect rewarded Bentley for her evasiveness and dishonesty, since no matter what she said, or claimed she did not recall, it could not be disputed or challenged.

Mr. Kleinman: I do not want to burden the Court...but we have the most unusual condition with this witness. She has refused to give me any definite recollection of anything that she has said or what was said to her before the grand jury or before the Congressional committees...She puts it as being due to lack of memory.

Judge Kaufman: She says that she has testified before so many bodies, grand juries and investigative committees, that she cannot remember what she told any particular body.

Mr. Kleinman: And, therefore, I think that it is our duty today now to determine whether she did tell the grand jury anything about Brothman in 1947...

Judge Kaufman: I have allowed you a wide latitude, but you have not shown anything inconsistent or even anything that comes close to being inconsistent. Even if she did or she did not tell anything about Brothman in 1947, it has not been established that what she has testified to here was inconsistent with what she testified to before the grand jury.

Mr. Kleinman: She testified, you remember...She said that she told the FBI about Brothman in 1945 or 1946, but she cannot tell us whether she testified before the 1947 grand jury about Brothman.

Judge Kaufman: Your request might very well be for the FBI statements...I will not permit you to examine the grand jury minutes nor do I see any necessity for me to examine them, in the absence of any showing before me that there is anything inconsistent.

Mr. Kleinman: I take exception to your Honor's ruling...Now my next request, which your Honor has already anticipated, is that I ask to have...available to

me the records of what the witness Bentley told to
the FBI as to the defendant Brothman.

Judge Kaufman: Of course that request indicates to
me just how absolutely baseless is your former request
for the grand jury minutes, and for the same reason I
deny that request.

Judge Kaufman's actions were unparalleled. After
he teasingly recommended the FBI statements as a
possible means of showing Bentley's inconsistent testimony, he denied the request of Brothman's lawyer for
them. Bentley's statements, no matter how false or
contradictory they may have been, were suppressed by
the judge to protect Elizabeth Bentley from exposure
as the dishonest witness she was.

HARRY GOLD

Harry Gold took the witness stand and was questioned by U.S. Attorney Saypol. After Saypol established that a notation on a white card in Gold's handwriting that was found in the cellar of his home was competent evidence to support Gold's oral testimony that he met Brothman for the first time on September 29, 1941, Saypol asked Gold to describe that meeting.

A. Brothman made inquiries of me. Abe asked me about the Soviet agent who had preceded me, and whom he identified as a woman called Helen. He also asked about the welfare of the Soviet agent who had come before Helen...

Mr. Saypol: When he mentioned Helen and John, had you ever met either of them?

A. I never met Helen or John...

But if Gold came as a replacement for Helen, it was reasonable for Brothman to assume that Gold knew Helen and John, who was actually Elizabeth Bentley and Jacob Golos. After all, even at the trial Gold did not dispel the impression he gave Brothman that he was sent to him by them.

Mr. Saypol: Did you say anything at that time to Abe about your personal, your marital status?

A. I told Abe that I was married, and had a wife and two children, twins.

Mr. Saypol: Was that true?

A. That was a lie...

Judge Kaufman: On your meetings with Abe, did

you ever say anything to Abe about your Soviet superior?...

The Witness: I told Abe I had a Soviet superior. I did not identify him by name. I only indicated I acted under orders from this Soviet agent...

Mr. Saypol: At a meeting with Brothman in December, you had a conversation with him?...

A. I had a talk with Abe sometime around the middle of December of 1941.

Mr. Saypol: What did you say and what did he say?

A. I told Abe that in order to facilitate and expedite the transfer of information to the Soviet Union, that I had effected arrangements through my Soviet superior...

Mr. Saypol: Let me interrupt for just a moment. You have used that phrase "Soviet superior." At that time, were you mentioning the name Sam to him or were you referring to him as your Soviet superior?

A. I never mentioned the name Sam to Abe...

Judge Kaufman: I must ask you Mr. Saypol, at this point, to address your questions to the witness in such a way that he does not testify to what Sam said to him or what he said to Sam until I am convinced that there has been a meeting between Sam and the defendant Brothman...

Kaufman was instructing Saypol on how to question Gold. He wanted Saypol to show that a meeting took place between Sam and Brothman. To reach this end, the judge not only suggested the questions he wanted Saypol to ask of Gold, but advised Gold of the answers he expected to receive from him.

Judge Kaufman: He can say "I went to Sam. I saw

him at such a time."

Mr. Saypol: That is exactly what I am going to do now.

Judge Kaufman: And after he saw Sam, he saw Brothman. I don't want details...

Kaufman's statement that he "didn't want details" was camouflage language to cover the detailed instructions he had given Saypol to present testimony that Gold first saw Sam before he saw Brothman.

Mr. Saypol: Thereafter, when did you see Brothman next?

A. I saw Abe again sometime between Christmas and New Year's of 1941...

Kaufman was still not satisfied with Saypol's efforts in establishing the proper sequence in the interrelationship of Gold, Brothman, and Sam. The judge impatiently questioned Gold for Saypol, interjecting the answer concerning Sam that he insisted on receiving from him.

Judge Kaufman: After you met Sam, what did you tell Mr. Brothman?...

A. I told Abe that a report giving great praise to the Buna-S work had been received.

Kaufman: Did you tell Mr. Brothman who gave you that report?

A. Yes, I did.

Kaufman: And who did you say gave it to you?

A. I said it was my Soviet superior...

Mr. Saypol: Do you remember the occasion of a meeting with Brothman at which you received a report on mixers?

A. Yes, I do.

Mr. Saypol: When did it take place?

A. Sometime in November of 1942...

Mr. Saypol: As the result of the conversation which you had with Sam, and following the conversation with Sam, did you then have a meeting or a conversation with Brothman?

A. I had a meeting with Abe following my talk with Sam, and I told Abe that a very important Soviet dignitary, a Russian official, was soon coming to this country, that he was making a special trip here for the explicit purpose of meeting with Abe and talking to him...

Mr. Saypol: Subsequent to that talk with Abe, did you arrange a meeting?

A. I did.

Mr. Saypol: Where did the meeting take place?

A. It took place in the Lincoln Hotel, 45th Street and Eighth Avenue. The time was sometime in December of 1942...

Mr. Saypol: What time did he arrive?

A. Well, after we had been in the room for about 20 minutes, there came a knock at the door and I opened it to admit Sam...

Mr. Saypol: Under what name did you introduce him to Abe?

A. I told Abe that this man was George—just George, that's all...

Judge Kaufman: Let me ask you something: Was George introduced as your Soviet superior or as the man that was coming from Russia that you had told Abe was coming from Russia?

The Witness: I introduced George as a Soviet dignitary who had come over especially from Russia...

How could Brothman know or be expected to know that Gold was referred to him by a Sam, a Soviet superior on September 29, 1941—when in December of 1942, Brothman did not even know a Sam even existed, and for the first time met a so-called agent code-named George who, according to Gold, was really Sam? The government testimony connecting Brothman with Sam Semenov was not remotely credible.

Mr. Saypol: Now, do you remember the 29th of May, 1947?

A. I don't remember the 29th of May, but I remember an occasion a day or so prior to Memorial Day of 1947.

Mr. Saypol: Do you recall on that day at about three o'clock where you were?

A. A little before three I was in the Elmhurst laboratory...

Mr. Saypol: Tell us what happened that day at that time?...

A. I went to Queens Plaza...and went up to the Brothman offices...that was a routine procedure with me...

Mr. Saypol: What happened when you got into the office? Who did you see?

A. Abe came forward...

Mr. Saypol: What did he say?

A. He said, "Look, Harry, the FBI was just here. They know everything. They know all about me. They know that you were a courier. It must have been that bitch, Helen."

Mr. Saypol: What else did he say?

A. "They even have pictures of you and I together. You have got to tell some story to cover me up. They are coming to see you this afternoon. Did you know John?"...I replied that I did not know John. Abe then said, "You have got to tell the same story I did to cover me up."...He then launched into a description of a picture that he said had been shown him by the agents of the FBI...

Mr. Saypol: Did he describe to you what the person in that picture which had been shown to him—what that person looked like?

A. Abe told me that the picture was that of a man with a wizened face, a wry grin, a receding hairline and curly hair, what there was of it.

Mr. Saypol: What else did he say to you?

A. Abe told me to identify that picture as John Gollush. He told me to make up any story to conceal the true facts as to how we had actually met, and said that I should tell the FBI that I actually met him, Abe, through Gollush...

But according to Gold's own testimony, Brothman could not have known what Gold told the FBI. Whatever Gold said had to be different from what Brothman said. Any detail of how he was introduced by Golos to Brothman by definition had to differ from what Brothman said, since Brothman did not give Gold any details, he could not possibly know what Gold would say. "Tell some story to cover me up" had to be a story that differed from Brothman's.

Saypol then asked Harry Gold what time the FBI arrived at his laboratory.

A. Sometime after four o'clock, about four o'clock I would say, just about four. After I had been there about twenty minutes, two men entered. It was a large man and a smaller one. They looked around and they asked for Harry Gold. I came forward and said that I was Harry Gold. They said that they represented the United States Government. They wanted to talk to me...

The two agents, Shannon and O'Brien, showed me several pictures. Among those was one of a man with a wizened face, a wry grin, receding hairline and curly hair. They asked me whether I knew this man, just as they had asked me about the other pictures, whether I knew any of the others. I identified the man as John Gollush...

Conveniently, the FBI agents did not ask Gold about Golos's bright red hair, his blue eyes, or his short stature, nor did the Government claim that Brothman told Gold any of these physical details to prepare him for the FBI agents' visit.

Mr. Saypol: I show you Government's Exhibit 2 in evidence, Mr. Gold. Do you recall whether that was the picture that was shown to you by Agents Shannon and O'Brien (handing)? Is it a clear likeness?

A. This is a picture that I was shown.

Mr. Saypol: That is the man whom you had identified as John Golos or John Gollush, although you had never in fact seen him before?

A. I had never see him before. I have never seen him.

Mr. Saypol: All right, continue.

A. In the course of my talk with Agents Shannon and O'Brien, I told them a completely false story involving how I had allegedly met Abe through John Gollush...

Mr. Saypol: Was it true or false that you had first met Brothman in 1940, in October of 1940?

A. It was false.

Mr. Saypol: When actually did you first meet Brothman?

A. On the night of September 29, 1941...

There was no reason for Brothman to say he met Gold in 1940 rather than 1941. Nonetheless, every lie Gold told became Brothman's lie. But there was actually only one issue and one goal of the prosecution: to establish that Golos did not introduce Gold to Brothman so that Gold's relationship with Elizabeth Bentley and Jacob Golos could remain unexposed.

Judge Kaufman: Let me get back to something you just said, that so-called instructions or advice from Brothman was the only reason that you had for making those statements to the FBI.

A. That is correct.

Judge Kaufman: Don't you really have reference to the fact that the type story that you were telling, in fact, was dictated by Brothman?

The Witness: That is correct.

Judge Kaufman: As distinguished from the reasons so-called. I do not know whether you see my point, Mr. Saypol.

Mr. Saypol: Well, as I see it, Brothman told him to tell a false story that he had told, and directed him to conform his story with his.

Mr. Kleinman: Your Honor, I submit it is improper for these—

Judge Kaufman: Disregard that statement of Mr. Saypol's. Continue.

Kaufman pretended to be correcting Saypol when it was he who was reinforcing Saypol's questions and coaxing the jury to believe that Brothman had instructed Gold to lie before the grand jury.

Mr. Saypol: I merely tried to answer your Honor's query. I think I see it eye to eye with your Honor.

Judge Kaufman: Proceed...

Mr. Saypol: Did the defendants Moskowitz and Brothman arrive at the laboratory thereafter?

A. Yes they did...

Mr. Saypol: What was said?

A. The greater part of the conversation was between Abe and myself and we reassured each other—kept reassuring each other, that very likely the FBI did not know as much about us as we had at first feared...

Mr. Saypol: What was the subject of the conversation amongst the three of you; what did you talk about and what did you say?

A. First Abe asked me to tell him the story, what sort of story I had told to the agents. And I related in detail the completely fictitious story involving Carter Hoodless and the American Chemical Society and John Gollush.

Brothman's asking Gold what he had told the agents indicated that he had no idea beforehand what Gold would be saying to them. To create a conspiracy, Brothman, who had already testified, would have had to ask Gold to falsify his testimony to match his. They would have had to make plans, define objectives, and rehearse their testimony. This did not occur. Gold was free to say anything he wished. Furthermore, unless there was constraint of some kind by means of force or fear to testify falsely, conspiracy to commit perjury could not be charged. If anyone should have been in fear, it was Brothman. It was evident in the questions he asked Gold; Brothman was aware that Gold was a liar who could say anything.

Mr. Saypol: About that time, do you remember driving to Pennsylvania Station with Abe?

A. Yes, I do...I was going home to Philadelphia for the week-end...

Mr. Saypol: When did you return?

A. I returned a day or so later. It was, I think, the last day of the Memorial Day weekend...I went directly to Sunnyside to Abe's home...

Mr. Saypol: What did you and Brothman and his wife do, where did you go?

A. We went to Peekskill where Abe had a summer home at that time, some distance out of Peekskill, New York...

Mr. Saypol: Did you have some conversation with him that night about a visit that had been made to your home in Philadelphia?

A. I told Abe that while I had been home for the weekend, in fact shortly after I had arrived, I had been visited by two Philadelphia agents of the FBI. These men had made inquiries about any blueprints of the Hendrick Company which I had told agents Shannon and O'Brien might still possibly be in my possession, and the two men had conducted a very cursory search of the house. It wasn't even a search. They just asked about the blueprints and I took them around the house and said there weren't any. Abe was greatly concerned about this. He was critical of the fact that I had even admitted to the agents, Shannon and O'Brien, the fact that there might be blueprints, and also to the Philadelphia men that there was the possibility of such blueprints...

Part of the FBI memo describing that visit to Gold's Philadelphia home read:

> *On May 31, 1947, Special Agents William B. Welte and Fred C. Birkby contacted the home of Harry Gold, 6823 Kindred Street, Philadelphia...*
>
> *Harry Gold appeared cooperative and looked through his personal effects, which he stores at his parents' home, to determine whether any of the blueprints mentioned in referenced teletype were still in existence. He was unable to locate any such blueprints.*

Mr. Saypol: I want you to go back a period of some six weeks after that Declaration Day weekend. Do you recall some incidents one night when you were coming toward New York from Elmhurst, or when you were coming from New York to Elmhurst, either way?

A. When I entered the firm's offices, Abe told me that he had that day received a subpoena from a federal grand jury sitting in New York to appear and testify before them...

Mr. Saypol: Do you recall a conversation sometime after that, perhaps a day or two, with Miss Moskowitz concerning this subject?

A. Yes.

Mr. Saypol: What was the conversation?

A. Miriam told me that she was concerned because, at that time, Abe had stated that he had considered changing the story he had originally told to the agents of the FBI; that is, considered changing it when he would tell it to the grand jury. And she said that she was going to try and get him to stick to the original story...

Mr. Saypol: Sometime thereafter...did you and

Moskowitz and Brothman meet for dinner again?

A. Yes, we did...

Mr. Saypol: Did Moskowitz say anything?...

A. Miriam told me that she and Gibby Needleman together had succeeded in persuading Abe from his desire to—which she had told me about several days before—to change the original story which he had given the agents of the FBI, and that between the two of them, with mostly Gibby being effective, that Abe had been persuaded to tell the same identical story he had previously given just before Memorial Day of 1947.

If Gibby Needleman, a lawyer whom Brothman, Moskowitz, and Gold consulted, did what Gold said he did, it was perplexing why he was not indicted. According to Kaufman and Saypol's reasoning, he should have been. If obstruction of justice occurred, Needleman did more, not less, than what Miriam Moskowitz was charged with doing.

Mr. Saypol: Now I project you to the morning of Brothman's appearance before the grand jury. Do you remember that?

A. Yes, I do.

Mr. Saypol: Did you see Brothman before he left to go to the grand jury?

A. Yes, I did.

Mr. Saypol: Did you have any talks with him then?

A. Abe told me at that time or asked me rather—he asked me whether there was anything at all that I should tell him now before he went up before the grand jury. I should tell it to him that morning. He said that he didn't want to go up before the grand jury and hear before them for the first time of some incriminating incident or bit of evidence that might serve to trip him up. He said, "It is better if I hear it from you now."

Gold was describing Brothman as worried about what Gold would say, rather than asking Gold to conform his testimony to his. Brothman wanted to protect himself from Gold. Brothman was worried that his truthful statements could be made to sound like lies.

Mr. Saypol: Did you see him after his appearance before the grand jury?

A. Yes, I did.

Mr. Saypol: Describe the circumstances...and what was said...

A. I asked Abe whether there had been any mention of my name. He said, No, there had not; my name had not been brought into any of the questions he was asked.

If indeed Brothman wasn't asked any questions about Gold, how could Gold make his testimony conform to Brothman's testimony concerning Gold's relationship with Bentley and Golos?

Mr. Saypol: Do you remember the night before you were to appear before the grand jury?

A. Well, before that and sometime in between—I can't place it accurately—sometime in between the time that Abe told me about the subpoena having come to the lab and sometime before the night that I appeared before the grand jury, Abe gave me a transcript, a copy, of the grand jury testimony he had given to the grand jury. It was a copy...he told me that I should read it over and use it for a guide. But I hardly glanced at it because he had also said, after he had appeared before the grand jury, that he had left out certain things...

Gold's saying that he hardly glanced at the statement was his denial that he had entered into the conspiracy. Furthermore, once Gold admitted that the statement Brothman provided was incomplete, he was saying that he could not very well rely on Brothman's summary, since information was left out.

All Brothman asked from Gold was a true story. Brothman never mentioned Carter Hoodless. Brothman never said that Gold met Golos at a chemical society meeting in Philadelphia. Those details were all Gold's invention. But even if we accept the government's version, there was simply nothing for Gold to alter or conform, since Brothman said that the grand jury did not question him about Gold's relationship with Bentley and Golos; they didn't even mention Gold's name.

Mr. Saypol: Did you tell the grand jury the same sort of a false story as you told to Agents Shannon and O'Brien...regarding the time and circumstances under which you and Brothman first met?

A. Yes, I did...

Mr. Saypol: How long did you remain with Brothman and Associates in their employ?

A. I remained with the Brothman firm up until June of 1948...

Mr. Saypol: About the time that your relationship, your employment with Brothman, terminated, do you remember an incident when both Brothman and Moskowitz were absent from their places of business for some short interval?

A. Yes, Abe and Miriam, late in May of 1948, went on a business trip to Switzerland together.

Mr. Saypol: How long were they gone?

A. About a week or ten days...

Mr. Saypol: When did they return?

A. Very early in June of 1948.

Mr. Saypol: What happened with respect to your employment by the Brothman firm?

A. I left the employment of the Brothman firm right after Abe returned...

Mr. Saypol: The last time you saw Brothman...what words did he tell you? If you remember?

A. Well, he said to keep the story clearly in mind... regarding the fictitious story we had originally told...

Mr. Saypol: You may examine, Mr. Kleinman.

Mr. Kleinman: Well, how about your feeling with respect to your own country, Mr. Gold, the United States—did you consider whether or not you were helping or hurting the United States?

A. I could not see that I was in any way harming the United States.

Mr. Kleinman: And that was while you were doing this industrial espionage, is that right?

A. That is while I was doing the industrial espionage...

Mr. Kleinman: All that was necessary at that time, Mr. Gold, was for anybody to go over to an engineering place like Hendrick and ask for or request just what you have there on that blueprint, and he could have gotten it for a fee, is that right?

A. That is correct, but I asked that question in November of 1935, and I got an answer...they said that they had an experience to the effect that people would give them information, would sell them a process, American firms would sell them a process, and that they would take it over there and put it in operation, and they would find that somewhere down the line, someone from the top man or someone down the chain of command had sabotaged the thing.

Mr. Kleinman: You mean by that, Mr. Gold, our American engineers were attempting to sabotage the Soviet people?

A. I am repeating what I was told...

Mr. Kleinman: All right. The next question is, did you believe that our American industrialists and engineers were sabotaging the Soviet people by giving them these spurious plans and blueprints?

A. I knew that there were many people in the United States who disliked the Soviet Union.

Mr. Kleinman: You did not answer my question, Mr. Gold. Did you believe that story when it was given to you?

A. Yes, I believed the story...

Mr. Kleinman: However, the information was available to anyone who could read the engineering books, is that right?

A. That is exactly what they didn't want. They could purchase all the books they wanted at Barnes & Noble. They were interested in processes in proven operation in the United States. They wanted them exactly as they were in a plant and exactly as they were working in a plant...

Mr. Kleinman: Did you intend any harm to the people of the United States?

A. I did not. Russia was an ally at that time...

Mr. Kleinman: When were you arrested in connection with the charges you pleaded guilty to in Philadelphia?

A. I went into voluntary custody on the 22nd of

May, 1950...

Mr. Kleinman: When did the FBI see you in the month of May?

A. They came to see me on the 15th of May.

Mr. Kleinman: You were not then arrested?

A. No, I was not....

Mr. Kleinman: When did you first admit to the FBI that you were a spy?

A. On the 22nd of May.

Mr. Kleinman: That was some seven days after they started to question you?

A. That is correct...

Mr. Kleinman: Returning for a moment to the question of the nickel catalysts, on which we had some testimony, didn't you perform several experiments for Brothman either in your laboratory at Penn Sugar Company or some other place?

A. Yes, I did...

Mr. Kleinman: When?

A. Sometime in either very late 1942, possibly early 1943. I am not sure of the dates, either.

Mr. Kleinman: Were you assisted in that work by somebody in the laboratory?

A. Yes, I was.

Mr. Kleinman: What is that person's name?

A. Morrell Dougherty...

Mr. Kleinman: How long have you known Mr. Dougherty?

A. Twenty-one years...

Mr. Kleinman: Is Mr. Dougherty married or a single man?

A. He is married.

Mr. Saypol: At this time I will start imposing an objection.

Judge Kaufman: He said he was married.

Mr. Saypol: I am talking about the general line of questioning. I don't see its connection here.

Judge Kaufman: I don't either...

Mr. Kleinman: Whenever you went to New York, did you do so during the working day or at night?

A. I did go sometimes during the working day. When I saw Abe, it was mostly at night. It was the longer trips that I utilized my time off for. Trips to see Abe I made in the evening, most of them. There were a few that I made during the day.

Mr. Kleinman: When you went off on these longer trips, who covered your work for you?

A. Who covered my work for me?

Gold's repetition of questions was his internal polygraphic response. Questions concerning Morrell Dougherty disturbed him.

Mr. Kleinman: That is what I asked.

A. Morrell Dougherty.

Mr. Kleinman: Did you tell him where you were going?

A. No, I did not.

Mr. Kleinman: Did you tell him the reason for the trips?

A. I did not tell him the reason for the trips. I always invented an excuse as to where I was going, but it was never the place where I said I was actually going...

Mr. Kleinman: When you first met Abe, you told him about your family, didn't you?

A. On orders from Sam...

Mr. Kleinman: You started to tell Abe from time to time some rather intimate details of your marriage, didn't you?

A. Oh, yes...

Mr. Kleinman: Not only did you make up a wife and family, Mr. Gold, but you also made up a story about the death of your brother...Did you in that story include details of your brother having been a paratrooper and having died in a paratroop jump?

A. I can't recall...

Mr. Kleinman: These stories that you told Abe about your family and children and brother, they continued until the time the FBI first spoke to you in May of 1947. Is that right?...

A. Yes...They continued until the FBI spoke to me, the very first day, in 1947.

Mr. Kleinman: That was the first time that you told Brothman that there was no truth in any of these stories you had told him, is that right?

A. That is correct...

Unknown to Brothman's attorney, Judge James P. McCranery had ordered a psychiatric examination of Harry Gold, before the day he sentenced Gold to a thirty-year term. The psychiatric report, dated December 9, 1950, described Gold as a neurotic and hostile personality with traits adding up to an "imbalance."

Mr. Kleinman: Did you continue to see your Soviet superior in 1946?

A. I did not.

Mr. Kleinman: Or in 1947?

A. I did not.

Mr. Kleinman: Or in 1948?

A. I did not...

Harry Gold was incapable of testifying truthfully. The FBI and the U.S. Attorney's Office had several statements in Gold's handwriting that attested to his meetings with his Soviet supervisor, Anatoli Yakovlev, in February and December of 1946.

Mr. Kleinman: In September, 1947, there were some negotiations going on with the Stanton Company and with A. Brothman Associates?

A. That is right...

Mr. Kleinman: You stated that there arose continually, or periodically at least, states of emergency. Were these matters also a financial emergency?...

A. The financial emergency was that there was simply no money for salaries...

Mr. Kleinman: The Stanton contract was the only thing that indicated a hope of relief from these financial difficulties in 1947. Is that right?

A. In 1948, 1947 or 1948, okay.

Mr. Kleinman: It was promised that you would become and be made a member of the firm with a proprietary interest if you remained. Isn't that right?...

The Witness: Yes, I was promised, but a number of promises of a like nature were made starting from 1946 on. The situation was this. When there was no money, I was a partner. When there was money, I became an employee, and that didn't happen to me alone...

Mr. Kleinman: There came a time when Abe Brothman went to Switzerland?

A. That is correct...

Mr. Kleinman: While Brothman was in Switzerland you went to the offices of A. Brothman and Associates as distinguished from the laboratory, is that right?

A. I went there on a couple of occasions...

Mr. Kleinman: Did you look through the office files

for anything in reference to the Stanton agreement or the Stanton contract?

A. I did not.

Mr. Kleinman: Did you have any occasion to go through the office files for anything?

A. I did not. Oscar did...

Mr. Saypol: Oscar who?

Mr. Kleinman: Oscar Vago, I assume.

The Witness: Vago.

Mr. Kleinman: Did Oscar tell you that he did?

A. Oh, yes.

In the event that Oscar Vago, Gold's co-employee at the Brothman firm, had any idea about appearing as a witness for Abraham Brothman and Miriam Moskowitz to dispute Harry Gold's testimony, and in so doing upset the prosecution's plans in other scheduled anti-Communist trials, Irving Saypol had a solution. He arranged for Vago to appear before the grand jury. Asked before the grand jury if he had gone to Hungary without his wife in 1929, and remained there until 1932, Vago replied that he had.

Vago was indicted for perjury on September 20, 1950. Unfortunately he had lied when he testified that he was outside of the United States for four years; it was only two months. He also lied when he claimed that his wife did not accompany him; she did. For these lies Vago was held in $50,000 bail, the equivalent of at least a million dollars today, even though he returned to the grand jury a week later to recant his testimony.

Vago, who was arrested only a few days before the Brothman trial began, would be treated without mercy. His attorney could not get his bail reduced. Finally in June 1952, after both the Brothman-Moskowitz and

Rosenberg-Sobell trials were over, Judge Sylvester J. Ryan, after finding Vago guilty of perjury on technical grounds, suspended his sentence. Vago had spent nearly two years in prison. In releasing him Judge Ryan criticized the prosecution, noting that Vago had lied only to avoid being deported, since his student visa had expired and he was in the United States illegally. The judge recognized that Vago's indictment had nothing to do with his involvement in any of the pending espionage trials. The cruelty dispensed to this man was one more in the chain of heartbreaking acts of inhumanity that Irving Saypol dispensed during his tenure as a government prosecutor. Saypol achieved his purpose here: Harry Gold could say anything he wished concerning Oscar Vago without fear of contradiction.

The cross-examination resumed.

Mr. Kleinman: Did you put in the call to...Brothman?...Did you tell him that there was no money, that you wanted money?

A. Oscar Vago had sent two cablegrams to Abe in which he said in effect, "We are starving. For God's sake, send us some money."...

Mr. Kleinman: However, Brothman did return within a few days...did he not?

A. Yes, he did...

Mr. Kleinman: Was there a discussion as to how much money he owed you or the firm owed you for back pay?

A. There was a discussion at a later date...he owed me around $3800 or $4000...

Mr. Kleinman: Now, to come down to May 29, 1947...Did Brothman state that he had made a statement to the FBI agents?

A. Yes...

Mr. Kleinman: Brothman did not say to you, "Tell the FBI that it was through Carter Hoodless that you met Golush," did he?

A. Brothman said to make up a story, any story, so I made up a story...

Mr. Kleinman: Between the 22nd of July and the time that you received your subpoena, did you have any further talks with Mr. Brothman about his testimony before the grand jury?

A. I cannot recall any...

Mr. Kleinman: Did you indicate to Abe in your talks with him any desire on your part to tell the grand jury the truth when you appeared before it?

A. I had no opportunity...The first thing that Abe did was to tell me that all he wanted me to do was to tell the same story that he had told the grand jury so as to cover him up.

But Gold never knew what story Brothman told the grand jury. All we know is that Abe Brothman was not sure what he was going to tell the grand jury. And finally after he did testify, all he told Gold was that he did not mention his name. Whatever Brothman swore to on July 22, 1947, was not forced upon Gold when he testified on July 31, 1947. Gold had nothing to conform his testimony to.

Mr. Kleinman: Did Abe threaten you?

A. No, he did not.

Mr. Kleinman: Did Abe intimidate you?

A. No, he did not...

Judge Kaufman: Are you about finished now?

Mr. Kleinman: Nearly, your Honor. I have maybe another fifteen minutes. I think I should be through with him in about ten minutes perhaps. Do you want me to continue or wait until tomorrow? It has been a long day, Judge, and I am coming to the end of my cross-examination.

Judge Kaufman: All right. You will assure me that it will be no longer than ten minutes tomorrow?

Mr. Kleinman: I started with fifteen, Judge, and I cut it down to ten, but I will promise you not to be repetitious.

Judge Kaufman: I know what happens overnight. You will think of certain questions to ask that have not been asked. Well, we will recess until ten-thirty tomorrow morning, ladies and gentlemen.

WITNESSES

On November 21, 1950, after Harry Gold had completed his testimony, Fred C. Birkby, a special agent of the FBI, was called as a witness for the government. Birkby was questioned by U.S. Attorney Foley.

Mr. Foley: Did you on June 3 and June 6 of 1950 conduct a search of the home of Harry Gold?
A. Yes, I did...
Mr. Foley: On what day did you search the living room?
A. June 3, 1950.
Mr. Foley: On what dates did you search the cellar?
A. June 3 and June 6, 1950...
Mr. Foley: In your search of the closets, did you find a folder?
A. Yes, I did.
Mr. Foley: A red folder?
A. Yes, I did.
Mr. Foley: What did that folder contain on the outside?
A. On the outside, it was marked "A.B. Stuff."...
Mr. Foley: What did you find in that folder?
A. The folder contained some blueprints, some papers with mathematical and chemical data, and a small white card.
Mr. Foley: Do you remember anything about the card?
A. The card contained some handwritten material including what appeared to be a license number...
Mr. Foley: What date did you find it?

A. On June 3, 1950.
Mr. Foley: What is the license plate number on that card?
A. 2M9088. [sic; 2N9088]

Birkby was the same FBI agent who had visited and searched Harry Gold's home back on May 31, 1947, and found nothing of value. Yet he was specifically called in to search Harry Gold's cellar on June 3, 1950; and this time he miraculously discovered Gold's handwritten notation with Sam's instructions to meet Brothman that a swarm of FBI agents could not find after two weeks of intensive searching.

Joseph P. Walsh, a New York City patrolman, was then called as a witness for the government and questioned by U.S. Attorney Roy Cohn.

Mr. Cohn: I would like you to examine Government's Exhibit 22 for identification, Patrolman Walsh...does it indicate that a summons, a parking summons, was given to Abe Brothman?
A. Yes.
Mr. Cohn: And on what date?...
A. August 15, 1941...
Mr. Cohn: Does that also contain the license plate number of the car on which Brothman was given a ticket?
A. Yes.
Mr. Cohn: And would you read that license plate number to his Honor and the jury?
A. 2N9088...
Judge Kaufman: I might tell the jury that the purpose of this testimony was not to establish...that Mr. Brothman was guilty of the hideous offense of

receiving a parking ticket...But the purpose of it was to establish that he had a car in August of 1941 with the license plate 2N9088...

Judge Kaufman was giving irrelevant testimony an aura of legitimacy, for the jury was persuaded to believe that evidence was mounting against Abraham Brothman. Brothman's license plate number, which he never denied having, was utilized as evidence against him merely because Gold had written it on a piece of paper. A false document from a false witness was being supported by the victim's truthful statements found within the document's contents.

Benjamin G. Dann, a business associate of Abraham Brothman, was called as a witness by William Kleinman, the lawyer for the defense.

Mr. Kleinman: And by whom are you employed, sir?
A. Hendrick Manufacturing Company...
Mr. Kleinman: Did you deal in any classified material?
A. Not that I knew of.
Mr. Kleinman: Were any of those drawings or proposals secret in their nature?
A. Not to my knowledge...
Judge Kaufman: I take it that Mr. Kleinman is attempting to establish that it was just a normal business transaction that was being engaged in between Gold and Brothman. That is the purpose of this testimony, Mr. Kleinman, isn't that right?
Mr. Kleinman: Yes, sir...

Judge Kaufman's tone denigrated Kleinman's defense that Brothman had engaged in normal business transactions with Hendrick Manufacturing Company and Harry Gold. U.S. Attorney Irving Saypol then began his cross-examination of the witness, Benjamin G. Dann.

Mr. Saypol: This is a question, Mr. Dann, which implies no personal reflection, but is somewhat as a matter of course in connection with the progress of this trial. As an official of Hendrick Company, can you tell us was it customary to effect the payment of Communist party dues in the course of your business as a means of sales persuasion?
A. No—
Mr. Kleinman: I object to that...
Judge Kaufman: He answered.

Kleinman then requestioned Benjamin Dann.

Mr. Kleinman: Is there anything about the litera-ture that you saw, that has been called to your atten-tion or about any of the blueprints, that attempted to describe or designate any product, article, or process which was secret or confidential?
A. Not that I know of...
Mr. Kleinman: Your Honor, I should like to make an offer of proof...The offer of proof is this. We have subpoenaed the Public Library and we have here the original publications in which there appeared these matters which I had marked for identification as hav-ing been published material of Brothman...
Judge Kaufman: This is in furtherance of your contention that there was nothing secret about these processes; they were published articles.
Mr. Kleinman: That is right, and common knowledge that people could have gotten by a little research...

WITNESSES

Judge Kaufman: I am going to tell the jury in my charge that it makes no difference whether they were secret or not secret...

Theodore R. Olive was then called as a witness for the defense.

Mr. Kleinman: Where are you employed?
A. The magazine Chemical Engineering...
Mr. Kleinman: Did you from time to time publish articles of which Mr. Brothman was the author?
A. Yes, sir...
Mr. Kleinman: Did there come a time when Mr. Brothman gave you a report on this manufacture of Buna-S synthetic rubber which contained various mathematical computations and designs of the plants for the production of synthetic rubber?
A. Yes...
Mr. Kleinman: I offer that in evidence...
Mr. Saypol: My objection is based on its immateriality.
Judge Kaufman: I will receive it, but I want the jury to know now, and I will further instruct them again tomorrow, that with respect to the charge in this indictment, it is not material whether or not the reports or blueprints or any of the material that was given to Gold or Miss Bentley were secret processes or novel processes, or anything of that character. This is not the charge here...

Kaufman adjusted to the evidence that there was nothing secret by saying it would not matter anyway. The jurors were instructed in a very real sense to convict Brothman and Moskowitz. They were told not to try to figure out why or what charge they would be convicting them of; that was a technical area that they must leave up to Judge Kaufman.

Kaufman continued:

The point in this case is that they conspired to obstruct and impede justice, and all of this background was introduced for the purpose of establishing the true relationship between the parties. In other words, to show that they did actually obstruct justice, that the conspiracy was successful...

But a conspiracy to obstruct justice meant just that. And yet no evidence was produced to show any obstruction of justice, other than Saypol's bare statement that the government was delayed in an espionage invesitgation for three years, without explaining in what manner the government had been delayed or obstructed.

SUMMATIONS

On November 22, 1950, William Kleinman presented to the jury his summation for the defense.

Mr. Kleinman: I have asked you to scrutinize the testimony carefully, and I have asked you to look at the witnesses carefully, and I am sure that you will agree with me that the prosecution's case hangs basically and primarily upon the testimony of the witness Harry Gold. It is true that we have the testimony of Elizabeth Bentley, we have the testimony of Mr. Shannon, and there was offered in the case the grand jury testimony, but I am sure that you will agree with me that you must decide the guilt or the innocence of Abe Brothman and Miriam Moskowitz basically and primarily upon the testimony of Harry Gold...

Ladies and gentlemen, who, who had the most at stake, who was the courier...It was Gold. And yet Gold wants you to believe that...when the FBI came into the picture, that he said nothing, and that Brothman said to him, "You've got to tell a story to get me out of this."...

Who was an accomplished liar, I might say to the point of giving indications of not only being a schizophrenic but a pathological liar? Who could have built up such a story about a wife, about the courtship of a girl, the meeting of others, the close details about a marriage that never took place, about children that never existed...Who could have built up such a story except the most accomplished pathological liar? What was the purpose of all that?...

What kind of a man does these things and how can you believe a man like that? You are asked to believe him now beyond a reasonable doubt...

At the beginning of the case, I was terribly worried that you might get an idea that there was something so awfully mysterious about these blueprints...

There was nothing mysterious about these blueprints. They dealt with standard objects and standard processes. They dealt with things that Mr. Brothman had originated which were published, which were matters of common knowledge which anybody with the least bit of knowledge could have gone to any of the textbooks and found out about, which you could have gotten from publications in the public library...

There is nothing in this case against Miriam Moskowitz except that Gold testified..."that she was concerned because, at that time, Abe had stated that he had considered changing the story he had originally told to the agents of the FBI; that is, considered changing it when he would tell it to the grand jury. And she said that she was going to try and get him to stick to the original story."...If the original story was a true one, surely he should not change his story, but is that any proof that she knew whether the original story was true or false when she advised him not to change his story when he appeared before the grand jury? Again, all you have is the testimony of Gold on this thing...

You will recall...he made mention of the fact that his former employer in New York owed him four thousand dollars...You see, it always rankled in his breast that he was fired, that he was thrown out of his place, and perhaps that his former employer owed him money.

But what motivates a man like that? I said at the outset that he had a disordered mind, a devious mind, nothing that you and I can understand. He is not a

*person we understand. But yet you are required under
our law not only to understand him, but to believe
him beyond a reasonable doubt before you may convict
Brothman, before you may convict Miss Moskowitz...*

The Government then presented its summations.
Irving Saypol argued:

*The defendants, Abraham Brothman and Miriam
Moskowitz, are charged in the indictment with having
conspired and agreed together and with each other
and with others, to defraud the United States of
America in the exercise of its governmental function
of administering and enforcing the criminal laws of
the United States of America, and to influence, obstruct and impede the due administration of justice...*

*Abraham Brothman, it is charged...corruptly endeav-
ored to influence Harry Gold, who was a witness
before the grand jury on July 31, 1947, and actually
he did influence him. Furthermore, he obstructed, he
influenced and he impeded the administration of justice...*

*Was Brothman telling the truth to the grand jury
when he denied to them that he had any connection
at all with the Communist Party or was that story, as
the indictment charges, a false story?...*

*And isn't the truth that Brothman's meetings with
these people was in his capacity as a Communist, as a
supplier of blueprints, documents and information,
complete details of processes, for the use and benefit
of the Soviet Union?...*

*The true story was bared in this courtroom in the
testimony of Miss Bentley, in the testimony of Harry
Gold. Their testimony is proven truthful beyond possible contradiction by a little white card, Government's*

Exhibit 10, found many years after it was written and used, in a cellar in Philadelphia...

The story is proven and supported by the silent but significant records of the Police Department of the City of New York as to the license number of Brothman's automobile nine years ago in 1941...

The truth of the testimony offered here by Miss Bentley, Gold and others, is conclusively established by the failure of the defense to produce one solitary word contradicting any of this testimony.

Mr. Kleinman: I must make an objection to that...

Judge Kaufman: Overruled. I will deal with that later properly myself...I think Mr. Saypol is fully familiar with the rules and with the dangers of trespassing the rules. Proceed...

Thus Judge Kaufman let stand Saypol's remark that the defense had not submitted one word contradicting Gold's testimony. Kaufman's stance encouraged Saypol to continue in the same vein.

The one issue at this time, as far as Gold is concerned, is whether or not he told the truth. His truthfulness is established by the testimony of the other witnesses, by documents, and even more eloquently by the fact that not one word Harry Gold has spoken in this courtroom has been contradicted by any evidence produced by the defense.

Mr. Kleinman: I object to that...

Judge Kaufman: Denied...

When the judge denied Kleinman's objection for the second time before the jury, he in effect endorsed Saypol's comment as that of his own. By his actions, Judge Kaufman let the jurors know that he wanted them to believe that Gold was a truthful witness whose testimony had not been contradicted. Saypol continued.

The FBI then went out to see Gold at the labora-tory. Gold, following Brothman's direction, told his lying story and added to it the concocted explanation of how he had met John Golush, as induced by Broth-man...

Later on, Miss Moskowitz said that Brothman should stick to the same false story he had told the FBI. She said at that time that Brothman had shown signs of a desire to make some changes in his tale when he went before the grand jury. To block this, Miss Moskowitz vowed that she would use her powers to persuade Brothman to tell the identical false story to the grand jury.

Gold testified before the grand jury on July 31st... He spoke about John Golush, this man who Gold had actually never met. He gave the grand jury a story and information about John Golush that he could have gotten from only one person, the defendant Brothman...

As the Court will undoubtedly tell you, whether or not Brothman was giving the Soviet Union secret or confidential information, or whether Brothman was giving the Soviet Union established plans and process-es which the Soviet Union wanted in the very form in which it was desired, is not the crux of this case.

The charge here is obstruction of justice. That obstruction was perpetrated to retard an investigation of espionage to conceal the activities of these parties on behalf of the Soviet Union...

The jury retired from the courtroom, and Kleinman

asked Judge Kaufman to explain to the jury that:

The testimony of Harry Gold, who is an accomplice, is to be scrutinized and acted upon with great caution, and is to be subject to grave suspicion...

If the jury does not believe the testimony of the witness Harry Gold, they must acquit the defendants...

Mere association, suspicious circumstance, or even opportunity to commit a crime are not of themselves sufficient grounds upon which to base criminal responsibility, and the jury may not convict the defendant Miriam Moskowitz if they come to the conclusion that the evidence against her amounts to mere association, suspicious circumstance or opportunity...

There is no direct proof in this case that the defendant Miriam Moskowitz knew whether the defendant Brothman's statement to Special Agent Shannon and his testimony before the grand jury on July 22, 1947, was true or false...

Judge Kaufman refused Kleinman's request, however, and made his own statement to the jurors. After first reading them the substance of the indictments brought against Brothman and Moskowitz, Kaufman stressed:

The obstruction of justice statute is one of the most important laws ever adopted. It is designed to protect witnesses in federal courts and also to prevent a miscarriage of justice by corrupt methods.

This appraisal of the special quality of the obstruction-of-justice laws was Judge Kaufman's message to the jurors that as patriotic Americans he expected them to bring in a guilty verdict. Judge Kaufman continued his statement to the jurors:

The grand jury was investigating espionage and subversion in 1947. They had the right to know the true facts...if Harry Gold's present story is true, that grand jury might have uncovered the espionage activities of Harry Gold and others at that time, in 1947, and the grand jury had a right to know the true facts.

As I have said, the grand jury had a right to get the true and unadulterated story. In considering the guilt or innocence of the defendants...you must first consider whether a false story as to their relationships was told by Brothman and Gold to the grand jury in 1947. If you find that a false story was told, you must determine whether the false story was the result of an agreement or an understanding. If so, who were the parties to this agreement or understanding, that is, who were the members of the conspiracy?...

To find Moskowitz guilty...you must find beyond a reasonable doubt that the relationship between Gold and Brothman was other than that testified to before the grand jury; that Moskowitz knew the relationship between Gold and Brothman to be other than that testified to before the grand jury, and that she was a member of the agreement to give false testimony before the grand jury, that is, that she cooperated in the mutual understanding or agreement...it is the Government's contention that her conduct indicated that she knew the true or actual relationship...

But Moskowitz, who came to work for Brothman years after the events concerning Brothman and Gold's meetings occurred, could not have known what took place between them. Whatever she knew was hearsay under any circumstances; it was not possible for her to know the actual facts of an occurrence that happened years before she arrived. Given the temper of the time, however, Harry Gold had the power to destroy anyone the government prosecutors selected for him to destroy.

After deliberating, the jury returned to the courtroom.

THE FORELADY: We, the jury, find the defendant Abe Brothman guilty of counts 1 and 2, and the defendant Miriam Moskowitz guilty as charged.

Judge Kaufman: Ladies and gentlemen, I want to thank you for your thorough and patient deliberations. I think your verdict was an intelligent one, and I think it was a proper verdict in accordance with the evidence in this case.

I think that your verdict was a complete vindication, as far as I am concerned, of the jury system...

I want to say to you, Mr. Saypol, that you have my congratulations upon a job well done. I think the evidence was exceptionally well presented. You had your problems because, as I understand, there was a most serious problem as to whether or not any indictment under our statutes could be found, and that it was due to your ingenuity in searching the statute books and finding the obstruction of justice statute, because there was a serious question about the statute of limitations having run on the matter of espionage itself...

Kaufman recognized and appreciated the efforts made by Saypol to find a technical way to bring charges against Abraham Brothman and Miriam Moskowitz—even though there was apparently no legitimate way to bring them. Kaufman also recognized that the statute of limitations may have run on all the charges as they were brought.

Mr. Saypol: The tributes, of course, I appreciate. Really they belong not to me. They belong to the Department of Justice, they belong to my able staff, particularly Mr. Cohn and Mr. Foley and Mr. Donegan, the Special Assistant to Attorney General McGrath, and to the Federal Bureau of Investigation, with whom I have worked closely and well.

Judge Kaufman: I want to say in reference to the FBI in this case that it is a revelation to me, because I have worked with the Bureau in years past as an Assistant United States Attorney and as Special Assistant to the Attorney General, but it gives me great mental security, and I am sure it does you ladies and gentlemen, that we have an agency such as the FBI in operation, guarding our internal security. Their work is truly amazing, particularly their work on Mr. Gold. It is just amazing. I think that Mr. Hoover and the Bureau should be congratulated in their work on this case, and I ask you to please advise him of my statement.

All that was missing from the proceeding was the singing of the National Anthem. Judge Kaufman continued:

Mr. Kleinman, I think it is proper also to say that you have the appreciation of the Court for the way you demeaned yourself throughout this trial. You were an advocate all the way. It is most unfortunate that we do not have more lawyers, particularly in this type of case, who can demean themselves as you did.

THE BROTHMAN-MOSKOWITZ TRIAL

You fought for your clients every inch of the way, you let nothing get by, and yet you acted as an advocate should, and you have the appreciation of the Court.

Mr. Kleinman: Your Honor is very kind to say so. Thank you...

SENTENCING

November 28, 1950, was the date scheduled for sentencing. On that day Irving Saypol addressed the court:

Mr. Saypol: Proceeding to Abraham Brothman first...He was considered to be a member of the Communist Party at large. I do know that on one occasion he addressed a meeting of a Communist Club in the Chelsea district, expounding his views...

Turning now to the defendant Miriam Moskowitz... There is information that she, too, was an active Communist, attending meetings in 1948 and 1949 of a Communist Party club in the Chelsea district. She is named in the first count alone with Brothman, the conspiracy count...

In the light of the fact that the defendant Miriam Moskowitz was not concerned as far as we know with offenses related to espionage, it is recommended as to her on the first count that she be sentenced to the maximum term of imprisonment of two years...and also fined the maximum of ten thousand dollars...

As to the defendant Abraham Brothman, it is recommended on the first count the same punishment be imposed upon him. As to the second count, that the maximum available there likewise be imposed, that is, five years, together with a five thousand dollar fine...

Mr. Kleinman: I have been instructed by my clients not to make any presentation outside of the evidence in this case. I have been specifically instructed not to make any argument to your Honor based upon any feeling of sympathy; and I, therefore, under instructions from my clients, refrain from advancing any such

115

arguments or suggestions to the Court at this time of sentence...

Since what we say here will gain some publicity, I only make this suggestion. I know that your Honor will not confuse this case with the spy investigations, the atomic bomb revelations, Gold's activities as a spy, and—

Judge Kaufman: It is merely a question of degree...

Kaufman's bias could not be contained. His every effort from the beginning of the trial to the end was to do as much harm as possible to Abraham Brothman and Miriam Moskowitz.

Mr. Kleinman: The information that the defendant Brothman gave...I think it was even told to the jury, were matters of common knowledge open to the public...

Mr. Saypol: May I just add a word...If these defendants had not indulged in their shenanigans in 1947, Harry Gold, what he stood for and what he did, might have been discovered three years earlier...

If anything, the testimony Brothman provided led to Gold and should have resulted in his investigation. Brothman provided evidence that Gold was intertwined with so-called Communist espionage agents: Jacob Golos and Elizabeth Bentley. Brothman actually led the FBI to Gold, Golos, and Bentley. But the government was impelled both to maintain the secrecy of Gold's undercover role and justify what appeared to be its own bungling in not pursuing Gold. By way of Judge Irving Kaufman and the prosecutors Irving Saypol and Roy Cohn, the government manufactured false charges against Abraham Brothman and Miriam

Moskowitz, claiming it was misled by them.

Judge Kaufman: The defendants in this case have not only been convicted of obstruction of justice, but what aggravated the case here is the fact that the obstruction of justice, serious by itself, was laid in the background of espionage. I said in my charge to the jury that the obstruction of justice is one of the most serious crimes on the statute books, because only by safeguarding the purity of the judicial process can it be protected. I believe those were my exact words. When you destroy the courts, you have made the first inroad, I believe, to the destruction of your country.

When the verdict came in, I said it was beyond my comprehension that anyone would commit an offense of this character against this country; and what is strange about this is that the very country that these defendants sought to undermine, and the evidence was clear and the verdict of the jury was clear on that particular point, that the very country that they sought to undermine gave them a fair, a painstaking and impartial trial, something they could not have obtained from the country they sought to aid.

Kaufman was using Harry Gold's very words—the words in which he commended the judge and lawyers when he was sentenced to a thirty-year jail term. Kaufman continued:

The parents of these defendants came to America seeking a haven from oppression, so that these defendants—their children—could be brought up in a wholesome atmosphere, an atmosphere which recognized that God had created a human being, the greatest thing which God has ever done...

There are so few safe havens remaining on earth today, and it seems to me that these defendants sought to undermine the staunchest supporter of freedom in the world today. I cannot understand. I said that when the verdict came. I repeat again I just cannot comprehend why these defendants and others seek to destroy that which protects them from tyranny.

The matter of imposing sentence, you know, Mr. Kleinman, is never a pleasant task for any court. It is almost a God-like function. You sit and pass sentence upon a fellow human being. In this particular case, I must say that I have deliberated. I have spent a great deal of time giving a great deal of thought to the matter of sentence, and I have come to but one conclusion, and that is that I regret that the law under which these defendants are to be sentenced is so limited and so restricted that I can only pass the sentence which I am going to pass, for I consider their offenses in this case to be of such gross magnitude. I have no sympathy or mercy for these defendants in my heart, none whatsoever.

The sentence of the Court is as follows: The defendant Brothman, therefore, is sentenced on count 2 to five years imprisonment and five thousand dollars fine. On count 1, he is sentenced to two years in prison and ten thousand dollars fine, the sentence on count 1 to commence upon the expiration of the sentence on count 2; the defendant to stand committed until the fines are paid.

The defendant Moskowitz is sentenced to two years on count 1 and a fine of ten thousand dollars, to stand committed until the fine is paid.

At this juncture, another lawyer, Albert Sattler,

appeared on behalf of Brothman and Moskowitz.

Mr. Sattler: On behalf of the defendants, we respectfully ask your Honor to admit the defendants to bail pending an application to the Circuit Court of Appeals pending appeal.

Judge Kaufman: On what ground?...You never called them to my attention during the trial?...You mean by my failure to charge some of your requests?

Mr. Sattler: Yes, sir.

Judge Kaufman: If I remember, I think you only called two or three to my attention.

Mr. Sattler: Yes, but I think as the record appears the requests which were submitted to your Honor asked that you specifically charge certain things and you specifically denied them, and the record so discloses...

Judge Kaufman: How did they get into the record? Those were my notes.

Mr. Sattler: They appear in the record.

Judge Kaufman: They should not be in the record. I don't know how they ever got in there. Those were notes and should not be part of the record. Those were notes for my personal benefit when you came to the bench, and should not be in the charge. I think the stenographer extended himself on that and gratuitously put in something that should not be there, and the Court will strike it out. This is the height of—something or other! I have never heard of anything like that. He takes my notes off the bench and puts them in the record. That is to be stricken out...

Judge Kaufman's denials of the defense lawyers requests were so blatantly prejudicial that he had them deleted from the record. Because of the judicial power of intimidation he possessed, Kaufman could get the stenographer to do anything he wished. So he simply had a portion of the stenographer's typed minutes deleted. Kaufman continued, instructing Saypol:

Mr. Saypol, will you please take that up with the stenographer, that portion that should not be in the record. Those were my personal notes...The stenographer was over-ambitious and over-extended himself. He was a very capable stenographer. He just is not a lawyer and does not know what is to go in and what isn't...I certainly do not want anything in the record that contains my personal notes as to just what I am doing to every charge.

Mr. Sattler: The impression I got was that you were making specific rulings on each request.

Judge Kaufman: No, that was a matter of convenience to me.

By this means Kaufman prevented a number of appeals arguments from being raised.

Judge Kaufman: I think I have made myself clear on that. I believe if you check with Mr. Kleinman, he will tell you the understanding, and that that was the procedure we agreed upon, and I want the stenographer instructed to correct the record accordingly.

With respect to your application for bail the application is denied.

On July 26, 1951, the United States Court of Appeals upheld the convictions of Abraham Brothman and Miriam Moskowitz on conspiracy to defraud the government of its function of enforcing Federal criminal laws, but reversed Brothman's conviction of obstruction of justice, lessening his sentence by five years.

ELIZABETH BENTLEY

OUT OF BONDAGE

The government prosecutions moved rapidly. The Brothman-Moskowitz trial had begun less than three weeks after Alfred Slack was sentenced in Septembcr 1950. Now, on December 18, 1950, less than three weeks after Miriam Moskowitz and Abraham Brothman were sentenced, the trial of the U.S. government versus William Remington was ready to begin.

Remington, an economist working for the U.S. Department of Commerce, made a fatal error without realizing it. He defended himself against Elizabeth Bentley's charges that he was a Communist by successfully suing her for libel. In so doing, he thoroughly discredited her.

Early on, Bentley's credibility was not as yet of critical importance to the government. But once the year 1950 arrived, and the U.S. Attorney General had decided to use Elizabeth Bentley as a witness in the government's case against the Rosenbergs and Morton Sobell, it was essential that her credibility be restored. The main case against the Rosenbergs and Sobell was in jeopardy of being lost unless Abraham Brothman and Miriam Moskowitz as well as William Remington were convicted of the charges pending against them. Saypol and Cohn succeeded in convicting Brothman and Moskowitz, now Remington remained.

William Remington did not deny Bentley's claim that he gave her information. He just denied that there was anything improper about doing so, since nothing he gave her was secret. As he said, "It was all printed data, or information released by the government in bulletin and other ways."

Remington explained that he was introduced to a man named Jacob Golos, who said that his name was John and that he was a writer. In March 1942, Remington had dinner with him and his assistant who called herself Helen Johnson. Helen Johnson was actually Elizabeth Bentley. At dinner Remington said Golos told him that Bentley did research for him as well as for a group of writers who contributed to a publication called *P.M.* Remington testified, "I was flattered that a writer of books should need my help." Remington said that Bentley met him on several occasions and often brought him Communist literature. But, Remington reported, he became suspicious of Bentley when he learned that she was not connected with any writer at *P.M.*

We are talking about 1942, supposedly before Bentley turned government informer. Yet she and Golos were using assumed names, and lying to their contact. The implication is that whether or not Remington was a Communist, he had a reasonable instinct that warned him of something not right about Bentley and Golos. There would be no need for Communist spies to overstate their Communism by claiming to be connected with a liberal publication like *P.M.*, if they were not so connected. It was only if they were pretending to be Communists that they would make a great show of leftist affiliations. And indeed, Bentley and Golos's purpose was to entrap Communists; they engaged in this purpose with a single-minded determination. They, like Harry Gold, went around the country hunting their Communist prey.

Elizabeth Bentley claimed to have been a Communist, and a member of the Communist Party, for three years, from 1935 to 1938. But her story was that after 1938 she left the Communist Party. This was her explanation when evidence surfaced showing that after she graduated from college, she joined an Italian Fascist organization in Italy, an odd act for an avowed Communist. She accounted for this inconsistency by saying that she joined because membership in that particular group enabled her to get discounts on purchases. Bentley testified, "We all belonged to it, not from a point of ideology...but simply because we got cut rates on various things."

Before using Elizabeth Bentley as a government witness, U.S. Attorney Roy Cohn decided that a biographical sketch should be obtained from her. On October 23, 1950, the FBI gave him the report of Special Agent John J. Danahy after he interviewed her on October 13. Danahy wrote:

> *Miss Bentley was informed of the requests of Mr. Cohn and this matter was handled very delicately by the Agents. Miss Bentley, as usual, took it in stride and advised that there*

had been some occasions when she had been indiscreet and that if this information became known to the ·defense, it would, of course, be rather embarrassing to her...

After her indoctrination into the Communist cause, she stated that she became a real Communist and...on many occasions shared her room with male Communists. She related that on some very few occasions she probably had sexual intercourse with some of these individuals, but that for the most part it was just an accommodation in order to give these people some place to sleep.

She related that it would, of course, be almost impossible for her to have a jury believe that while she was living at a certain address if fifteen or twenty men stayed at her home at different intervals over a period of a month or two that with a few exceptions this was merely an accommodation.

She stated that...she had been indiscreet on some occasions but stated definitely that she was not promiscuous.

Elizabeth Bentley was a fascinating and enigmatic personality. She told much about herself in a book she had written: an autobiography, *Out of Bondage*. The reader of this book is left with astonishment that the government would have been desperate enough to use a witness like her. The book begins:

As the S.S. Vulcania sailed into New York Harbor that July day in 1934, I leaned on the deck rail and looked at the skyline wistfully. It was good to be back in my own country after a year's study in Italy, I thought, and yet what, really, was I coming back to? I had no home, no family. Nor was there much prospect of finding a teaching position.

After Bentley told of joining the Communist Party,

she described her initial meeting and relationship with Jacob Golos, the man she called Yasha.

I had been told he was a leading agent of the Communist International, that I could trust him implicitly, and that I should obey his orders without question...

Although short in stature, he was powerfully built with a large head, very broad shoulders and strong square hands. His eyes were startlingly blue, his hair bright red, and I was intrigued by the fact that his mouth was very much like my mother's...

We usually met in small, out-of-the-way restaurants where we would not be seen, and after eating drove around in his car. He would look over the material I had brought, listen to what I had to report and then, going over the situation with me, point out what was important and what trivial and tell me what to look for in the future. Undoubtedly my "greenness" at undercover work exasperated him, but he was always very patient. He would carefully explain why I had done the wrong thing and then proceed to set forth the correct methods. My amateurish attempts to listen at closed doors and search wastebaskets especially annoyed him...

It was on a cold, snowy night in December that I discovered I was in love with him...

His hand touched mine, I looked at him, and then quite suddenly I found myself in his arms...

"I love you very much," he said, "yet there is the shadow of pain in my heart because I know what lies before us."

I didn't understand what he meant...

"I can see that you are puzzled," he said. "But then you don't understand the situation we are

in...You and I have no right, under Communist disci-
pline, to feel the way we do about each other."

The whole fabric of my world seemed to be col-
lapsing around me.

"But that's absurd," I cried. "They have no right
to demand that!"

"Yes," he said gently, "they do. If personal rela-
tionships are allowed to get in the way of the move-
ment, we shall never achieve our goal...

"There is only one way out," he explained reluc-
tantly, "and that is to stick together and keep our
relationship unknown to everyone. It will be a hard
life for both of us. We will not be able to live to-
gether; we will only be able to see each other occa-
sionally...Do you think you would be able to do
that?"...

I had already made my decision. Here was the man
whom I admired, loved, and trusted. I belonged with
him, no matter how hard the road ahead might be.

Elizabeth Bentley's description of her love affair
with Jacob Golos, who was married at the time to
Celia Golos and had a girlfriend named Caroline Klein,
only accentuated the power of her vivid imagination.
Even if we believe that Golos actually told her that
Party discipline prohibited select members from falling
in love, we can see that what he said to her was
intended to keep her from getting too close to him.

One night Yasha came to see me looking white and
strained.

"I'm afraid it's happened. Our offices were raided
this morning by the Department of Justice and they've
planted agents at the front door to question anyone
who comes in. It's very lucky that I told you under

no circumstances to come up there. Otherwise you might have been involved."...

"I've been served with a duces tecum subpoena," he said wearily, "and that means I've got to appear in court with all my files and documents. There's not time to destroy anything, and some of that material is going to involve our comrades badly. Why didn't I get rid of it before?"...

The indictment of World Tourists went before the Federal Court in New York and the trial began. It seemed to drag on endlessly, first in New York and later in Washington. Yasha was on the stand hour after hour. The American authorities were trying to get him to admit that he had been mixed up in illegal activities, but solidly and unwaveringly he stood his ground...

But the frightful strain was telling on Yasha. His red hair was becoming grayer and sparser, his blue eyes seemed to have no more fire in them, his face became habitually white and taut. When he came to see me, he would fall on the couch, trying to catch his breath after the three flights of stairs he had climbed...

What was aging Yasha was not alone the grueling trial but the sense that he had let down his old comrades. The files which the Department of Justice had seized in their World Tourists raid proved conclusively that Earl Browder had gone abroad under a pseudonym and with the aid of faked papers. He was arrested on the charge of passport fraud. This seemed to upset Yasha more than anything else.

"Earl is my friend," he kept saying, over and over. "I have known him for many years and I like him. It is my carelessness that is going to send him to jail."

According to Bentley's version, it was the material that Golos and perhaps even she had provided that led to the imprisonment of Earl Browder, the head of the Communist Party in the United States. Bentley describes Golos as asking rhetorically, "Why didn't I get rid of it before?" The answer was implicit in the question; Golos simply informed on Browder and provided the government with the information they needed to convict him.

Over the years the FBI had been receiving extensive information from a confidential informant identified as T-1 who was able to obtain information from World Tourists, Incorporated, It is not overreaching to surmise that Elizabeth Bentley, who was confidential informant T-1 after 1946, was the same T-1 who had been providing the FBI with data from World Tourists for several years before 1946.

It was shortly after November 1945, when Bentley was said to have first begun working for the FBI, that she was given the code name Gregory, while still maintaining the same T-1 designation. The name Gregory was with little doubt used by the FBI to identify information received from her after her status with them had changed in early 1946.

The FBI and J. Edgar Hoover had been interested in World Tourists, Inc. and Jacob Golos for quite some time. On August 18, 1941, Hoover sent a teletype to the New York office: "Advise by return wire whether World Tourists, Incorporated now out of existence." A teletype reply the next day said, "World Tourists, Inc. still operating...Surveillance of J. N. Golos contemplated near future." Since J. Edgar Hoover was personally interested in Jacob Golos and World Tourists, Inc., as far back as 1941, it is not logical to believe that the FBI knew nothing about Elizabeth Bentley, a woman supposedly so close to Golos, until late 1945, when she first reportedly came to the their attention. Bentley's story continued.

We were convinced that our telephones were being tapped, hence our conversations over the wire were purely business ones. Every so often a Communist electrician would check the walls of Yasha's office, inch by inch, to make sure that no dictaphones had been planted. To be doubly secure we never talked there unless the radio was turned on or one of us sat and continually jiggled the telephone receiver to break any sound waves that might be picked up by a hidden microphone. In general, we made it a policy not to keep too many incriminating documents in our possession. Those which it was absolutely necessary to preserve were carefully placed in the World Tourist safe (only Yasha and I had the combination), and a complicated set of booby traps was rigged up to insure against tampering.

Bentley then explained that in mid-1941 Golos made an important contact with a group of Communists who worked for the government in Washington.

Jubilantly he came to my office one day to announce that he had just had a long and satisfactory conference with the leader of the group, who had come up to New York.

"Who is he?" I asked curiously, knowing that I shouldn't ask such a question. But Yasha was quite willing to tell me.

"His name is Nathan Gregory Silvermaster and I used to know him quite well in the Party way back in the early thirties. He's a trusted comrade whose

record of revolutionary activity dates very far back—almost as far as mine."...

"He sounds like a good person," I said thoughtfully.

"He is, and so is his wife Helen, whom you will soon meet... "I am trying to persuade them to accept you as an intermediary. Your job is to sell yourself to Helen—make friends with her and give her the feeling that you are completely reliable...

It sounded like a tall order. The next day, however, found me in Washington on my way to 5515 35th Street, NW...The door of 5515 was opened by a slight, wiry woman of about forty, with dark brown hair done in a knot at the back of her neck and rather wary brown eyes set in a face that seemed more Polish than Russian...

Optimistically I hoped that I had made a good impression on her, but I had a strong feeling that she was still very suspicious.

A week or so later Yasha informed me that the Silvermasters had agreed to accept me as their contact, albeit somewhat reluctantly.

"You'll have to let them get used to you gradually," he said with a sigh. "Greg is satisfied with the arrangement but Helen suspects you of being an undercover agent for the FBI. We've tried to argue her out of that idiocy, but she's the kind of woman who relies heavily on feminine intuition and she insists her hunches are invariably right."

I laughed ruefully. It was bad enough to spend a good share of my time dodging the FBI without being accused of working for them. Yet, looking back on the episode now, I wonder whether Helen didn't have a deeper insight into human nature than all the rest of us...

It was in the summer of 1942 that I finally met Earl Browder. He had taken a summer cottage on a lake near Monroe, New York, where he could rest and do some writing. As Yasha and I drove into the front yard, Earl was standing on the front steps, nonchalant in baggy trousers and a sport shirt, with his pipe in his mouth...

Earl's wife Raissa came bustling in from the kitchen with plates and napkins, shouting imperious orders in Russian...She acknowledged her introduction to me briefly, almost without interest, and then launched into a long conversation with Yasha...I wondered to myself just why Earl, who seemed so nice, could ever have been attracted to her. What I did not then know was that Raissa, even as far back as the Revolution, had been a powerful figure in the GPU organization in Russia and that she still worked for it. One of her duties was to keep her husband in line and make reports on him. Browder had evidently had no choice in his marriage; the powers-that-be in Moscow had issued the orders and he had had to follow them.

Bentley did not have the remotest basis for claiming that Earl Browder had been ordered by the Russian Communist Party to marry Raissa, or that Browder was kept under Party control by his wife. The truth is that Bentley was not a well woman. The FBI and the U.S. Attorney's office had known since 1948 that she was mentally unbalanced. Nevertheless, they repeatedly maintained that she had never been treated for a psychiatric disorder. It was not until March 1958 that an FBI report admitted, "She received psychiatric examination" in a Hartford hospital ten years before.

In her book Bentley said that one day Golos told her that the Communist Party wanted to separate the two of them.

Anger seethed through me. They couldn't take me away from Yasha. I wouldn't let them do it!

"Over my dead body!" I said violently...

"They can't do that to you!" I said savagely. "Just let me at them and I'll tell them a thing or two...They may be able to kick other people around but they've never run into an American. Ordinarily we're peaceful people, but when we get mad, we can be plenty tough."...

Soon afterward Yasha won a partial victory...I was not to be taken away from Yasha, and I would be able to continue on helping him with the other agents in Washington. I greeted the news with a whoop of joy. Now things were going to be all right...

Sometimes in the midst of his pacing Yasha would stop and stare at me savagely. Then in the tone of a man being tortured beyond his endurance, he would cry out, "If I turn traitor, turn me in!"

Bentley's reference to Golos's mentioning his fears of becoming a traitor to the Russians was a curious comment. Bentley, after describing how Golos died on a Thanksgiving evening in 1943, then told about her last meeting with a Russian espionage contact, whom she identified as Al.

"I bring greetings from Moscow," he said expressionlessly. "And now I think we should have dinner."...

"Where would you like to eat?" I asked steadily.

"Anywhere that is not near the Soviet Embassy," he said. "After all, I am a high official there and I

should not like to meet anyone I know."...

"We'll go to Naylor's on the waterfront; at this hour of the evening there won't be many people."...

"I hope the food is good," he said thoughtfully. "Americans are such stupid people that even when it comes to a simple matter like cooking a meal, they do very badly." My face must have gone white, for he suddenly looked at me with the impersonal interest of a scientist viewing a germ under the microscope. "Ah, yes, I had forgotten for the moment that you, too, are an American. But then you are very different from the rest of your fellow countrymen—you, at least, have brains...

"You are very fortunate. A great honor has just been bestowed on you. The Supreme Presidium of the USSR has just awarded you one of the highest medals of the Soviet Union—the Order of the Red Star."

I stared at him.

"The Red Star," I said dazedly.

"I don't blame you for being overwhelmed," he said. "It's an honor that few people receive." He pulled a clipping, in color, from his pocket. "This is a facsimile of the decoration," he said precisely. "The original will arrive very shortly. But you can take my word for it that this medal is one of the highest— reserved for all our best fighters."...

"The Red Star entitles you to many special privileges...you could even ride on the street cars free."

Jacob Fass claimed in an affidavit for the FBI that Thomas Black told him that he had "been awarded the order of Lenin." David Greenglass said that Julius Rosenberg had received a citation from the Russians that "had certain privileges with it in case he ever went to Russia." J. Edgar Hoover, in his article, "The

Crime of the Century," wrote, "The Soviets, to be sure, had 'honored' Harry Gold...Gold had been awarded the Order of the Red Star for his outstanding work on behalf of the USSR...One of the privileges of the award was free trolley rides in the city of Moscow!"

Never once was the remotest evidence given of the existence of these awards. It was the cultic language of Hoover, Bentley, and Gold.

Bentley continued:

He stopped for a moment; then, seeming to sense that I was not too impressed by this, he went on: "Besides, you are a member of the most powerful organization in the Soviet Union; we are the ones who really rule the country. Just wait until you pay a visit to Moscow; you will be wined and dined and treated like a princess. We know how to reward our people for what they have done."

A wave of revulsion and nausea swept over me; I thought for a moment I was going to be violently ill. Hastily I pulled on my coat and got to my feet.

"I'd better leave now, Al," I said unsteadily. "I'm afraid I'll miss the last train."

As he handed me into a cab, Al took my hand and kissed it.

"Goodbye, darling," he said.

I didn't answer, for I think if I had I would have spit in his face. So this was what the top leaders of the Communist world movement were like! A slow rage crept into me; I knew then what I was dealing with. We have all been fooled...

The conclusion was inescapable; I must go to the FBI and tell them what I knew about Soviet undercover work in the United States...From now on I would be a notorious person—the "Red Spy Queen."

HARVEY MATUSOW

Three years after Bentley's book was received, another, very different book appeared: *False Witness* by Harvey Matusow. Like Bentley, Matusow was a former Communist who wrote about what prompted him to turn on his former associates, falsely accusing many of them of being Communists. Money, not fame alone, was an important consideration.

Once Matusow saw the benefits that false testimony, especially against Communists, could bring, he embarked upon a career of providing statements to the news media that he admitted he just made up. When Matusow was asked by a reporter from the Hearst publications, "How many student Communists are there in the United States?" he replied, without any basis at all, "There are 3,500 in the New York schools."

Matusow wrote, "Seeing myself on television and hearing reports of my doings on the radio all built up my ego. I considered myself a success. I had my identity. I was a national figure."

Having established himself as a professional witness on Communism in education, Matusow was besieged with requests for his services. William Jansen, superintendent of the New York City schools, hired him as a paid consultant in February of 1952.

Matusow said, "As consultant-investigator I contributed much to the intimidation of teachers...I signed affidavits incriminating people, some of whom were later suspended."

Matusow's services were soon in demand by others. Even the New York City Police Department sought him out. He was also approached by Dr. John Jacob Theobold, president of Queens College. Matusow, who quit college, was flattered. "Here was I a professional witness-informer being sought out by the distinguished president of a college." Professor Theobold visited him at his cold water flat in Greenwich Village. Matusow described Theobold as "determined upon cleansing his school of all 'non-American' ideas. He didn't want Communists or pro-Communists on his campus and was looking to me for help."

Matusow reflected: "I was on the lowest rung of the ladder of life...And yet with all this the president of a college, the superintendent of the largest school system in the country, the police commissioner of the most respected police department in the nation looked to me for counsel and advice."

He described how his career as an informer advanced:

> My testimony before the House Committee on Un-American Activities was successful enough to entice other committees to call me as a witness...
> The Senate Internal Security Subcommittee headed by Senator Pat McCarran of Nevada was the major recipient of my testimony...I was quite cognizant of the absurdity of my testimony. But I wanted the headlines and I knew the committee also wanted them.

Matusow's sworn statement accusing a certain black actor was enough to cause the studio to cancel the actor's contract and blacklist him in Hollywood. Matusow wrote, "The basis for my statement on this actor, who was a Negro, was that I had known him to have associated with certain Communist Party members. The truth was I had never seen him at a Communist Party meeting and had no knowledge whether he was a Communist Party member or not..."

HARVEY MATUSOW

About his dealings with Roy Cohn, Matusow said:

After my first meeting with Roy Cohn...the United States attorney prosecuting the second Smith Act case against Communist Party leaders...I agreed to be a witness at the trial...

Preparing my testimony was not an easy task for Roy Cohn or me. We both knew that I had to supply stories telling where the defendants said "violent overthrow of the government."

Roy Cohn and I started to pour over the documents, picking out quotations...

Cohn worked feverishly hard in getting me to memorize my lines so I would not miss my cue. This was not difficult for me. I loved play acting...

I had to testify in regard to "facts" implicating each defendant, and show that the defendant was guilty as charged. I could not give opinion, as I had done before Congressional committees. I had to remember conversations, or speeches that the defendants had made...

I related a conversation with the defendant Alexander Trachtenberg. He, being a book publisher, had discussed a book by Andrei Vishinsky, The Law of the Soviet State...

The defense counsel bitterly objected to the admission in evidence of this book, but...I succeeded in getting into the record...that Trachtenberg had referred to a passage which "incited" revolution. This was not so.

Shortly before this book went to press, I signed an affidavit describing how I had testified falsely at this trial...The following is an excerpt from the affidavit:

> *The question of my testimony concerning the book* The Law of the Soviet State, *by*

Andrei Vishinsky, was first raised by Roy Cohn, Assistant United States Attorney, who worked with me in preparing my testimony...

I informed him that Trachtenberg had discussed the price of the book. Cohn stated that this would not be sufficient to lay the necessary foundation for its introduction in evidence. Cohn pointed to a passage in the book and told me that that passage was important in proving the Government's case. He then asked me if I had discussed anything with Trachtenberg which would tie him with this passage, and I said, "No," I had not. Nevertheless, thereafter, in several sessions with Cohn, we developed the answer which I gave in testimony, tying Trachtenberg to that passage. We both knew that Trachtenberg had never made the statements which I attributed to him in my testimony.

Matusow also related the circumstances that led to his trip to Salt Lake City in October of 1952 at the invitation of the Senate Internal Security Committee. At that Senate hearing, he claimed that the Mine Mill Union had plotted to cut off copper production for the Korean War. Matusow wrote:

It was here that I had my first face-to-face encounter with Clinton Jencks, a man who was once a friend, and whom I later helped convict in a Federal court...

I was no more than two or three feet from him and was asked to repeat my charges...

I testified that I had three conversations with him in which he told me he was a Communist Party member. Actually, there was no basis whatsoever for this statement of mine; and in January, 1955, the lawyers for Jencks's defense received from me a sworn statement to that effect.

My testimony alone had convicted Jencks—there were no other witnesses who could say Jencks was a Communist and had violated the Taft-Hartley Law.

Harvey Matusow tried as best he could to expose a sickness that had enveloped him and so many others. He concluded his book and this unfortunate stage of his life with a sworn confession.

Affidavit of Harvey M. Matusow in the case of United States of America vs. Clinton E. Jencks, January 20, 1955.

HARVEY M. MATUSOW, being duly sworn, deposes and says:

1. I make this affidavit in support of the motion by the defendant for a new trial, and to do what I can to remedy the harm I have done to Clinton E. Jencks and to the administration of justice.

2. I appeared as a witness for the Government against the defendant in the course of the trial in this Court in January, 1954, on an indictment charging Mr. Jencks with having filed a false non-Communist affidavit with the National Labor Relations Board on April 28, 1950...

3. The matters I testified to were either false or not entirely true, and were known by me to be either false or not entirely true, at the time I so testified...

Matusow's efforts were ignored. Finally he was arrested, convicted, and jailed, not for providing false statements in his prior testimony, but for his later retractions which the courts held were false.

WILLIAM REMINGTON

At William Remington's December 1950 trial there were many witnesses to testify to his loyalty, and indeed he was loyal. He merely had certain leftist beliefs that were strictly in the cerebral sphere.

Remington was respected by his co-workers as a fair-minded person, who generally advocated positions unfavorable to Russia, though he may, when he was a youth, have associated with Communists.

To Remington's shock, the government presented as its first witness Ann Moos Remington, his former wife. She testified strongly against Remington—too strongly, claiming that Elizabeth Bentley visited her every two weeks to collect Party dues while she was married to Remington, and that she saw her husband give Bentley "some pieces of paper" which were "top secret." She said her husband told her in 1938 that he was a Communist. She also testified that she and her husband attended Communist Party meetings.

Under cross examination she was unable to recall any other people who attended these Communist Party meetings. She admitted that she did not know how dues were computed and she and her husband had no dues book. She also acknowledged that when she and her husband attended a Marxist class in economics in New York, her husband challenged the doctrine of the Communist speaker so forcefully that the two of them had to leave quickly.

One key setback for Remington's lawyer, William Chanler, was the rulings of Judge Gregory K. Noonan, who refused to allow the defense to see Ann Remington's grand jury minutes which bore stark evidence of the intensive questioning she underwent for five hours before she finally agreed to testify against her ex-husband.

There was another curious but not innocuous fact concerning Judge Noonan. He was a close friend of Judge Irving Kaufman. Indeed, they were more than friends; they had been partners in a highly successful law firm before they were both appointed to the federal court. Judge Noonan's appointment was no doubt owed in some degree to Judge Kaufman. While he was still practicing as an attorney, Kaufman held the powerful position of confidential coordinator of Federal patronage and consequently had the power to recommend Noonan for judgeship.

Before the trial could get underway it was learned that Irving Saypol had been intimidating witnesses called by Remington. Saypol was seeing to it that they were first called before a grand jury controlled by his prosecution team. Witnesses called in Remington's behalf were terrified by these tactics. Chanler's office bitterly charged that the government was using the grand jury "for the sole purpose of intimidating potential defense witnesses." Chanler described Saypol's tactics in a December 28, 1957, article written by Fred J. Cook.

> We had gone up to New Hampshire, and we located two witnesses, both Communists, who knew the makeup and membership of the Communist Party and the Young Communist League of the state. One, a woman, was a party official with access to all the membership records. She had checked them and told us that Remington's name definitely did not appear anywhere...we told them we would call them when we needed them. Then, I suppose, I made a mistake. I telephoned them from my office, using my regular phone, and told them to come to New York. The next

morning when they arrived, two FBI agents were waiting on the station platform with subpoenas for them to appear before the Grand Jury. They were so frightened that they notified us they would claim their constitutional privilege and refuse to testify. And so we had to let them go back to New Hampshire, unheard.

But William Remington was the victim of an even greater outrage. John Giland Brunini, the foreman of the grand jury, who had been so effective in making certain that Remington was indicted, it came out, was closely involved with Elizabeth Bentley and had done "editorial work" on her autobiography, *Out of Bondage.* Chanler produced two witnesses who testified that Bentley and Brunini had a contract, entered into before Remington was indicted, that guaranteed him part of the profits of the book. One of the witnesses, Eileen Collins, the publicity director of the publishing house, testified to her knowledge of the contract. Mrs. Collins said that these facts had troubled her conscience, and that at her urging, a law student who was a friend of hers called Judge Noonan's chambers and told his clerk these facts. Judge Noonan at the time stated, "This is the first time I ever heard of it." Whether or not Judge Noonan heard it for the first time or not was immaterial; he was hearing it now. John Brunini and Elizabeth Bentley were helping prosecute William Remington for a financial reward.

During the trial it became clear how Saypol had managed to get Remington's ex-wife to turn against him. Saypol asked Remington, "Now will you say whether it is true or not that you committed adultery with another woman named Jane?" Remington answered, "Yes." Though his extra-marital affair occurred, as he testified, "after my wife and I were estranged," it still was painful enough when heard by Ann Moos Remington to have her testify vindictively against him.

Remington was convicted on February 7, 1951, and sentenced to five years in jail. He remained free on bail until August 21, 1951, when his case was heard on appeal and his conviction reversed. But Irving Saypol, Roy Cohn, and the government could not accept the reversal. In early 1953 Remington stood trial again, not for the old charges of espionage or Communist affiliation, but for lying in his testimony when he denied the government's charges. Instead of going to trial on the old case, the government just claimed that it lost the case on appeal only because Remington lied.

For the second trial, Myles Lane was the prosecutor, and the judge was Vincent L. Leibell. The trial moved quickly to a conclusion. On January 27, 1953, Remington was convicted of two counts: lying when he denied passing documents to Bentley, and lying about his membership in the Young Communist League. This time Remington failed on appeal.

Later Remington's lawyer, Chanler, in an interview, explained what led him to appeal the first conviction. He spoke to the attorneys for Remington's ex-wife, who told him that the circumstances of her appearance before the grand jury were so peculiar she would not even discuss them with them. Finally Chanler was given access to the grand jury minutes. They showed, he said,

> that for three hours, Ann Remington's story was the same, generally, as her ex-husband's. In essence, it was this: she and Bill, at one time...had friends who were Communists, but they had never been members...Bentley, she

said, had never figured much in their lives.
This was the gist of her testimony before the
Grand Jury. Then, Brunini, the foreman—the
man who helped Miss Bentley with her
book—really took over. He accused Ann
of lying and trying to protect her husband...she
protested that it was late and that she would
like to go out and have some lunch and
consult her lawyer. Brunini told her she could
get something to eat when she told the truth;
that everyone knew that her husband had been
a Communist.

The misconduct that occurred secretly behind the
closed doors of the grand jury was surpassed only by
the monstrous conduct of Irving Saypol. An FBI report
dated October 31, 1950, written by Special Agent J.
G. Spencer shows that Saypol and his assistant
Thomas Donegan, the same assistant who represented
Bentley in a civil matter years before, knew all along
that the grand jury foreman, John Giland Brunini, was
working closely with Elizabeth Bentley. The report
also demonstrated the FBI agent's serious concern in
regard to this matter; it read:

After some deliberation between Donegan
and Saypol, Saypol suggested that Miss Bentley
be asked to come to his, Saypol's office as
soon as possible that morning, October 30...
During the conference Miss Bentley was
interrogated by Mr. Donegan and Mr. Saypol
concerning her relationship with John
Brunini...who incidentally is also a resident of
the Shelton Hotel where she is presently
residing...
The seriousness of this situation is of
course concerned with the fact that Brunini
was the foreman of the Grand Jury that
indicted Remington, and during the progress of
the Grand Jury Brunini met Bentley socially,
talked about her writing a book, arranged a

publisher for her, obtained an advance of $2,000, and subsequently collaborated with her during the trial, and at the present time is editing this book. Donegan volunteered that during a recent conversation he had had with Brunini regarding this incident, Donegan asked Brunini if there had been any intimate relations between himself and Miss Bentley, and he denied that such was the case.

At the conclusion of the conference both Mr. Saypol and Mr. Donegan agreed that Miss Bentley should be moved to a different hotel.

Regarding Brunini's tactics with Remington's wife before the grand jury, Chanler said that Brunini told Ann Remington, "We have teeth but we do not like to use them." Chanler continued,

Time and again, the other woman was thrown in her face...finally after a whole hour of this, she came around and gave out the version she told from the witness stand...we were not allowed to keep those Grand Jury minutes, but I made an affidavit of what was in them, and this went up to the Appeals Court...it was this that formed the basis for Judge Leonard Hand's strong dissent.

William Remington was sentenced to three years in jail. While in jail he was beaten over the head with a brick by a fellow inmate, and he died on November 25, 1955, at the age of 37. He was scheduled to be released the following August. Commenting on the murder, acting warden Fred Wilkinson said, "You'll get pretty much the same reaction concerning loyalty in a prison climate as in any other community."

Robert G. Thompson, one of the Communist leaders sentenced by Judge Medina in the Smith Act trial, fared better than Remington. Thompson, who had won the Distinguished Service Cross for his bravery during

World War II, was only severely beaten by a fellow inmate while in jail.

JUDGE KAUFMAN IN PERSON

Moving ahead some thirty years to mid-March 1984, Judge Irving R. Kaufman, among his countless honors, was now chairman of the President's Commission on Organized Crime. Kaufman had been appointed to that post by another patriotic warrior against Communism, the President of the United States, Ronald Reagan. The Commission was in the process of investigating organized crime's influence over legitimate banks.

James Frattiano, a notorious criminal, testified that he had killed nineteen people and that he knew a Mafia member who had hidden a million dollars in his mattress. That is all Frattiano said.

Kaufman's technique had not changed in all these years. He used Frattiano to colorfully repeat, as the Commission traveled from city to city, the facts about his murders and his knowledge about the existence of the great organized Italian crime ring known as the Mafia. Frattiano's testimony had nothing to do with exposing the methods by which banks help legitimize organized crime's illegal cash. Yet Kaufman and the committee he headed created the impression that Frattiano, his murders, and the Mafia were all part of a massive money-laundering scheme involving national banks of the United States.

Decades before, Kaufman used Elizabeth Bentley in almost the same manner. She helped intensify the paranoia of our nation, convinced as we were that Communists or even liberals were loyal only to Russia and ready to commit espionage against us. Bentley's "expert" testimony confirmed that American Communists were the equivalent of Russian spies.

Elizabeth Bentley had been fighting Communism for

years before the rest of the nation was ready to join her. The war against Communism, however, did not begin with her; it had raged as far back as the Palmer Raids of 1919, when thousands of Communists, Communist sympathizers, and aliens were arrested. Our successful capitalists dreaded Communism's appeal. It could mean the end of all they acquired. After all, it had happened in Russia; it could happen in America. Communism was a danger that had to be eradicated.

But in the late 1930s and early 1940s we had joined with our ideological enemy to wage war with an even greater enemy, fascism. We and the Russians won, and there were amicable feelings between our two nations. It took time to sour them. But as 1948 moved into 1949, our newspapers began pounding Elizabeth Bentley and J. Edgar Hoover's message that Communists were the equivalent of Russian spies working for Russia and that Russia was not our ally but our enemy. Still most Americans were not convinced this was so. It took more time. Then on September 25, 1949, President Truman announced that an atomic explosion had occurred in the Soviet Union. Fear gripped our nation. The Russians had the atom bomb. Now, it was not just J. Edgar Hoover and Pat McCarran battling Communism. Senator Joseph McCarthy became a national figure, the public became obsessed, and Communists were hunted in the United States as oppressed people have been hunted throughout the history of mankind. This was the setting for the beginning of the trial of Julius and Ethel Rosenberg and Morton Sobell.

THE TRIAL OF THE ROSENBERGS AND SOBELL

THE INDICTMENT

The trial of the United States of America versus Julius Rosenberg, Ethel Rosenberg, and Morton Sobell began on March 6, 1951.

Judge Irving R. Kaufman announced to the jurors, "Mr. Schaefer will now read to you the indictment in this case."

Then the judge explained to the jury that punishment would be decided by him alone. He told them, "That is completely within my jurisdiction, not within the jurisdiction of the jurors."

Irving Saypol made his opening statement.

The indictment returned by the Grand Jury is a simple one...It is charged that the three defendants, the Rosenbergs and Sobell, from 1944, until the time when they were indicted by this Grand Jury some

151

months ago, conspired and agreed with each other and also with other conspirators, including Harry Gold, David Greenglass, David's wife, Ruth Greenglass, and one, Anatoli Yakovlev, an agent and official of the Soviet Union, and with others...to deliver information, documents, sketches and material vital to the national defense of our country, to a foreign power, namely, to Soviet Russia...

The evidence will show that the loyalty and the allegiance of the Rosenbergs and Sobell were not to our country, but that it was to Communism, Communism in this country and Communism throughout the world...

We will prove that the Rosenbergs and Sobell, acting separately and in concert, engaged in a ceaseless campaign to recruit promising members for their Soviet espionage ring. They were ever on the lookout for those whose state of mind and sympathies were such that the Rosenbergs and Sobell thought they would be ripe for a proposition to betray this country by stealing its secrets and giving them to the Soviet Union, to advance its cause and the cause of world Communism...

The evidence will show how at the behest of the Rosenbergs, Greenglass stole and turned over to them and to their co-conspirator Harry Gold, at secret rendezvous, sketches and descriptions of secrets concerning atomic energy and sketches of the very bomb itself...

At this point, Alexander Bloch, who was assisting his son in representing the Rosenbergs, objected to Saypol's statements.

Mr. A. Bloch: If your Honor please, I move for a

mistrial in this case upon the ground that the opening statement of the learned United States Attorney was inflammatory in character and introduced an element which is not pertinent to the case or relevant to it, to wit, Communism, and made other inflammatory and damaging statements which are not part and should not be part of an opening.

Judge Kaufman: Your motion is denied...

Mr. A. Bloch: I object to Communism being mentioned at all on the ground that there is no causal connection between Communism and the crime charged in the indictment. If it is done for the purpose of showing motive, they have to show that there is some causal connection...

Mr. Saypol: It will be shown...

Judge Kaufman: I accept Mr. Saypol's statement that he will show that causal connection...The objection is overruled...I am admitting this testimony on the theory of motive...

But why would Communism necessarily be a motive? A belief in Communistic principles would not necessarily mean that a Communist would be loyal to Russia simply because Russia was a Communist country. The government was using primitive bias as a substitute proof for motive.

MAX ELITCHER

Max Elitcher was the first witness called; he was the government's chief witness against Morton Sobell, the young scientist who had fled to Mexico at about the time of Julius Rosenberg's arrest and was charged with having conspired with Rosenberg to transfer secret government information to the Soviet Union. Elitcher and Sobell had known each other for years. They had gone to school together and lived only a few feet from one another. What could have made Elitcher, who considered Sobell his closest friend, testify against him?   Elitcher was at one time a member of the Communist Party. In order to obtain employment for the U.S. Navy he had to deny that he was ever a member of the Party. Elitcher was eligible to receive a five-year prison term for having obtained his job by false pretenses. This was one of the reasons that may have prompted him to claim that he was approached by Sobell and Rosenberg to engage in espionage.

Before the jury took their seats in the jury box, Saypol asked Judge Kaufman to exclude all witnesses from the courtroom, the usual procedure undertaken to prevent witnesses from hearing each other's testimony and making it the same. Saypol, however, asked that an exception be made as to the agents of the Federal Bureau of Investigation.

Emanuel Bloch, in his desire to be as accommodating as possible to the government authorities, agreed to allow FBI agents who participated in the case to remain in the courtroom during the trial. Bloch's concession, however, could only hurt his clients, since the FBI agents could match their testimony to that of the other witnesses whenever it suited them.

Max Elitcher was called to the stand as the first government witness. He was questioned by United U.S. Attorney Irving Saypol:

Mr. Saypol: Do you know the defendant Julius Rosenberg?

A. Yes, I do.

Mr. Saypol: Do you see him here in court?

A. Yes, I do...

Mr. Saypol: Where were you living in 1944 in the summer?

A. At 247 Delaware Avenue SW in Washington.

Mr. Saypol: About that time did you see the defendant Rosenberg?

A. Yes I did.

Mr. Saypol: Tell us the circumstances under which you saw him.

A. Well, one evening, it was early, before supper, I received a phone call from a person who said he was Julius Rosenberg.

Judge Kaufman: When was this?

The Witness: In June, 1944...He said that he was a former classmate. I remembered the name, I recalled who it was, and he said he would like to see me. He came over after supper, and my wife was there and we had a casual conversation. After that he asked if my wife would leave the room, that he wanted to speak to me in private. She did and he then said...that there were many people who were implementing aid to the Soviet Union by providing classified information about military equipment, and so forth, and asked whether in my capacity at the Bureau of Ordinance would I have access to and would I be able to get such information and would I turn it over to him...

Mr. Saypol: Is that the first time you met him?

A. After school, yes...

Mr. Saypol: I take it then that Rosenberg, Sobell, and you studied engineering at City College together?

A. Yes...

Mr. Saypol: After your graduation some time in 1938, did you move to Washington?

A. Yes...

Mr. Saypol: When did you see Rosenberg next?

A. In the summer of 1945...

Mr. Saypol: When did you see him next?...

A. He called me again in September of 1945...

Mr. Saypol: Did you see him?

A. Yes. He came over to the house...

Mr. Saypol: What did he say?

A. Well, the war was over and he was saying that even though the war was over there was a continuing need for new military information for Russia, and again was trying to get my views about it, whether I would want to contribute in the future...I said I would see and if I had anything and I wanted to give it to him, I would let him know...

Mr. Saypol: Thereafter did you see Rosenberg?

A. Yes, I did...

Judge Kaufman: When was this?

The Witness: Either the end of '46 and possibly '47, the date I don't know...I told him about my new work...and he then interrupted and told me...there was a leak in this espionage, and because of that there were precautions being taken by him. He told me it would be best if I don't see him, if I don't visit him, that I don't come to see him until he lets me know or until someone informs me. Otherwise—I think that was the substance of the conversation...

Mr. Saypol: About that time, where had Sobell been working?

A. At G.E.

Mr. Saypol: Did his employment change then?

A. Well, sometime in 1947 he took a position at the Reeves Instrument Corporation...I met him more than once at Reeves.

Mr. Saypol: Do you recall the occasion when you had lunch with him?

A. Yes...End of 1947. I don't remember the month.

Mr. Saypol: At this luncheon conversation, what was said?

A. Well, there was this request for names or information about any engineering students that I might know, who were progressive...I told him I didn't know anybody. However, if somebody came along I would tell him about it...

Mr. Saypol: Then, did there come a time when you went to work for the Reeves Instrument Company, too?

A. Yes.

Mr. Saypol: When was that?

A. In October 1948...

Mr. Saypol: Now...at the time you first came to work for Reeves or immediately preceding that, did you have any conversation with Sobell about your plans?

A. Yes. I had been informed—well, my plans for leaving the Bureau of Ordinance started some months before I left...However, when I finally did decide to leave, which was about in June of 1948, again on the occasion of a visit to New York on business, I called him and told him that I was planning to leave the Bureau; that I had definitely decided to do so. He said, "Don't do anything before you see me. I want to talk to you about it, and Rosenberg also wants to speak to you about it." He made an appointment for me to meet Rosenberg at 42nd Street and Third Avenue, which I did...

Mr. Saypol: What did Rosenberg say to you?

A. Rosenberg asked about my plans to leave...I told him I had decided to leave Washington. He said that that was too bad; that he was sorry to hear it, because he had wanted me to stay there, at the Bureau of Ordinance; he wanted me—he needed somebody to work at the Navy Department for this espionage purpose, and he wanted me to change my mind...Sobell was along and I recall that he agreed with Rosenberg in his trying to convince me to stay down at the Bureau of Ordinance...Sobell left and Rosenberg and I had dinner together...

Mr. Saypol: What was the conversation in the course of that dinner?

A. Well, among other things, we continued to talk about this espionage...he asked whether I knew of places where important military work was done...He also told me about the fact that money could be made available for my education, if I so desired...

Mr. Saypol: Now, there came a time when you drove to New York with your family?

A. That is correct.

Mr. Saypol: When was that?

A. The end of July or the beginning of August. Just about the end of July...I was coming up to look for a place to live and my family and I drove up to New York. We were going to stay at the home of the Sobells during the search for a home, a permanent home.

Mr. Saypol: Did you come to Sobell's home with

your family?
A. Yes, I did.
Mr. Saypol: Did you talk to him? Did you see him there?
A. Yes, I did...
Judge Kaufman: This is the end of 1948.
The Witness: No, June-July of 1948. Well, on the way up...

Elitcher was apparently not sure of the date, and Saypol later tried to correct him by supplying it. None of the defense lawyers objected to Saypol's coaxing testimony, not having realized how important it was for the government to establish that Elitcher's visit to Sobell and subsequent drive to Catherine Slip occurred on or after July 30, 1948, the date when Elizabeth Bentley's role as a government informer was officially announced.

Mr. Saypol: Just a moment. Excuse me. I think the witness said the end of July or August.
The Witness: Yes.
Mr. Saypol: Go ahead.
A. On the way up to New York, upon leaving Baltimore we had stopped to buy some dishes and we went off the main road and on coming back I noticed that I was being followed...

Once it was determined that Max and Helene Elitcher were planning a trip to New York City in late July 1948, an FBI memo dated July 29, 1948, requested that they be followed to "ascertain where the Elitchers attempt to obtain their apartment in NY." Surveillance began on Friday, July 30, the day the couple left their apartment in Washington, DC.

First it was the agents of the Baltimore office who watched them. At 1:49 P.M. the Philadelphia agents took over. At 4:55 P.M. surveillance was turned over to the agents of the New York office at 97th Street and Riverside Drive.

A July 30 FBI report signed by Special Agent in Charge Edward Scheidt included a teletype he had sent that stated, "Max and Helene Elitcher...extremely alert for surveillance." Scheidt said the couple should be followed only for the purpose of finding out where they would stay that night; then surveillance should be discontinued. The Elitchers first went to his father's residence at 1571 Lexington Avenue, and why the agents who were following them did not consider that their resting place was not explained. Only when the couple left his father's place and went to Morton Sobell's home did the FBI decide to end surveillance.

Another teletype sent by Special Agent Scheidt the same day said:

> *Evening of July thirty Max and Helene Elitcher proceeded to home of M. Sobell (164-17 73rd Ave, Flushing, New York)...ascertaining if Sobell has telephone in home and if so consideration being given to request technical surveillance in attempt to follow Max Elitcher's efforts in locating apartment New York.*

Scheidt then wrote to the New York Telephone Company asking them for Morton Sobell's telephone number. Scheidt reported on August 5 that they had advised him, "There is no telephone listed for 164-15 or 164-17 73rd Avenue, Queens, NY."

But Sobell lived at 164-17 73rd Ave. Sobell's telephone number was OL8-0829 and both Sobell's address and telephone number were listed in the 1948 New

York City telephone directory. The FBI, which spent a fortune in time and effort following Elitcher to his destination, now made a point of terminating the project.

The question is why. The answers are not easy to come by, but what is certain is that the FBI was following useless and counterproductive procedures. The FBI agents at their worst could not have been so incompetent. More had to be involved. Was Elitcher working undercover for the FBI? If so, it might explain how, in June of the following year, he was able to board the *USS Mississippi* in Norfolk, Virginia to inspect top-secret Navy equipment. There seems to be no other way to explain how a prime espionage suspect could be given such free access to secret government installations. Elitcher, when interviewed about this event, did not deny that it occurred. In fact, the information received from him led to the investigation of Lietenant Commander Morton Prager, the party who gave him permission to visit the installation.

Elitcher, the evidence strongly suggests, was being used to test the adequacy of national security by exposing weak links in the military. In all likelihood, Gold was used in a similar capacity. For example, on May 31, 1950, the FBI received a report from David C. Evans, a reputable citizen who claimed that he recognized Gold from a newspaper photo as the same person he saw at White Sands, New Mexico, when a rocket was launched on September 15, 1949. Evans said that Gold was in the company of two Army photographers. The reports concerning Elitcher's visit to the *USS Mississippi* and Gold's visit to a government rocket launching site were not actively pursued by the FBI in Elitcher's case and attributed to a mistake in identity in Gold's case.

THE TRIAL OF THE ROSENBERGS AND SOBELL

Max Elitcher continued his testimony.

Elitcher: I then proceeded on to Sobell's. When I got there, we had one child and we put the child to bed, I called Sobell aside and told him that I thought that I had been followed by one or two cars from Washington to New York. At this point he became very angry and said that I should not have come to the house under those circumstances...However, he didn't seem to believe that I had been followed...

He finally agreed that I would stay. However, a short time later he came over to me and said he had some valuable information in the house, something that he should have given to Julius Rosenberg some time ago and had not done so; it was too valuable to be destroyed and yet too dangerous to keep around. He said he wanted to deliver it to Rosenberg that night. I told him it was foolish under the circumstances; that it was dangerous, it was a silly thing to do. However, he insisted and said that he was tired. He asked me to go along...Upon leaving I saw him take what I identified then as a 35 millimeter film can.

No reference was made to it. He took it. When we got into the car he put it in the glove compartment. We drove—he drove over to Manhattan along the East Side Drive and he parked outside the Journal American Building. He left the car...He took this can out of the glove compartment and left and I drove up the street and down and parked facing the East River Drive on Catherine Street [Slip] and waited for him there. He came back approximately a half hour later, or perhaps a little shorter, and as we drove off I turned to him and said, "Well, what does Julie think about this, my being followed?"

He said, "It is all right; don't be concerned about

it; it is O.K." He then said Rosenberg had told him that he once talked to Elizabeth Bentley on the phone but he was pretty sure she didn't know who he was and therefore everything was all right. We proceeded back to the house.

It was essential to the government prosecutors that Elizabeth Bentley's name be mentioned by Max Elitcher. Once her name had come up in connection with Julius Rosenberg, she could appear as a witness and testify that the Communist Party of the United States took orders from the Communist Party of the Soviet Union. Her testimony on this theme was considered so critical that the government prosecutors did not believe they could win their cases without her. But for Elitcher's mention of Bentley's name to sound credible, he had to say he had heard it after July 30, 1948, the day when her name was first announced to the public. That is why the trip to Catherine Slip on July 30, 1948, the very day the FBI decided to not follow Elitcher for just another ten miles after following him for over two hundred miles, was appended to Elitcher's testimony.

Mr. Saypol: Just a moment. At that time was the name Elizabeth Bentley under discussion?

A. Well, it had been in the newspapers just prior to that time...

Mr. Saypol: In the time that you worked with Sobell at Reeves Instrument Company, or at any time, did you ever see Sobell take any papers or documents?

A. Well, in the course of his duties, I did, as far as I know, I saw him take—he had a briefcase, and he did take things out of Reeves Instrument. I

163

presume that they had to do with work...

Emanuel Bloch, the attorney for Julius and Ethel Rosenberg, then began his cross-examination of Max Elitcher.

Mr. E. H. Bloch: And when was the first time that you spoke to the FBI?
A. In—it was July of 1950...

Elitcher's appraisal of the time he first spoke to the FBI was not very convincing. He had probably been cooperating with government officials for years before July 1950. On April 24, 1948, J. Edgar Hoover gave direct orders for an investigation of Max Elitcher. But then an FBI teletype dated May 12 stated,

> *All investigation in this case suspended at the direction of the Bureau.*

A few weeks later yet another FBI memo reported that on July 8, 1948 authority was given to install a tel-mike at Elitcher's residence at 247 Delaware, Washington, DC. It does not call for deep intellectual penetration to see that the investigation of Elitcher was discontinued because he was cooperating with the FBI, even to the point of allowing them to tap his phone to record calls from the outside.

There is additional evidence to support the contention that Elitcher was a long-time government informer. In 1941, he dated a woman named Bernice Levin, and when he visited New York City in 1947 and 1948 he resumed the relationship. Elitcher admitted to the FBI that he had been romantically involved with Levin. If Elitcher's relationship with her was merely an adulterous liasion, it would require no further discussion. But it was not that simple. Bernice Levin had been supposedly forwarding infor.dation to Elizabeth Bentley. The FBI noted:

> *On September 20, 1948 Elizabeth T. Bentley, former self-confessed Soviet espionage agent, furnished to Special Agents Thomas G. Spencer and Lawrence Spillane, the following signed statement concerning Bernice Levin:*
> *"Sometime in the Fall of 1941 when I was making my first trips to Washington, DC, at the request of Jacob Golos, the latter informed me that Bernice Levin, who was employed in the War Production Board, was a person I should contact and who would furnish information to me...*
> *"After I first contacted Miss Levin she started to give me information...*
> *"To the best of my recollection the information supplied by Miss Levin was concerned principally with production figures of items and materials which came to her attention while in the employ of the War Production Board."*

The greater likelihood is that Elitcher, rather than Rosenberg, was the one who knew Bentley. Bernice Levin was Elitcher's girlfriend in 1941, during the period when she was said to be actively passing information to Bentley. The probability is that Elitcher knew Golos as well. The evidence suggests that Elitcher was solicited by the FBI in the same manner that Bernice Levin, William Remington, and a host of others were recruited and enveloped in Bentley and Golos's counter-espionage operation of uncovering spies working for the U.S. government. Elitcher, it is suggested, was at some time, in the 1940s, placed in a vulnerable position, and offered alternatives of cooperating with the government or undergoing indictment. For Elitcher, the choice was not difficult.

Elitcher was the hunter, rather than the hunted. He searched out Sobell; he turned Rosenberg's innocent visits into an attempt to obtain information for the Communists. It was Elitcher who chased after a very reluctant Julius Rosenberg. Elitcher seemed to enjoy the perverse excitement of having a friend and at the same time informing on him.

Bloch re-examined Elitcher.

Mr. E. H. Bloch: Did you make any written statements, either to any members of the FBI, who questioned you, or to Mr. Saypol, or any members of the staff?

A. Yes.

Mr. E. H. Bloch: On how many occasions?

A. Three...

Mr. E. H. Bloch: Did you pass any information, secret, classified, confidential or otherwise, of the Government of the United States, to the defendant Julius Rosenberg, at any time?

A. I did not...

Mr. E. H. Bloch: As a matter of fact, from your own story on direct examination, you rejected all overtures on the part of anybody to try to enlist you in stealing information from the Government; isn't that correct?

A. Well, I didn't reject them. I went along. I never turned over material, but I was part of it, I mean...I was part of discussions concerning it until 1948...

Mr. E. H. Bloch: You didn't, though?

A. I did not...

Mr. E. H. Bloch: Let me ask you: Did you ever

sign a loyalty oath for the Federal Government?

A. I did.

Mr. E. H. Bloch: When?

A. I think it was sometime in 1947. I don't remember the time or the time of year...

Mr. E. H. Bloch: At the time you verified that oath, did you believe that you were lying when you concealed your membership in the Communist Party?

A. Yes, I did.

Mr. E. H. Bloch: So you have lied under oath?

A. Yes...

Mr. E. H. Bloch: Now, when for the first time did you see a member of the John O. Rogge firm?...

A. I would say about a week after the first interrogation...

Mr. E. H. Bloch: Now, you had merely the most casual relationship or acquaintanceship with Julius Rosenberg during your student days, isn't that right?

A. Yes.

Mr. E. H. Bloch: And you didn't see him, you say, from the time of your graduation in 1938?

A. That is correct.

Mr. E. II. Bloch: Until June, 1944?

A. That is my recollection...

Mr. E. H. Bloch: And then you say he telephoned you sometime in the early part of June 1944 and asked to come to see you, is that right?

A. Yes...

Mr. E. H. Bloch: And then you say Rosenberg, not having seen you for six years, hardly knowing you, launched into an overture to you to engage in getting information?

A. Yes...

Mr. E. H. Bloch: Did you mention the name of Bentley when you were first brought downtown for *questioning in June 1950 to this building to the FBI agent?*

A. I did not...

Mr. E. H. Bloch: Who was the first one who suggested the name "Bentley" to you?

A. I believe—

Before the question could be answered, Judge Kaufman interrupted, instructing Elitcher to provide the answer the judge sought, namely, that Elitcher mentioned Bentley's name on his own volition.

Judge Kaufman: Did anybody suggest Bentley to you, or did you state the name on your own volition?

A. Well, I don't recall. I believe that someone during some interrogation said did I have anything to do with Bentley, but it wasn't in relation to this particular testimony that I gave about the trip...

Mr. E. H. Bloch: In other words, the word Bentley or the name Bentley was projected into your mind by somebody either in the FBI or on the prosecuting staff of the United States Government, is that correct?...

A. Yes...

Mr. E. H. Bloch: Do you remember when it was first mentioned?

A. I do not...

Mr. E. H. Bloch: Do I understand that you signed three statements?

A. Yes...

Mr. E. H. Bloch: So that in the first statement you didn't mention this particular conversation where Bentley's name was mentioned by Sobell and in the second statement you didn't mention this particular conversation where Bentley's name was mentioned? Is that an accurate statement?

A. That is correct...

Mr. E. H. Bloch: When did you testify before the grand jury the first time?

A. The middle of August.

Mr. E. H. Bloch: Did you testify on more than one occasion before the grand jury?

A. Yes.

Mr. E. H. Bloch: How many occasions?

A. Two times. Twice...

Mr. E. H. Bloch: Now, when you testified before the grand jury for the first time did you mention the word "Bentley"?

A. Well, I don't remember whether I actually testified to it before the grand jury, whether that question was asked. I had—

Judge Kaufman: You had what?

The Witness: I had already told the FBI about this trip.

Mr. E. H. Bloch: I am going to ask you a very simple question. Did you mention the name Bentley at any time during your interrogation before the grand jury the first time you testified before the grand jury?

Judge Kaufman: Don't answer. It has been answered. He said he wasn't asked, but he had already told the FBI about it before.

Kaufman was encouraging Elitcher to lie and when Elitcher did not promptly comply, Kaufman did the lying for him. Elitcher did not say that he was not asked the question before the grand jury; Kaufman said it. Elitcher testified that he did not remember "whether that question was asked." To make this episode even more disturbing, Kaufman, after Elitcher said, "I had already told the FBI about this trip," led the jury to believe that Elitcher mentioned Bentley's name to the FBI, when it was apparent that Elitcher was referring to the trip he took in Sobell's car to Catherine Slip, not to his mention of Elizabeth Bentley's name.

Mr. E. H. Bloch: Who recommended you to Mr. Rogge's office?

A. No one...

Mr. E. H. Bloch: Did Mr. Rogge tell you that David Greenglass was a defendant in this case?

A. Well...They told me they were defending Mr. Greenglass...

Mr. E. H. Bloch: And you didn't ask Mr. Rogge or...any member of this firm anything about any duality...in representing you on the one hand and a defendant in this very same situation on the other?...

The Witness: Well, we went down to Mr. Rogge's firm with our recommendation...

Mr. E. H. Bloch: When you say "we," you mean you and your wife?

A. Yes. My wife was with me...

Mr. E. H. Bloch: Now, prior to the time that you went down to Mr. Rogge's office was any mention made here in the Federal Building by anybody, whether it be a Federal man or whether it be a member of Mr. Saypol's staff or whether it be you, about Mr. Rogge?

A. No.

Mr. E. H. Bloch: Was his name ever mentioned?

A. No.

Mr. E. H. Bloch: Prior to the time—

A. No...

Mr. E. H. Bloch: And, sir, you are, are you not,

presently unemployed?
  A. That is correct.
  Mr. E. H. Bloch: Were you fired?
  A. Well, I was asked to resign...
  *Mr. E. H. Bloch: Did you buy a new automobile
within the last two weeks?*
  A. Yes.
  *Mr. E. H. Bloch: When you bought that automobile
did you have any worry in your mind about any future
prosecution by the Government against you?*
  Mr. Saypol: I fail to see the relevancy...
  Judge Kaufman: I will let him answer.
  Mr. Saypol: Will your Honor hear me?
  *Judge Kaufman: You say there is no relevancy. I
am inclined to agree with you but I am going to let
him answer.*
  *Mr. Saypol: Will your Honor let me state on the
record my objection? I think the cross-examination is
taking a turn which is wholly unfair to the prosecution. First there is an implication that the United
States Government recommends lawyers and witnesses
to defendants...*
  *The Witness: The question was whether I was wor-
ried? Yes, I was...*

Saypol was telling Elitcher not to mention that
anyone related to the U.S. Attorney's office referred
him to O. John Rogge. Although the question that had
been posed by Bloch had nothing to do with Saypol's
complaint of irrelevancy, Saypol was anticipating
Bloch's direction. He was terrified of what Elitcher
might say if he were again asked who referred him to
O. J. Rogge. Saypol was telegraphing an urgent message to both Elitcher and Kaufman to be very careful
with this line of questioning. It could lead to the

revelation that he or his staff had referred Elitcher and other government witnesses to lawyers who were former prosecutors.

As shocking as this may sound, prosecutors frequently did send informers, prosecution witnesses, and friends to lawyers they favored, and they almost always took a share of the fee collected. This was customary procedure, with a third party usually making the contact in order to protect the referring prosecutor from exposure. The legal fees paid to O. John Rogge were very likely shared with Irving Saypol.

Edward Kuntz, Morton Sobell's lawyer, then began his cross-examination of Max Elitcher.

Mr. Kuntz: In June, 1944, you said you had a conversation with Rosenberg?

A. Yes...

Mr. Kuntz: Well now, the invitation to you was to get Government documents, was it not?

A. Yes.

Mr. Kuntz: Now let's see whether you accepted it with or without qualifications. Did you go and get any Government documents?

A. No...

Mr. Kuntz: Right after you had the conversation with Rosenberg in early June '44, did you communicate in any way with Sobell?

A. I don't recall any such communications...

Mr. Kuntz: Afterward, you didn't see Sobell for some time, did you?...

A. I saw him in '45.

Mr. Kuntz: When?

A. At his wedding.

Mr. Kuntz: Did he say anything to you about getting documents from the United States Government?

A. No...

Mr. Kuntz: And then the next time you saw Sobell was in '46, up in Schenectady; is that right?

A. Yes.

Mr. Kuntz: Sobell didn't invite you up there, did he?

A. No...

Mr. Kuntz: Now, on each occasion that you had a conversation with Rosenberg or with Sobell, where they made invitations to you, did you accept those invitations to commit espionage?

A. I accepted the invitations, yes.

Mr. Kuntz: Did you get any documents from the United States Government?

A. No.

The line of questioning was important. Elitcher's saying that he had accepted the invitation to commit espionage was meaningless. His "yes" answer had no verifiability. Had he answered "no" it would have been just as meaningless. Saying "yes" and not participating in espionage activities was certainly less culpable than saying "no" and engaging wholeheartedly in espionage. Yes or no answers to what Elitcher believed he was doing should have been rejected as meaningless. The testimony developed during the trial established beyond dispute that Max Elitcher never once transferred a secret of any kind to Sobell or Rosenberg, who supposedly solicited and harassed him for four years without success.

Mr. Kuntz: Did you hand any documents of the United States Government to Sobell?

A. No...

Mr. Kuntz: I just wanted to spend a few minutes'

time, if you please, on this occasion when you came up from Washington in the car with your family, and I think that was in June of '48, am I right?

A. It was in July...

Mr. Kuntz: The same day you were being followed by FBI agents, weren't you?

A. Yes...

Mr. Kuntz: Mr. Elitcher...If I remember correctly, between 1942 and 1948 you only saw Sobell on a very few occasions; is that right?

A. Yes.

Mr. Kuntz: This occasion of your trip to Catherine Slip, that loomed rather important in your mind, did it not?

A. Yes...

Mr. Kuntz: But you didn't tell this to the FBI on the first visit?

A. No, I did not.

Mr. Kuntz: Were you trying to conceal it?

A. At the time, perhaps.

Mr. Kuntz: In other words, you were trying to lie to the FBI, weren't you?

A. No. I omitted it, but I didn't—all right, I lied...

Mr. Kuntz: You only mentioned Miss Bentley to the FBI after the FBI suggested that name; isn't that true?

A. Yes...

Judge Kaufman: Well is that the fact?...

A. Well, not right after, in time...

Judge Kaufman: Well now, I wish, Mr. Witness, that you would explain an answer, if it requires explanation, and that you don't answer simply yes or no, because I am beginning to get a bit confused here. Now what is the answer to that?

Judge Kaufman was ordering Elitcher to change his testimony, and he did.

A. *During the early questioning, they mentioned Bentley; they might have mentioned other names, too, saying, "Did you have anything to do with Miss Bentley"? I said no. That was the end of that. There was no further questioning by the FBI about the name Bentley until I brought up the name of Bentley myself, at a later period.*
Mr. Kuntz: What you are trying to say is, they did not direct your mind to this particular incident?
A. That is correct...

Elitcher simply withdrew his previous testimony relating to Elizabeth Bentley.

Mr. Kuntz: Let's take it from there. Didn't you answer my question only a few minutes ago, when I asked you whether it wasn't a fact that you told about this conversation with Bentley after the FBI mentioned Bentley? Didn't you tell us that?
A. Yes, but much later.
Mr. Kuntz: Didn't you tell this jury that only two or three minutes ago?
The Witness: I am now confused, sir...The name Bentley was brought up by the FBI agents and I said I had nothing to do with Miss Bentley. At a much later period, I told them that the name Bentley had been mentioned to me by Sobell.
Mr. Kuntz: I move to strike out the answer.
Judge Kaufman: It will stand.
Mr. Kuntz: It is not responsive, and I ask the witness to answer the question I propounded. I submit

it is in answer to something but not the question I propounded.

Judge Kaufman: Don't raise your voice to me.

Mr. Kuntz: I am sorry, Judge; I am sorry, Judge; it means nothing. It is my customary way, your Honor...

Kuntz knew very well when it was time to be humble. The meanness of Judge Kaufman was not something to test.

This meanness did not belong to Judge Kaufman alone. All Kuntz had to do was look back little more than a year before—to see the way Judge Medina handled Communists and their lawyers in his court. Medina not only sentenced ten of the convicted Communist Party leaders to five-year terms, he held their lawyers in contempt and sentenced them to terms of up to six months in jail, though it was he who instigated the contempt.

Two of the lawyers, who were from New York, Abraham J. Isserman and Harry Sacher, had their names forwarded to the Bar Association of New York for disbarment proceedings—at the insistence of Irving Saypol. They were disbarred. The other three lawyers were also disbarred in their states. It took several years of appeals before they were finally reinstated, and by that time their careers were ruined.

Destruction of the Communist Party in America required the destruction of lawyers who would represent Communists. As a result, the American Bar Association recommended expelling lawyers who were Communists or believed in Marxist-Leninist doctrines. Various state bar associations throughout the country set up committees to institute disciplinary proceedings against lawyers who had Communist affiliations. It was several years before the courts reversed themselves and decided that it was wrong to punish a lawyer for representing a Communist or a similarly unpopular client. Before the courts reached that decision, accused Communists often could not even find a lawyer. One Communist leader had to defend himself in a New York trial, because he had been turned down by over two hundred lawyers. It was under these conditions that Edward Kuntz, Harold Phillips, Alexander Bloch, and Emanuel Bloch undertook the defense of Ethel and Julius Rosenberg and Morton Sobell.

Judge Kaufman: All right, I think the subject has been exhausted.

Kaufman saw to it that questions which brought out Elitcher's dishonesty and the influence exerted upon him by the FBI and the Attorney General's office were discontinued.

The following discussion took place at the bench, outside of the hearing of the jury.

Mr. E. H. Bloch: The defendant Julius Rosenberg now asks the Government to produce for use in this trial, and with respect to further cross-examination of this witness, the following: All written statements signed by this witness and delivered to the authorities of the United States of America...

In support of my application, your Honor, I contend that...there were prior contradictory statements made in some or all of those documents or material that I have mentioned, and in the testimony that he gave before the grand jury on the first occasion, to warrant the granting of the application...

Judge Kaufman: Well, I don't agree with you, at least insofar as that first statement to the FBI, and if I did, I would do it in the fashion that has at least been indicated by some of the cases. I think that I should examine that first FBI statement. I believe that is the only statement where it has been pointed out that there may be some inconsistency, and I would examine that, and if I find that there is an inconsistency in a substantial manner with what has been testified here in the trial, then, of course, I will have to take the next step on it...

Mr. Phillips: May I add to this request, while you are examining the first statement there, you might just as well examine the other statements from the same standpoint, as long as it is discretionary with you, as to the rule.

Judge Kaufman: May I say to you, Mr. Phillips, the cases have held that in the first place there should not be an undue burden placed upon the Court to examine everything. I am...willing to give you the benefit of the doubt in examining this statement, and I shall examine this statement...

Mr. Saypol: May I know if there are any other discrepancies that counsel pointed to?

Mr. E. H. Bloch: Yes, I think the June 1944 incident.

Mr. Saypol: You mean, as to when the first meeting with Rosenberg took place, when Rosenberg called him to his home?

Mr. E. H. Bloch: Yes.

Mr. Saypol: There is a conflict?

Mr. E. H. Bloch: Yes.

Mr. Saypol: I don't know how that is material.

Judge Kaufman: My own opinion is that it is immaterial...You see, his testimony today is unusual...he told the FBI several months before June '44, but his recollection today is that it was June.

Kaufman made nothing of the fact that the date supplied to the defense, listing the time when a supposedly criminal act occurred, was false and misleading. The judge considered outright lies merely mis-recollections of the truth.

Irving Saypol next began to re-examine Max Elitcher.

Mr. Saypol: There has been some examination here concerning statements, questioning of you by agents of the Federal Bureau of Investigation, by myself and by members associated with me. Do you remember the first day that the agents of the FBI called upon you at your place of employment?

A. Yes, I do.

Mr. Saypol: I think that was July 20, 1950, was it not?

A. I don't know the date. It wasn't in July.

Mr. E. H. Bloch: If you say that is the date we will accept that as the date, Mr. Saypol.

Elitcher said that he was not questioned by the FBI on July 20, 1950. He even denied that he was questioned for the first time in July at all. Yet Bloch was so respectful of Saypol or intimidated by him that he voluntarily discounted Elitcher's contradictions of his own testimony.

Mr. Saypol: In the course of cross-examination of you by Mr. Kuntz, he asked you a question whether or not it was a fact that you had lied to the agents in regard to Bentley. Did you deliberately make a misstatement of fact to the agents with the intent to deceive them?...

A. No, I did not.

It was obvious that during a recess Saypol reviewed Elitcher's answers with him and persuaded him to give very different answers to certain questions. Elitcher after recess decided that he was no longer a liar.

Mr. Saypol: Do you wish to make an explanation in regard to the answer you have given when you said that you lied?
A. When I said that, I meant that I had not revealed to them this trip, the fact that I had been followed to New York and what resulted at Sobell's house, and going down to Rosenberg's house, going down to the East Side and the mention of Bentley. When I said I had lied I meant that I had not told them that story at that particular time. Otherwise I didn't lie to them...

Bloch cross-examined Max Elitcher.

Mr. E. H. Bloch: Now, didn't you testify on cross-examination by Mr. Kuntz just before the luncheon recess that you deliberately omitted mentioning this automobile ride that you took with Sobell from your home in Flushing to Catherine Slip and the conversation that you are alleged to have had with Sobell where Bentley's name was mentioned?
A. Yes, I omitted to say that.
Mr. E. H. Bloch: You deliberately omitted to say that, did you not?
A. Yes...
Judge Kaufman: This witness is excused, but I would like to have him available Monday morning in

the building in the event that I deem it necessary that he be recalled on the matter of these statements...

DAVID GREENGLASS

David Greenglass, Ethel Rosenberg's younger brother, was then called as a witness for the Government. After being first sworn, he was questioned by U. S. Attorney Roy Cohn.

Mr. Cohn: Now, in 1943 did you enter the Army of the United States?
A. I did...
Mr. Cohn: Now am I correct in stating that during the next year, July 1943 to July 1944, you were stationed at various posts, Army posts throughout the United States?
A. I was...
Mr. Cohn: After your two weeks' orientation at Oak Ridge, Tennessee, were you then assigned to report to some other place in the United States?
A. I was.
Mr. Cohn: Where was that?
A. Los Alamos, New Mexico...
Mr. Cohn: About when did you report to Los Alamos?
A. August, 1944...
Mr. Cohn: Were you told at the time the nature of the work being done at the Manhattan Project?
A. No.
Mr. Cohn: Was the fact that it was secret reaffirmed to you?
A. It was...
Mr. Cohn: You knew that the information as to who Dr. Bohr out there was was secret?
A. I did...

Mr. Cohn: Now, was one of the scientists who was present at Los Alamos and whose name and presence you came to know Dr. Walter Koski?

A. That is correct.

Mr. Cohn: I believe Dr. Koski is here in court. Would you rise, Dr. Koski?...

Mr. Cohn: Did you specifically work in the machining of a flat type lens mold and other molds which Dr. Koski required in the course of his experimentation on atomic energy?

A. I did...

Mr. Cohn: Now am I correct in stating that during the entire period of your stay in Los Alamos, 1944 to the time you were discharged in 1946, you worked in the machine shop and in the Theta shop on apparatus and equipment in connection with experimentation on atomic energy?

A. I did...

Mr. Cohn: Now did you have any discussion with Ethel and Julius concerning the relative merits of our form of government and that of the Soviet Union?

Mr. A. Bloch: Objected to as incompetent; irrelevant and immaterial, not pertinent to the issues raised by the indictment and the plea...

Judge Kaufman: I believe it is relevant...in view of the fact that the indictment charges conspiracy to commit espionage in that matters of national defense which would be advantageous to Russia is charged in the indictment I think it is most relevant...

Mr. Cohn: Talking about Socialism over capitalism, did they specifically talk about Socialism as it existed in the Soviet Union and capitalism as it existed here?

A. They did.

Mr. Cohn: Which did they like better? Did they tell you?

The Witness: They preferred Socialism to Capitalism.

Judge Kaufman: Which type of Socialism?

The Witness: Russian Socialism...

Mr. Cohn: Mr. Greenglass, when you went out to Los Alamos, was your wife out there with you?

A.   No, she wasn't...She came to visit me on our second wedding anniversary.   It was November 29, 1944...

Mr. Cohn: Now, was there any time...when you had a conversation with your wife concerning the atom bomb?

A.   I did...

Mr. Cohn: Will you tell us, Mr. Greenglass, what your wife said and what you said.

A.   My wife said that while she was still in New York, Julius Rosenberg invited her to dinner at their house at 10 Monroe Street...He then went on to tell Ruth that I was working on the atomic bomb project at Los Alamos, and that they would want me to give information to the Russians....

Mr. Cohn: What did you tell your wife?

A.   I told my wife that I wouldn't do it.   And she had also told me that in the conversation, Julius and Ethel had told her that Russia was an ally and as such deserved this information...So later on that night after this conversation, I thought about it and the following morning I told my wife that I would give the information...

Throughout the trial the Greenglasses were described in court and in the newspapers as a young couple dominated by the Rosenbergs: Ruth Greenglass an unwilling participant in espionage, and David Greenglass a dupe who joined the Young Communist

League in order to play handball. Ruth Greenglass, quoted by Louis Schaeffer of the *Daily Fowards* in an article, September 2, 1950, said, "There was a time when David and I were partial toward Communism. But we were never embittered or intolerant toward people who did not agree with us. But Ethel was quite different. She did not buy from a butcher or grocer unless he were an open sympathizer toward Soviet Russia. She considered everyone who was against Communism her personal enemy."

There is evidence to dispute Ruth's self-portrait in the letters she and David wrote one another while he was in the Army.

> *[Letter dated April 28, 1943, from David Greenglass to Ruth Greenglass]*
> *There is a vital battle to be fought with a cruel, ruthless foe. Victory shall be ours and the future is socialism's.*

> *[Letter dated May 2, 1943, from Ruth to David]*
> *All I can say is that I am sorry I missed so many other May Days...Perhaps the voice of 75,000 working men and women that were brought together today, perhaps their voices demanding an early invasion of Europe will be heard and then my dear we will be together to build—under socialism—our future...*

> *[Letter dated December 27, 1943, from David to Ruth]*
> *Dearest, you are no snob, what you say is true and there are only two ways to look at it. Either convert our friends or drop them.*

J. EDGAR HOOVER AND NIELS BOHR

The questioning continued.

Mr. Cohn: Would you tell us as you recall it, what your wife asked you?

A. She asked me to tell her about the general layout of the Los Alamos Atomic Project, the buildings, number of people and stuff like that; also scientists that worked there, and that was the first information I gave her.

Mr. Cohn: You say she asked you for that information, is that right?

A. She asked me for that information. When I gave it to her she memorized the information...She told me that she was instructed not to write it down, but to memorize it.

Judge Kaufman: Instructed by whom?

The Witness: Instructed by Julius.

Mr. Cohn: In giving to your wife the names of the scientists working at Los Alamos on that occasion can you now recall any of the names which you furnished to her?

A. I gave her Oppenheimer's name, I gave her Bohr's name and Kistiakowski's name.

The whereabouts and identity of certain scientists was considered classified information since the special knowledge they possessed, if learned, could enable a foreign government to deduce the direction of the U.S. Government's plans. Oppenheimer and Kistiakowsky were scientists working at Los Alamos whose presence there was not considered classified. Niels Bohr's presence, however, since he was so closely associated with atomic energy, was considered top-secret. But David Greenglass did not give his wife Bohr's name. The presentation of this false evidence had the full participation of U.S. Attorneys Irving Saypol, Roy Cohn, and Myles Lane. No less involved in the falsification of Greenglass's testimony was the director of the FBI, J. Edgar Hoover. In Greenglass's original statement, given to the FBI when he was arrested on June 15, 1950, he said that he "furnished Gold with information concerning the identity of a world-famous scientist...working at Los Alamos under an assumed name," but he did not mention Bohr's name. Interviewed repeatedly during June and July of 1950, Greenglass never identified Bohr.

Ruth Greenglass, when she was questioned on August 7 by U.S. Attorney Myles Lane in the presence of two of Hoover's most reliable agents, William F. Norton and John Harrington, also failed to support her husband's claim that he provided her with Bohr's name. Ruth Greenglass's answers to Myles Lane's questions follow.

> *Q. Did he give you the name of any of the scientists working down there?*
> *A. Yes, Oppenheimer and Urey, I remember.*
> *Q. Any others?*
> *A. No...*

Not even Harry Gold supported David Greenglass's testimony. On August 1, 1950, when Gold was interviewed by Special Agents Norton and Harrington, Gold denied that Greenglass had told him that Niels Bohr was working at Los Alamos.

When the FBI originally claimed that Greenglass had said that he gave Harry Gold the name of a

187

world-famous scientist, they did not mention the scientist's name. Niels Bohr was the scientist finally chosen. That choice was announced in August 1950 when J. Edgar Hoover, referring to David Greenglass's signed statement of July 17, wrote to Assistant Attorney General James M. McInerney:

> *It is somewhat doubtful that the fact that Dr. Oppenheimer and Dr. Kistiakowski were employed at Los Alamos was considered by itself to be classified information by the Manhattan District...For your information, it was Dr. Bohr who was referred to by Greenglass in his statement...*

Hoover, however, knew that David Greenglass had not told anybody about Niels Bohr working at Los Alamos. Hoover obstructed justice and suborned perjury; he created an entirely false set of facts which he knew to be false.

JANUARY-JUNE, 1945

Mr. Cohn: After you furnished this information to your wife, did your wife return to New York?

A. My wife returned to New York and I had told her that I would be in New York in January on furlough, so she left for New York, knowing that I was going to be there...I arrived home January 1st, 1945...

Mr. Cohn: How long was your furlough?

A. It was a 15-day furlough with travel time...

Mr. Cohn: After your arrival in New York did there come a time when you saw the defendant Julius Rosenberg?

A. Yes, he came to me one morning and asked me to give him information, specifically anything of value on the atomic bomb, whatever I knew about it...And he told me to write it up, to write up anything that I knew about the atomic bomb.

The following took place at the bench, in the absence of the jury.

Judge Kaufman: Let me say for the record that I have examined three statements given by the witness Elitcher to the FBI dated respectively July 20, 1950, July 21, 1950 and October 23, 1950. I have as well read the grand jury minutes of Mr. Max Elitcher dated August 14, 1950 and January 31, 1951.

It is my feeling in the matter, that while I find no true inconsistency...I have determined that I shall turn over to the defense the statements given to the FBI respectively noted before, and the grand jury minutes...

I don't want a long protractive cross-examination

again to start...

Mr. E. H. Bloch: Yes, your Honor...As you can see...it would take probably about a half hour minimum to even read the statements without trying to digest them for inconsistency...I would like to make the suggestion to the Court, and ask a favor of the Court, that the witness Elitcher be asked to come back on some subsequent date, whatever date...

Judge Kaufman: No, no...You know the testimony. It only occurred on Friday. It is clear in your mind...We will recess at one o'clock until 2:30. That will give you an opportunity. It didn't take me long to read the statements; no more than a half hour tops...

Mr. Phillips: Will we have enough time in a half hour to read these?

Judge Kaufman: No. You will have an hour and a half. You don't eat for an hour. I don't. I eat for 10 minutes. I have a sandwich and coffee. You can arrange to have a sandwich and coffee brought in for you today, but we must move this trial along...In order to get this trial moving in an orderly fashion I have determined that you are to examine these statements I have referred to before and the grand jury minutes. You are to do so during the one and a half hour lunch period. I have read them. It didn't take me half hour to read them. You will have an hour and a half. I don't think you will have any difficulty whatsoever in crystallizing the particular thoughts you have in mind. So there it is...My own feeling in the matter is that this man really told a very good, honest, logical story, consistent with what he told here in court. That is my general feeling on the subject...

The jury was recalled and direct examination of

David Greenglass continued.

Mr. Cohn: Now, Mr. Greenglass, I think that on Friday afternoon before we adjourned, we were at the point where Rosenberg had returned to your apartment to get this information on the atom bomb that he had asked you to write down; is that correct?

A. That is correct.

Mr. Cohn: Will you tell us again—first of all, did you in fact furnish him with written information concerning the atom bomb?

A. I did.

Mr. Cohn: Will you tell us just what information you furnished him with on that day?

A. I gave him a list of scientists who worked on the project. I gave him some sketches of flat type lens molds, and I gave him some possible recruits.

Mr. Cohn: What kind of recruits?

A. For Soviet espionage...He said he wanted a list of people who seemed sympathetic with Communism and would help furnish information to the Russians...

Mr. Cohn: Now, Mr. Greenglass, have you, at our request, prepared a copy of the sketch of the lens mold which you furnished to Rosenberg on that day in January?

A. I did.

Mr. Cohn: Would you examine Government's Exhibit 2 for identification (handing) and tell me if that is the sketch which you prepared.

A. That is the sketch that I prepared...

Mr. Cohn: Did there come a time when you and your wife did in fact go to Rosenberg's home in response to the dinner invitation?

A. We did...When I got to the apartment with my wife, there was Julius and Ethel Rosenberg and a woman by the name of Ann Sidorovich...

Mr. Cohn: Now, had you ever met Ann Sidorovich before?

A. I had never met her before, no.

Mr. Cohn: Did you know any members of her family?

A. I knew her husband...

Mr. Cohn: Would you tell us exactly what happened on that evening, exactly what was said and by whom?

A. Well, the early part of the evening we just sat around and spoke socially with Ann and the Rosenbergs, and then Ann Sidorovich left. It was at this point that Julius said that this is the woman who he thinks would come out to see us, who will come out to see us at Albuquerque, to receive information from myself...

Mr. Cohn: What kind of information?

A. On the atomic bomb...

Ann Sidorovich was never arrested though, according to Irving Saypol, she was a courier for the Russians. The Government's failure to prosecute her or call her as a witness, when she would have no choice but to testify or plead the Fifth Amendment, had to be because she had denied that she was involved in the espionage Greenglass described. But the government did list Ann Sidorovich as their witness. This in effect precluded Bloch from calling her for the defense, since her listing by the prosecution led him to believe that she, like the Greenglasses and Elitchers, would be coerced to testify for the prosecution. FBI reports of interviews with Ann Sidorovich that later surfaced revealed that she would have been willing to testify if called as a witness by either side and was convinced the Rosenbergs were innocent.

Mr. Cohn: Now, was anything said about the reason for Ann Sidorovich being present at the Rosenberg home on that particular night when you were there?

A. Yes, they wanted us to meet this Ann Sidorovich, so that we would know what she looked like; and that brought up a point, what if she does not come?

Mr. Cohn: You mean, there was a possibility that somebody else would come?

A. That's right. So Julius...my wife and Ethel went into the kitchen and I was in the living room; and then a little while later, after they had been there about five minutes or so, they came out and my wife had in her hand a Jello box side...And it had been cut, and Julius had the other part to it, and when he came in with it, I said, "Oh, that is very clever," because I noticed how it fit, and he said, "The simplest things are the cleverest."

Mr. Cohn: Now, let me see if I understand that. Your wife had one side; is that correct?

A. That's right.

Mr. Cohn: Who kept the other side?

A. Julius had the other side.

Mr. Cohn: Was there any conversation as to what would be done with these two sides?

A. Well, my wife was to keep the side she had, and she was to use it for identification with the person who would come out to see us...

Mr. Cohn: During this evening, was any reference made by either of the Rosenbergs, to the material which you had turned over to Julius a couple of days before?

A. Well, we discussed the lenses—we generally

talked shop about what I had done at Los Alamos, and we discussed lenses all during this evening, and, you know, whatever was going on at Los Alamos, scientists...things of that nature; and he said that he would like me to meet somebody who would talk to me more about lenses.

Mr. Cohn: Did he tell you who this person he wanted you to meet was?

A. He said it was a Russian he wanted me to meet...

Mr. Cohn: Did anything further come of Julius's statement that he wanted you to discuss this lens with the Russians?

A. Yes.

Mr. Cohn: Tell us.

A. A few nights later—well an appointment was made for me to meet a Russian on First Avenue, between 42nd and 59th Streets—it was in that area.

Mr. Cohn: Who made the appointment?

A. Julius made the appointment.

Mr. Cohn: When was it in relation to the dinner meeting in January?

A. It was a few days after. I took my father-in-law's car and drove up there...Julius...introduced the man to me by first name, that I don't recall at this time, and the man got into the car with me. Julius stayed right there and we drove around...

Mr. Cohn: Now, about how long did this drive with the Russian last?

A. About twenty minutes or so...

Mr. Cohn: Did you see Julius any more on that night?

A. Yes, he came back—I mean, he was around there, and the Russian got out and they went off together, and I drove back home...

Mr. E. H. Bloch: *Now, if the Court please, just a second. I move to strike out the characterization of the man that he met, especially in the last answer, as "Russian."*

Judge Kaufman: *That is denied. The testimony, as I understand it, is that Julius said he wanted to introduce him to a Russian...*

Mr. Cohn: *About when did you leave New York and return to Los Alamos?*

A. *About the 20th.*

Mr. Cohn: *Did your wife go with you*

A. *She did not go with me.*

Mr. Cohn: *Did there come a time when she joined you at Albuquerque?*

A. *She did...*

Mr. Cohn: *When did you say it was that Harry Gold came to your house, Mr. Greenglass?*

A. *It was the third Sunday in June 1945.*

Mr. Cohn: *What time of day?*

A. *It was in the morning...There was a knock on the door and I opened it. We had just completed eating breakfast, and there was a man standing in the hallway who asked if I were Mr. Greenglass, and I said yes. He stepped through the door and he said, "Julius sent me," and I said "oh," and walked to my wife's purse, took out the wallet and took out the matched part of the Jello box...*

Mr. Cohn: *After you produced that did Gold do anything?*

A. *He produced his piece and we checked them and they fitted, and the identification was made...*

Mr. Cohn: *Now, after mutual identification was effected, did you have any conversation with Harry Gold?*

A. *Yes. I offered him something to eat and he*

said he had already eaten. He just wanted to know if I had any information and I said, "I have some but I will have to write it up. If you come back in the afternoon I will give it to you."...

Mr. Cohn: Tell us exactly what happened when he came back...

A. Well, when he came back to the house he came in and I gave him the report in an envelope and he gave me an envelope which I felt and realized there was money in it and put it in my pocket...

Mr. Cohn: Going back to these sketches which you gave to Harry Gold, do you remember just what sketches you gave to Harry Gold concerning a high explosives lens mold on that occasion?

A. I gave sketches relating to the experiment set up; one showing a flat—the face of the flat type lens mold...

After Greenglass identified court exhibit numbers 6 and 7 as the replicas of the sketches he gave to Harry Gold, questioning of him was interrupted to allow another witness, Walter Koski, to be called to the stand.

WALTER KOSKI

Walter S. Koski, called as a witness on behalf of the Government, being first duly sworn, testified as follows:

Mr. Saypol: Dr. Koski, what is your profession?

A. Physical chemistry...

Mr. Saypol: In 1944 did you become associated with the United States Government?

A. I did.

Mr. Saypol: In what capacity?

A. As an engineer at the Los Alamos Scientific Laboratories...

Mr. Saypol: You have been in attendance here and you have heard the witness, Greenglass's testimony, the defendant Greenglass's testimony, have you not?

A. I have.

Mr. Saypol: I show you Government's Exhibit 2, rather. Will you examine that, please?...Is that a reasonably accurate portrayal of a sketch of a type of lens, mold or lens that you required in the course of your experimental work at the time?

A. It is...

Mr. Saypol: In your special field as you knew it at the time, 1944 and 1945, did you have knowledge that the experiments which you were conducting and the effects as they were observed by you could have been of advantage to a foreign nation?...

A. To the best of my knowledge and all of my colleagues who were involved in this field, there was no information in text books or technical journals on this particular subject...

Dr. Walter Koski evaluated his work as highly creative. Whether it was or not was a question that was not satisfactorily answered at the trial.

Mr. Saypol: And up to that point and continuing right up until this trial, has the information relating to the lens mold and the lens and the experimentation to which you have testified continued to be secret information?

A. It still is.

Mr. Saypol: Except as divulged at this trial?

A. Correct...

Mr. Saypol: Will your Honor allow a statement for the record in that respect? The Atomic Energy Committee has declassified this information under the Atomic Energy Act and has made the ruling as authorized by Congress that subsequent to the trial it is to be reclassified...

Bloch began his cross-examination of Dr. Koski:

Mr. E. H. Bloch: Is it not a fact that a scientist would not consider Government exhibit 2, 6, and 7...until the scientist knew the dimensions of the lens or the cylincrical apparatus?

A. This is a rough sketch and, of course, is not quantitative but it does illustrate the important principle involved.

Mr. E. H. Bloch: It does omit, however, the dimensions?

A. It does omit dimensions.

Mr. E. H. Bloch: It omits, for instance, the diameter, does it not?

A. Correct...

Judge Kaufman: You say it does, however, set

forth the important principle involved, is that correct?

The Witness: Correct.

Judge Kaufman: Can you tell us what that principle is?

The Witness: The principle is the use of a combination of high explosives of appropriate shape to produce a symmetrical converging detonation wave.

Mr. E. H. Bloch: Now, weren't the dimensions of these lens molds very vital or at least very important with respect to their utility in terms of success in your experiments?

A. The physical over-all dimensions that you mention are not important. It is the relative dimensions that are.

Mr. E. H. Bloch: Now the relative dimensions are not disclosed, are they, by these exhibits?

A. They are not.

Mr. E. H. Bloch: That is all...

Kaufman tried to represent the sketches of the lens mold as valuable but Dr. Koski admitted that the missing relative dimensions were of critical importance. Saypol then re-examined Dr. Koski.

Mr. Saypol: The important factor from the experimental point of view is the design, is it not?

A. Correct.

Mr. Saypol: That was original, novel at the time, was it not?

A. It was...

Mr. Saypol: Would I be exaggerating if I were to say colloquially that one expert, interested in finding out what was going on at Los Alamos, could get enough from those exhibits...which you have before you to reveal what was going on at Los Alamos?

A.   One could...

Mr. Saypol: So that the sketches, particularly 2 and 6, do show relative dimensions in that they show the relations of each of the factors in the lens, one to the other?

A.   They do.

Mr. Saypol: That is all...

In this way, Koski was led to restate that relative dimensions were shown when they were not. Koski contradicted himsel, giving a conclusion contrary to the facts. The dimensions were missing, so by mathematical logic the relative dimensions had to be missing. Saypol misled the jury by using the broad words "relations" and "factors," enabling Koski to say that relative dimensions were shown and thus confusing the jurors.

A conference was then held between the lawyers and Judge Kaufman concerning the grand jury minutes and statements made to the FBI as they related to Max Elitcher's testimony. Bloch and Kuntz were willing to let the issue die. But Phillips, their colleague on the defense, was not so willing to discontinue pursuing the discrepancies he thought existed in Elitcher's statements. Judge Kaufman, however, was determined to obtain Phillips's consent on abandoning further questioning of Elitcher. When Phillips failed to give in, Kaufman simply ignored his protest.

Mr. Phillips: As for the defendant Sobell, frankly, I am not quite convinced that I would be doing my duty by answering one way or the other...I should like the indulgence of the Court to think it over between tonight and tomorrow.

Judge Kaufman: I am going to ask you to make your decision now. You have had one hour and 45 minutes.

Mr. Phillips: Do you know how much reading matter there is?

Judge Kaufman: I read it myself, Mr. Phillips.

Mr. Phillips: Did you read all the statements in an hour and a half?

Judge Kaufman: I read every word of it and I read it in about 35 minutes, having in mind the testimony while I was reading it...Do you want another five minutes?

Mr. Phillips: We are in disagreement at this moment.

Mr. Kuntz: I personally feel, as far as our client is concerned, I am satisfied with the record as it stands...

Judge Kaufman: Then, as I understand it, gentlemen, everybody is now in agreement that there is going to be no further use made of Court's Exhibits 1 to 5 and the witness Elitcher is excused; is that correct?

Mr. E. H. Bloch: Yes.

Mr. Phillips: By the way, I don't like the word "agreed"; we are not all agreed...and I make request of the Court to give me time until tomorrow morning to make up my mind as to what is in the best interests of justice to my client.

Judge Kaufman: I have given you one hour and 45 minutes...I personally read all of that matter in 35 minutes.

Mr. Phillips: Maybe I am not as quick-witted as the Court...

Judge Kaufman: Very well then, we will proceed with the next witness...

THE TRIAL OF THE ROSENBERGS AND SOBELL

Do you want the witness Greenglass?
Mr. Saypol: Yes, we have sent for him...

THE ATOM BOMB SECRET REVEALED

David Greenglass returned to the witness stand.

Mr. Cohn: Now you have told us about the visit of Harry Gold to you in June about the material that you turned over to him. When after that was the next occasion when you saw Julius Rosenberg?

A. It was on my furlough in September, 1945...

Mr. Cohn: Did you tell him what you had for him?

A. Yes. I told him "I think I have a pretty good"—"a pretty good description of the atom bomb."

Mr. Cohn: The atom bomb itself?

A. That's right...

The government at first assumed that Harry Gold's visit to Albuquerque, New Mexico, in September 1945 could establish an espionage meeting between him and Greenglass at that time. But the prosecution subsequently learned that Greenglass was not in Albuquerque, but on furlough in New York City at that time. So the government simply reconstructed Greenglass's story that he met with Julius Rosenberg in New York instead of with Harry Gold in Albuquerque.

Greenglass testified that he turned over his first lens mold sketch (exhibit 2) to Rosenberg in January 1945 and the other two sketches of the lens mold (exhibits 6 and 7) to Harry Gold in June 1945. Cohn continued questioning Greenglass about the information he gave Rosenberg in September 1945.

Mr. Cohn: Did you draw up a sketch of the atom bomb itself?

A. I did.

Mr. Cohn: Did you prepare descriptive material to explain the sketch of the atom bomb?

A. I did.

Mr. Cohn: Was there any other material that you wrote up on that occasion?

A. I gave some scientists' names, and I also gave some possible recruits for espionage.

Mr. Cohn: Now, about how many pages would you say it took to write down all of these matters?

A. I would say about 12 pages or so...

Mr. Cohn: Have you prepared for us, Mr. Greenglass, a replica of the sketch—I believe it is a cross-section sketch of the atom bomb—a replica of the sketch you gave to Rosenberg on that day?

A. I did.

Mr. Cohn: I show you Government's Exhibit 8 for identification, Mr. Greenglass, and ask you to examine it and tell us whether or not that is a replica of the sketch, cross-section of the atomic bomb?

A. It is.

Mr. Cohn: And how does that compare to the sketch you gave to Rosenberg in September, 1945?

A. About the same thing. Maybe a little difference in size; that is all...

Mr. Cohn: We offer this in evidence, your Honor.

Mr. E. H. Bloch: I object to it on the same ground urged with respect to Government's Exhibits 2, 6 and 7, and I now ask the Court to impound this exhibit so that it remains secret to the Court, the jury and counsel.

Mr. Saypol: That is a rather strange request coming from the defendants...And I am happy to say that we join him.

Judge Kaufman: All right. It shall be impounded...It will be sealed after it is shown to the jury...

Mr. E. H. Bloch: Let me say by way of explanation, Mr. Saypol, that despite the fact that the Atomic Energy Commission may have declassified this, I was not at all sure in my own mind, and I am talking privately, whether or not even at this late date, this information may not be used to the advantage of a foreign power...

Judge Kaufman: Let me ask you this. Perhaps we can even avoid this matter of clearing the courtroom if counsel stipulate right now that the matters that were described, as he is about to describe, were of a secret and confidential nature...

Mr. E. H. Bloch: If the Court please, after some conversation between counsel, we cannot find concurrence among ourselves and, although I have made my position, or at least I have given my thinking to the Court, I am willing in the interest of harmony of the defense, to yield to the reservations and misgivings of Mr. Phillips and Mr. Kuntz and let the trial proceed, and if the Court desires to keep this type of testimony secret I, for one, would have no objection...

Judge Kaufman: You would like to stipulate it?

Mr. A. Bloch: I would like to stipulate it as an American citizen and as a person who owes his allegiance to this country. I would like to stipulate it first to save the expense; I understand it would save quite an expense to the Government to bring all these people here.

Judge Kaufman: May I ask you gentlemen, Mr. Phillips and Mr. Kuntz, why aren't you stipulating this?

Mr. Phillips: For the reason that I do not feel that an attorney for a defendant in a criminal case should make concessions which will serve the People from the necessity of proving things, which in the *course of the proof we may be able to refute...*

Judge Kaufman: Mr. Bloch, I understand that you are willing to concede the testimony concerning that particular phase of it, is that correct?

Mr. E. H. Bloch: I was willing to do this, your Honor—I want to restate it very clearly. I thought that in the interest of national security, any testimony that this witness may give of a descriptive nature concerning the last Government exhibit might reveal matters which should not be revealed to the public.

Judge Kaufman: Therefore?

Mr. E. H. Bloch: And, therefore, I felt that his testimony on this aspect should be revealed solely to the Court, to the jury and to the counsel and not to the public generally...

Bloch's willingness to concede to not have the secrets of the Atomic Bomb exposed could have been his most important legacy. Criticism of Bloch's judgment in this instance was unfair. Bloch had no way of knowing for certain at the time that David Greenglass was providing worthless information. In the years since, many lawyers have insisted that it was incumbent upon Bloch to question in open court the value of Greenglass's atom bomb sketches, not to have them impounded. This was reasoning that could only be arrived at after it was known that Greenglass's information was without value. Realistically, the information was no doubt worthless. But what if it was not worthless? It would mean that Kaufman, with the help of Irving Saypol, was in effect giving the secret of the manufacture of the atomic bomb to every nation of the world, friend or foe, and even private individuals. Kaufman, with or without declassification, according to his own evaluation, openly transferred to virtually every foreign power information that was capable of being injurious to our nation.

Judge Kaufman: Ladies and gentlemen, in as plain and simple language as I can possibly put it to you...When the defendant is put on trial, under our form of government, I am happy to say, he is entitled to full confrontation, and that means confrontation of all the evidence which the Government contends to prove the guilt of the defendant or defendants...Mr. Benson, will you ask the press to come back before we bring the jury back...
Mr. E. H. Bloch: You want the press excluded.
Mr. Saypol: No, we want them in...

Bloch could not understand why Kaufman was calling the press into court. Phillips and Kuntz, while wanting to see the evidence so they could dispute it, didn't want the press. With only the jury hearing this sensitive information it possibly could have been kept secret; but certainly not if it was given to the press.

Mr. E. H. Bloch: My position is that I think the press ought to be excluded in the prohibition.
Judge Kaufman: In the prohibition?
Mr. E. H. Bloch: I believe so; otherwise I believe the purpose would be defeated, unless the press is enjoined to secrecy.
Judge Kaufman: No, they won't be enjoined to secrecy. They will be enjoined to good taste...Mr. Murphy, are there any members of the press who want to come in?
Mr. Murphy: I can get them in in a moment.
Judge Kaufman: Will you get them?
Mr. Murphy: Yes.

Judge Kaufman: May I say to the members of the press that I have considered the question of the press being present during the period of the taking of this part of the testimony.   My personal feeling in the matter is that all of this testimony that is anticipated has probably fallen into the hands of those from whom we are trying to keep the information...I personally can't be certain of that fact...However, there has been a discussion here between Mr. Saypol, and I take it representatives of the Atomic Energy Commission on the subject of whether the press should be present, and it has been resolved generally that the press should be here.   However, we are going to trust to your good taste and your good judgment on the matter of publishing portions of this testimony...

Mr. Cohn: Now will you tell us just what happened, Mr. Greenglass, after you handed this sketch and the descriptive material concerning the atomic bomb to Rosenberg?   What did he do, what did the others there do?

A.   Well, he stepped into another room and he read it and he came out and he said "This is very good. We ought to have this typed up immediately."...Ethel did the typing and Ruth and Julius and Ethel did the correction of the grammar...and at this time Julius told me that he had stolen the proximity fuse when he was working at Emerson Radio...

Mr. E. H. Bloch: If the Court please, I move to strike out that, the reference to stealing the proximity fuse, upon the ground that it is not related to the charge here.   It imputes to the defendants the commission of a separate crime.   I think it injects inflammatory and prejudicial material into this trial, and I ask that it be stricken.

Judge Kaufman: Did he tell you what he did with

that proximity fuse?

A. He told me that he took it out in his brief-case. That is the same briefcase he brought his lunch in with, and he gave it to Russia.

Judge Kaufman: All right. Strike out "stealing" and we will let this latter part stand.

Mr. E. H. Bloch: I respectfully except to your Honor's ruling.

Judge Kaufman: You must remember that the conspiracy charge is a general statement to turn over information to the USSR pertaining to national defense. It is not limited to atomic information...

Mr. E. H. Bloch: I respectfully except and I now ask for...a mistrial.

Judge Kaufman: Denied...

Greenglass was thus given the leeway to say anything that he wished concerning what Rosenberg told him, just as Elitcher was empowered to put words into Morton Sobell and Julius Rosenberg's mouths. Here Judge Kaufman, while he struck out the word "stealing," allowed the jury to consider that Rosenberg had given something called a proximity fuse to the Russians.

GREENGLASS AND RUSSIA

Mr. Cohn: After you were discharged from the Army at the end of February, 1946, where did you go?

A. I went back to New York City...I went into business with Julius Rosenberg and my brother...It was two businesses, G&R Engineering...and then the Pitt Machine Products Corporation.

Mr. Cohn: How long did you remain in business with Rosenberg and your brother?

A. Till August, 1949...

Mr. Cohn: Now, during those three years from February or March, 1946, until August of 1949, did you see Rosenberg at business from time to time?...

A. I did.

Mr. Cohn: Did you have any conversations with him?

A. I did...

Mr. Cohn: Try to tell us as best as you can, if you can remember, when or around when each conversation took place.

A. Well, in '46 or '47 Julius Rosenberg made an offer to me to have the Russians pay for part of my schooling...and that I should go to college for the purpose of cultivating the friendships of people that I had known at Los Alamos and also to acquire new friendships with people who were in the field of research that are in those colleges, like physics and nuclear energy...

Mr. Cohn: Did he tell you anything else concerning his activities along these lines?

A. He told me that he had people giving him information in up-State New York and in Ohio.

Mr. Cohn: Did he tell you why they were giving

him that information?

A. They were giving information to give to the Russians...

Mr. Cohn: Now, did Rosenberg ever say anything to you about any reward that he had received from the Russians for the work that he had been doing?

A. He stated that he had gotten a watch as a reward...

In David Greenglass's pretrial testimony, which encompassed numerous interviews with FBI interrogators, he never stated that Julius Rosenberg received or gave anything to "Russians." Irving Saypol and Roy Cohn, though they knew this, allowed, if not encouraged, Greenglass to testify falsely. The word "Russian" had an awesome effect on the jurors. It was repeated for their ears at every possible moment.

Mr. Cohn: Now, was there anything else that they received which they told you about?...

A. He said he received a citation.

Mr. Cohn: Did he describe the citation at all?

A. He said it had certain privileges with it in case he ever went to Russia...

Mr. Cohn: Now, I asked you yesterday afternoon if you remembered a visit you received from Rosenberg in February of 1950. Do you remember such a visit?

A. I do.

Mr. Cohn: How do you fix the date of that visit?

A. Well, it was a few days after Fuchs was taken in England.

Mr. Cohn: A few days after the news of Dr. Fuchs' arrest in England appeared in the papers; is that right?

A. *That is right...He came up to my apartment and awakened me...He told me, he said, "You remember the man who came to see you in Albuquerque? Well, Fuchs was also one of his contacts"; and this man who came to see me in Albuquerque would undoubtedly be arrested soon, and if so would lead to me...And Rosenberg said to me that I would have to leave the country...Well, I told him that I would need money to pay my debts back so I would be able to leave with a clear head...so he said he would get the money for me from the Russians...*

Mr. Cohn: *Will you tell us when the next conversation took place?*

A. *Well, my wife was in the hospital, she had been badly burned in an accident and it was about the middle of April, it was...before she came out of the hospital, Julius came to see me and he said I would have to leave the country and—well, that was about the gist of the conversation...*

Mr. Cohn: *Had he given you any money up to this point?*

A. *No, no money was given to me up to this point.*

Mr. Cohn: *When was the next conversation?*

A. *The next conversation was after my wife had gotten out of the hospital about May...it was probably a little before May, and he came up to my apartment in order to get some stocks from me, some shares that I had for a business enterprise I was in with him, and he at this time told me that I would have to leave the country as soon as possible, he would get the information for me to leave...*

So according to Greenglass, Rosenberg had been petitioning him to leave the country from February

1950 until at least May, promising him all that time to give him the money to flee. Why Julius would be so urgent in his request and yet not provide Greenglass with the money for so many months when he was supposed to have Russian money at his disposal, is difficult to understand.

Mr. Cohn: Now when was the next conversation with Rosenberg on this subject?

A.   Well, it was after my wife came out of the hospital after giving birth to our youngest child.

Mr. Cohn: About when was that?

A.   It was May—it was May 22nd or 23rd, something like that...

Mr. Cohn: Tell us what he said and what you said...

A.   He came into the apartment and he had a Herald Tribune in his hand with a picture of Harry Gold on it and he said, "This is the gentleman who came to see you in Albuquerque."...

I looked at it and I said I couldn't tell from that picture, and he said, "Don't worry, I am telling you this is the man and you will have to go out—you will have to leave the country," and he gave me a thousand dollars then and said he would give me $6000 more.   We then went for a walk...He said that I would have to get a tourist card.

Mr. Cohn: For what country, did he tell you?

A.   To go to Mexico.

Mr. Cohn: In other words, the first place you were to go to was Mexico?...

A.   He told me that in order to get the tourist card you have to have a letter or you have to be inoculated again at the border—a letter from the doctor saying you were inoculated.

Mr. Cohn: For what, did he tell you?

A. For smallpox.

Mr. Cohn: Did he tell you how he found that out?

A. He said he went to see a doctor and a doctor told him about it and I said I would attend to that. He then told me I would have to have passport pictures made up.

Mr. Cohn: Passport pictures?

A. Of myself, my wife and my family, and also he gave me a certain form letter to memorize and sign "I. Jackson" at the end of the letter. This letter was to be used when I get to Mexico City. I was to write to the Secretary to the Ambassador of the Soviet Union and state in that letter—I don't recall completely right now but something to the effect about the position of the Soviet Union in the UN...

David Greenglass, asked about how he was to make his escape to the Soviet Union, described:

I was to wait three days at some place...with a guide to the city in my hand...with my middle finger...between the pages of the guide—go to a place called Plaz de la Colon and look at the statue of Columbus there...I was then to wait until some man was to come up close to me and then I would say, "That is a magnificent statue," and that I was from Oklahoma and I hadn't seen a statue like it before, and this man was to say, "Oh, there are much more beautiful statues in Paris." That was to be our identification...I was to continue on to Vera Cruz and then to Sweden or Switzerland, one or the other. I would—in Sweden I was to go to the statue of Linnaeus in Stockholm and repeat—after sending a letter...to the Secretary of the Ambassador of the

Soviet Union, with the same type of letter and also "I. Jackson" as the signature again...

Mr. Cohn: All right. Now, did you write down these instructions or did Rosenberg write them down?

A. Nobody wrote them down. I was told to memorize them at this time and I did memorize them.

Nothing was said about what would happen had Greenglass forgotten one of these details. He was already uncertain about the instructions; he could not say for sure whether one of his destinations was Sweden or Switzerland.

Mr. Cohn: Did you have any further conversation with Rosenberg on that day?

A. Well, that was the end of the conversation on that day except that—he said that he probably—that he had to leave the country himself and he was making plans for it, and I said, "Why you?" He said that he was a friend—that he knew Jacob Golos, this man Golos, and probably Bentley knew him...

Considering that Jacob Golos had been dead since 1943, this did not sound likely. Greenglass was then questioned about certain passport photos that were found in his possession on the day of his arrest.

PASSPORT PHOTOS

Mr. Cohn: *Now was there any further conversation with Rosenberg on that occasion?*

A. Only that he asked me to memorize it and get eveything attended to—the passport photos.

Mr. Cohn: *What did he tell you about the passport photos; he wanted you to get those yourself, is that right?*

A. That is right.

Mr. Cohn: *Did he tell you exactly what he wanted to know with regard to the passport photos?*

A. Yes, he wanted five copies, five pictures, each with myself, by myself, my wife, and then my wife and the children and then myself with the children, and then I think all of us together, the family altogether...We went over to the shop and we had these pictures taken; and later that evening I picked the pictures up after they were done; and it was during the week—it was Memorial Day, and I remember I was off that night, Julius came over, and I gave him the pictures...

Mr. Cohn: *Now I think you told us that he had asked you to have five sets of pictures taken; is that right? Five poses, five sets each?*

A.   That is right...I had six sets of pictures taken.

Mr. Cohn: *How many did you give to Julius?*

A.   Five sets.

Mr. Cohn: *What did you do with the sixth set?*

A.   I kept it in the drawer.

Mr. Cohn: *Was that set after your arrest given to the FBI?*

A.   I gave it to the FBI...

PASSPORT PHOTOS

Ruth Greenglass's testimony was memorized quite differently. She contradicted David, saying she was the one who gave the passport photos to the FBI; she testified, "I gave the sixth set to the FBI."

Furthermore, the claim that the Greenglasses were instructed by Julius Rosenberg to get sets of photographs in order to obtain passports was not even conceived by the FBI or the U.S. Attorney's office until mid-August 1950. The first mention of the passport photos is in a remarkable FBI document dated September 8, 1950. It says, "Ruth Greenglass advised SA John A. Harrington that she had told her attorney O. John Rogge about the aforementioned passport photographer in August 1950 and had asked him to notify the FBI and that he had said that he would do so...Mr. Rogge advised SA Harrington that the above information is true and that he had simply forgotten to bring this matter to the attention of the FBI."

The Rosenbergs and their lawyers never saw that memo. They only heard Ruth and David Greenglass's testimony that the photos were given to the FBI in June 1950. They had no idea that Ruth had not mentioned this incident until August and that the FBI had first heard about it in September.

Walter and Miriam Schneir have done excellent work investigating the government's fraudulent presentation of the passport photos evidence. They published the so-called passport photos in their book *Invitation to an Inquest* (1967), where it could be seen that these were not passport photos, but ordinary family photographs. Two of the photographs, which were dated June 15, 1950, on the back, were merely part of the inventory of personal effects taken by the FBI from Greenglass's home on the day of his arrest. As

217

to the additional photographs, the government produced them months later.

Eleven years after the Greenglasses had testified, the Schneirs located the photographer's studio and visited the proprietor, who showed them a receipt. It was dated January 19, 1951, and was signed by Special Agent William F. Norton. It was for six negatives.

In other words, Norton merely took the six negatives from the photographer on January 19 and had them developed. He chose two of them, and on January 26, 1951, inventoried the chosen photographs by signing and dating them on the back. He then added them to the two photos dated June 15. The evidence strongly suggests that neither David or Ruth gave a set of passport photos to the FBI when David was arrested. They had only two photographs of themselves on hand. Furthermore, why would only two photographs be dated June 15, 1950, unless the others were not available? And why would the FBI agent go to the photographer's shop to pick up negatives unless he did not have the original prints?

The most logical conclusion was that the FBI manufactured the evidence. According to both Ruth and David, they both said they gave the FBI a set of passport photos; a set consisted of five photos. But the FBI received only two photos on the day it claimed to have received them.

The FBI's approach to evidence on the question of the passport pictures is illuminated by the following story, revealed years after the Rosenbergs were dead. In December 1952 Raymond L. Paradis, a cellmate of David Greenglass at Lewisburg Penitentiary, reported to the FBI that Greenglass told him he could get for him a false passport if Paradis ever desired to leave the United States. Greenglass identified the source of these false passports as Theodore Harris. The FBI reported:

> *Greenglass told Paradis to mention Greenglass's name to Harris and that Harris for a payment of $500 to $1000 would fix him up with the necessary papers. Greenglass also advised Paradis that at the time he was picked up by the FBI he had a passport on him.*

But the FBI concluded that in view of David's past cooperation with the bureau, this information had been fabricated either by Paradis to ingratiate himself with the Bureau or by Greenglass to impress Paradis. The Philadelphia FBI office did everything it could to stifle the report, claiming that it could be dangerous to Paradis if other inmates learned he was an informer.

Paradis described how knowledgeable Greenglass was about obtaining false passports. He said that Greenglass wanted to refer him to a lawyer in Mexico City, and he felt confident that he could get more information from Greenglass.

The Philadelphia office decided not to interview David Greenglass on the subject until April 29, 1953, the date Paradis was scheduled to be released. But the Washington office of the FBI, learning of Paradis's revelations in February 1953, overruled Philadelphia and ordered that Greenglass be interviewed immediately. Thus while the Philadelphia office had tried to sabotage Raymond Paradis's efforts, first slandering him as a braggart and then avoiding further meetings with him, the Washington office did even more to sabotage the investigation by interviewing David Greenglass on February 9 and alerting him to Paradis's objectives. In their report of this incident, the FBI scoffed at Paradis's allegations by stating, "It is recalled that at the time of Greenglass's arrest by Bureau agents in June 1950, no passport was found in his possession, although he had passport photos on him."

It was not until April 3, 1953, that Theodore Haralampoppoulos, who used the name Harris, was contacted by the FBI. Harris, who was always available since leaving Lewisburg prison in November 1952, was not sought out for several months. When he was finally interviewed, he did not contradict Paradis's claims, but merely refused to mention names. The FBI's questioning of him was as shallow as it was brief. The information that Paradis and Harris could have provided was lost and the strong inference that David Greenglass had a passport and had helped frame the Rosenbergs was submerged and forgotten.

$5,000 IS LESS THAN $1,000

Roy Cohn continued to question David Greenglass about Julius Rosenberg's visit to him in May 1950 when Rosenberg allegedly gave him $1,000.

Mr. Cohn: When had he given you the thousand dollars?
A. When he first came into the apartment and showed me that Harry Gold had been arrested.
Mr. Cohn: He had given you a thousand dollars in cash; is that right?
A. That is right.
Mr. Cohn: What did you do with that thousand dollars?
A. I gave it to my wife, who paid bills with it and spent it, generally...

Greenglass added that Rosenberg returned a week later and delivered $4,000 in a brown paper wrapping, placing it on the mantelpiece of his bedroom.

Emanuel Bloch proceeded to cross-examine David Greenglass.

Mr. E. H. Bloch: Now let me ask you this: You have testified you got a thousand dollars from Rosenberg in 1950...and you insisted upon that money to pay your debts, isn't that correct?
A. That is correct
Judge Kaufman: Excuse me, this thousand dollars that you got in 1950, I want you to get this clear in my mind, was that in payment for the information which you had at or about that time turned over to Rosenberg or was that in anticipation of your trip out

221

of the country?

The Witness: In anticipation of the trip out of the country...

Judge Kaufman was emphasizing to the jury the prosecution's theory that Rosenberg gave Greenglass the $1,000 for the purpose of leaving the country. Kaufman did not want any other answer from Greenglass, especially not that the $1,000 was money he believed Rosenberg owed him.

Mr. E. H. Bloch: When you, as you testified, finally told Rosenberg that you were not going to leave the country and you were going to stay right here...did you ever offer to give him back that thousand dollars?

A. I did not.

Mr. E. H. Bloch: Now then, I think you testified further that you received an additional $4000 from Rosenberg sometime in June, is that right—sometime in June 1950?

A. That's right...

Mr. E. H. Bloch: Do you know now that that $4000 or a major part of it went to pay your lawyer?

A. I do.

Mr. E. H. Bloch: Have you been told how much of that $4000 went to pay your lawyer?

A. Yes.

Mr. E. H. Bloch: All of it?

A. All of it...

Mr. E. H. Bloch: Did you have any doubts when you, as you testified, got a thousand dollars from Mr. Rosenberg in June 1950?

A. I did.

Mr. E. H. Bloch: But you took that money and

you used it to pay off household debts; isn't that correct?

A. Well...About that thousand dollars, I felt that I was given nothing for this thousand dollars; I had plenty of headaches and I felt the thousand dollars was not coming out of Julius Rosenberg's pocket, it was coming out of the Russians' pocket and it didn't bother me one bit to take it, or the $4000 either.

Mr. E. H. Bloch: You had no qualms at all about taking the $1000 or the $4000, did you?

A. Not at all.

Mr. E. H. Bloch: Even though that money, as you say, was given to you for purposes of flight?

A. That is right.

Mr. E. H. Bloch: You never offered to return that money?

A. I certainly did not...

Mr. E. H. Bloch: At any rate, at present you bear an affection for Ethel?

A. I do.

Mr. E. H. Bloch: Do you bear an affection for your brother-in-law, Julius?

A. I do...

Mr. E. H. Bloch: When was the first time after your discharge from the Army that the FBI came around to talk to you about your activities at Los Alamos?

A. In 1950, February...

Mr. E. H. Bloch: Where did these FBI representatives see or speak to you in February, 1950?

A. One man called me up on the phone and he said he would like to see me. He came to my house; he sat down at my table; I offered him a cup of coffee and we spoke—he did not say to me that he suspected me of espionage or anything else—he just *spoke to me about whether I had known anybody at Los Alamos, and that was the gist of the whole conversation. He walked out of the house maybe an hour later, and that is all there was to it...*

Mr. E. H. Bloch: Did he ask you any questions, either directly or indirectly, with respect to your knowledge of any illegal activity that occurred at Los Alamos while you were there?

A. I don't recall exactly what the whole conversation was about. It made very little effect on me...It didn't seem like anything—I mean—

Judge Kaufman: Were you asked to sign any paper of any kind?

A. No, not at all...

Mr. E. H. Bloch: Did he tell you what he came for?

A. Well, he wanted to know...It was very difficult to find out what he wanted. He didn't come out and say he wanted some information. He just talked around the point. I didn't get what he really wanted to find out.

Mr. E. H. Bloch: Was Los Alamos discussed?

A. Oh, yes.

Mr. E. H. Bloch: Did he say he was looking for people who might have conducted illegal activity in Los Alamos?

A. No, he didn't say that.

Mr. E. H. Bloch: What was the name of the FBI man?

A. I can't remember the FBI man's name.

Mr. E. H. Bloch: Did you ever see the FBI man since?

A. I have not seen him since...

Mr. E. H. Bloch: You didn't tell that FBI man at that time, that you had engaged in any illegal activity at Los Alamos, did you?

A. I didn't tell him, but I was pretty well on the verge to tell him...

Mr. E. H. Bloch: Did you mention to him anything about the fact that you had given secrets of the Los Alamos project to any unauthorized person?

Judge Kaufman: Don't answer that. He has already answered it.

Kaufman did not want Greenglass to be asked about the visit by the FBI in February 1950. Additional questioning could establish that Greenglass had been under the control of the government long before he was officially arrested. Further exploration into this area could also lead to perplexing questions as to why J. Edgar Hoover ordered an investigation of Greenglass on February 8, only days after Greenglass's one-hour meeting with the FBI agent who "just talked around the point." What became of Hoover's order and what other meetings occurred between the FBI and David Greenglass between that February date and his arrest in June would not be told.

Mr. E. H. Bloch: When was the next time you were interviewed by the FBI?

A. When I was arrested, June 15th...

Mr. E. H. Bloch: And when were you arraigned?

A. Do you mean the time? It was in the afternoon, I believe.

Mr. E. H. Bloch: And that was on June 16th...

A. That is right...

Mr. E. H. Bloch: Did you have counsel at that time?

A. I did.

Mr. E. H. Bloch: Who was your counsel?

A. O. John Rogge.

Mr. E. H. Bloch: And was Mr. Rogge there personally?

A. He was...

Mr. E. H. Bloch: Now, did you make a request for counsel at any time after you were taken down here to the Federal Building on June 15, 1950?...

A. Somebody said to me, "You ought to get a counsel—you ought to get a lawyer."...

Mr. E. H. Bloch: Did you call any relative on the evening of June 15th or in the early morning hours of June 16th from this building, telling him or them that you wanted counsel?

A. I did.

Mr. E. H. Bloch: And to whom did you speak?

A. I spoke to my brother-in-law, Louis Abel...

Mr. E. H. Bloch: Now, Mr. Greenglass, let's come back for a moment to the night of June 15, 1950, and the early morning of June 16, 1950. How many statements did you sign that evening and the following morning?

A. I signed one statement that evening and the following morning...

Mr. E. H. Bloch: Now, in that statement did you refer to the incident in Albuquerque, New Mexico, in the latter part of November, 1944, in which you had a conversation with your wife and in which she invited you to commit espionage?

A. I referred to it, yes. I also, in that statement, I gave a general outline of everything I was to say...and later statements. I had more memory of what I had done and I filled in more.

Mr. E. H. Bloch: Now, I understand that, but please, Mr. Greenglass, we are trying to find out specifically just what you said to the FBI.

Judge Kaufman: Yes, and I don't think you ought to go into such minute detail...Don't you think you are laboring the point, really?

Mr. E. H. Bloch: I honestly don't, your Honor. I feel in good conscience that it is my duty to ask these questions. Otherwise, I assure you that I wouldn't ask them. This is not going to take long, your Honor...

Kaufman just did not want Bloch to thoroughly cross-examine David Greenglass. The Judge was not confident that Greenglass could maintain credibility if he was questioned too carefully.

Bloch continued cross-examination.

Mr. E. H. Bloch: Was there anything in your statement which you signed on the evening of June 15, 1950 here in the Federal Building about the receipt of $1000 from Rosenberg in the year 1950?

A. I don't believe it was in the statement, no.

Mr. E. H. Bloch: All right.

Judge Kaufman: But you had told them about it?

To protect Greenglass, Kaufman wanted him to say that he had told the FBI about the $1,000. Greenglass complied.

The Witness: I had told them about it...

Mr. E. H. Bloch: Now, is it your testimony that you mentioned the $4000 to the FBI representatives that evening?

A. I did and I will tell you how I know, that, because when they searched the house they couldn't find it and I told them then later on that I had given it away.

If Greenglass were as truthful and cooperative as he says he was, why didn't he refer the FBI to his brother-in-law Louis Abel, who was holding the money? If Greenglass had told the FBI all of this, would the agents leave it out of their report when they were investigating a case that was so notorious? Greenglass had to be lying.

Mr. E. H. Bloch: Now, did you tell them that evening to whom you had given that money?

A. I don't remember that either.

Mr. E. H. Bloch: Didn't one of the FBI representatives when you mentioned the $4000 ask you where the $4000 is?

A. He must have. I just don't remember saying anything to him about where it was...

Mr. E. H. Bloch: But you are not sure?

A. I am not sure that I did or I didn't...

Mr. E. H. Bloch: And then you made attempts to get a lawyer; isn't that right?

A. That's right.

Mr. E. H. Bloch: You called up your brother-in-law and you told him, "Get a lawyer," didn't you?

A. That's right...

Not exactly. Greenglass hired O. John Rogge, a specific former U.S. Attorney, who was also Max Elitcher's lawyer, not just any lawyer.

Mr. E. H. Bloch: You involved your wife that night, did you not?

A. Well, I don't know sufficiently enough about the law to realize that I did involve my wife...

Mr. E. H. Bloch: Didn't you tell the FBI that

night that your wife came out to Albuquerque?

A. *That is absolutely true.*

Mr. E. H. Bloch: And made an invitation to you to commit espionage; you told them that, did you not?

A. *That's right.*

Mr. E. H. Bloch: You also told them, did you not, that she had accompanied you to Rosenberg's house in September, 1945; you told them that, did you not?

A. *That's right...*

Mr. E. H. Bloch: Did you tell the FBI about your wife's participation in the Jell-O box incident?

A. *I did...*

Not according to the FBI records, which first mention the Jell-O box incident on June 28, 1950, nearly two weeks after Greenglass was arrested. An FBI teletype dated June 30 stated that Greenglass's attorney, O. John Rogge, had advised the FBI that the means of identification between Gold and Greenglass was a torn box top. Another FBI report dated July 12 said that "Mr. Rogge suggested that Gold be questioned regarding the identity of the person who gave him the one-half box top." The details of the Jell-O box incident were not developed until several weeks after Greenglass was arrested.

Mr. E. H. Bloch: How many statements have you given to the FBI or any other of the Government agents or officials where you actually signed your name at the end of certain printed matter?

A. *I would say about six or seven...*

Mr. E. H. Bloch: Besides the six or seven written statements there were other occasions when you were asked questions and a stenographer took down the questions and your answers?

A. That is correct...

Mr. E. H. Bloch: During all of your months in jail did anybody go over with you any subject matter which related directly to those sketches that were introduced in evidence here as Government's Exhibits 2, 6 and 7?

Mr. Cohn: I don't know what Mr. Bloch means "go over with you." I think if he would clarify that—

Harvey Matusow, in his book *False Witness* (1955), vividly described what Roy Cohn meant by "go over with you" when he described how Cohn prepared him for trial. Cohn aggressively encouraged Matusow to provide false testimony. Matusow was not believed. Decades later, after Cohn's death, and after numerous other books described Cohn's methods, it was established beyond question that Roy Cohn frequently falsified evidence to insure himself of success in the courts.

Judge Kaufman: Try to clarify it for him.

Mr. E. H. Bloch: Did you draw any sketches for any of the FBI men or any agents of Mr. Saypol's staff prior to the time you came to testify here?

A. I did...

Judge Kaufman: These sketches that are in evidence, are they products of your own mind? By that I mean, were you helped by anybody on the outside in drawing those sketches?

A. Nobody, just myself.

It was noted in the FBI files that Greenglass was interviewed by representatives of the Atomic Energy Commission on February 2, 1951 in the office of U.S. Attorney Myles Lane. Nobody can say for certain what

Greenglass was questioned about, or whether he was instructed at the time by the AEC.

Judge Kaufman: Did anybody tell you to change any line here or change any line there?
A. Nobody told me anything like that.
Mr. E. H. Bloch: Did you ever get a B.S.?
A. I did not.
Mr. E. H. Bloch: Did you ever get an engineering degree?
A. I did not...
Mr. E. H. Bloch: Do you know anything about the basic theory of atomic energy?
A. I know something about it, yes...I am no scientific expert, but I know something about it...
Mr. E. H. Bloch: Did you ever take courses in calculus?
A. No...
Mr. E. H. Bloch: Or nuclear physics?
A. I did not.
Mr. E. H. Bloch: Or atomic physics?
A. I did not...
Mr. E. H. Bloch: Or advanced calculus?
A. I did not...

DR. SPINDEL AND DR. SCHWARTZ

Emanuel Bloch began to question Greenglass as to how he managed to obtain the information he supposedly forwarded to Gold and Rosenberg.

Mr. E. H. Bloch: Now you stated that after your wife came to visit you around November 29, 1944 until the time you got your first furlough in January 1945, you did get information outside that would come to you in the official discharge of your duties as a machinist, is that right?...
A. I did procure for instance the fact that Baker was Bohr from a man who happened to be a scientist...William Spindel.

Dr. William Spindel was not on the government's witness list. And with good reason; Spindel denied giving secret information of any kind to Greenglass. On March 15, 1951, FBI Agent Edward Sheidt wrote Saypol:

> *Dr. William Spindel...advised our Albany Field Office that he had read the testimony of David Greenglass in the* New York Times *in which Greenglass stated that Spindel advised him that Nick Baker was Niels Bohr. Spindel stated...that he is prepared to deny flatly that he ever furnished this information to Greenglass...*

Mr. E. H. Bloch: You told us about Bohr already. You said you got that information from this G.I., whose name is Spindel. Now I am asking you if you got any information from any scientist working on that project during that period?

A.   I was in the room when I heard discussions about implosion effect experiments, implosion effect of lenses, while some scientists were discussing it in the office of the building I was in...

Mr. E. H. Bloch: Now, I believe on your direct examination you told us, in substance that you snooped around to get information; isn't that right?...And you would make it your business to enter into a conversation or overhear conversations where you could pick up information?

A.   That is right...

Mr. E. H. Bloch: Now Mr. Greenglass, can you sketch for us every lens mold upon which you worked or which was constructed at the Theta shop in Los Alamos?

A.   Not every one but I can draw--sketch a good deal of them...

Mr. E. H. Bloch: You did not even know the formula for the curvature, did you?

A.   That is exactly correct...

Mr. E. H. Bloch: You had to be a scientist to know the formula, isn't that right?

A.   That is right...

Unknown to the Rosenbergs, the FBI had diligently attempted to find scientists who could support Greenglass's testimony that he received information from them. The FBI's efforts were a total failure.

An FBI memo of February 22, 1951, said that the Bureau had received a handwritten list from David Greenglass of sixteen "former employees at Los Alamos" who were "possible espionage recruits which he gave to Julius Rosenberg in January 1945, and a similar list furnished to Harry Gold in June 1945..." Not one of these so-called recruits supported Greenglass's contentions, a fact which was also kept from the Rosenbergs. Even Harry Gold denied receiving the names of recruits from Greenglass, thus directly contradicting his testimony.

Finally, when Greenglass claimed that he learned about the atomic bomb from yet another scientist at Los Alamos, Manuel Schwartz of Chicago, Illinois, this scientist also disputed Greenglass's claims.

On August 6, 1950, Schwartz made the following statement to FBI agents Rulon Paxman and Jeremiah Hurley:

> I was formerly employed on the Atomic Energy Project at Los Alamos...While on the project I believe I had knowledge of the following: critical mass of the atomic bomb; velocity of the shock waves from the atomic bomb; size of the atomic bomb; detonating device of the atomic bomb, which I comprehended vaguely; the inside make-up of the atomic bomb; the slow and fast explosives used in the atomic bomb.
>
> Near the latter part of 1944 or early part of 1945, I became acquainted with David Greenglass...Thereafter I saw Greenglass...for about one year. This was principally during 1945...
>
> Greenglass was working on something at the machine shop which in my opinion would give him knowledge of the outside proportions of the atomic bomb...
>
> It is my belief that Greenglass would not have understood the physics of the information in my possession pertaining to the atomic bomb and that causes me to believe that I would not have discussed this information with Greenglass.

The Attorney General's office, however, decided that with the help of Judge Kaufman, a jury would believe their contentions based on Greenglass's word,

without the testimony of Dr. Spindel, Dr. Schwartz,
or any one of Greenglass's sixteen supposed recruits.

FAMILY QUARRELS

Mr. E. H. Bloch: Now, up to the time of the formation of the Pitt Machine Products Co., Inc., did you borrow any money for your share of the business?...

A. I had some money and I put it in, and I borrowed some money and put that in, too...

Mr. E. H. Bloch: Now, while you were in business at 370 East Houston Street, did you have any quarrels with your brother-in-law, Julius?

A. Only business quarrels. It didn't amount to anything.

Mr. E. H. Bloch: Now, weren't there repeated quarrels between you and Julius when Julius accused you of trying to be a boss and not working on machines?

A. There were quarrels of every type and every kind. I mean there was arguments over personality, there was arguments over money, there was arguments over the way the shop was run...It was quarrels, just business quarrels...We remained as good friends in spite of the quarrels...

Judge Kaufman: And you saw him in 1950 after that?

The Witness: I saw him after that.

Judge Kaufman: Even after you left the business?

The Witness: That is right.

Mr. E. H. Bloch: You did not visit him very often, though, did you, during the years 1948 and 1949 and 1950?

A. No, I didn't...

Mr. E. H. Bloch: Did you ever come to blows

with Julius?

A.   No, I didn't.

Mr. E. H. Bloch: Do you remember an incident when you were sitting in the corner candy store at Houston and Avenue D when your brother Bernie had to separate the both of you?

A.   It slipped my mind.

Mr. E. H. Bloch: What slipped your mind?

A.   I mean I didn't remember it.

Mr. E. H. Bloch: Do you remember it now?

A.   I do...

Mr. E. H. Bloch: Did you hit Julius?

A.   I—I don't recall if I actually hit him...

Judge Kaufman: Subsequent to that, had you patched things up?

The Witness: Certainly. We were very friendly after that...I still felt I should leave the business, so I left, all in good faith—I mean...

Judge Kaufman: Now...When did you leave the business?

The Witness: In August, 1949...

Mr. E. H. Bloch: Mr. Greenglass, the fact remains, does it not, that you went out of that business in August, 1949, and never got a nickel for your shares?

A.   That's correct...

Mr. E. H. Bloch: And you wanted money, did you not?

A.   I did.

Mr. E. H. Bloch: And he refused to give you money, is that correct?

A.   That is correct. I wanted $2000 and he finally agreed that he would give me $1000 and when my wife made out the note to him to sign, he didn't want to sign the $1000 note. He said his word is good *enough and that he will pay me at such time when he will have the money available.*

Mr. E. H. Bloch: That was—

A. $1000 is the only thing he wanted to pay me. $1000...

Mr. E. H. Bloch: Now, did there then come a time when he came around and asked you to resign as a director and as an officer of the corporation?

A. He did...

Mr. E. H. Bloch: He kept coming around your house, did he not, and he was asking for your signature on that resignation?

A. Yes...

Julius Rosenberg's frequent visits to Greenglass during the year 1950 were obviously to obtain his signature on a resignation form, not to pay him anything and obviously not to give him the thousands of dollars that Greenglass claimed he gave him.

Mr. E. H. Bloch: How much money in all did you lose, of your own funds, in the Pitt Machine Products Co., Inc.?...How much?

A. I lost all of the money I originally put in...plus subsequent loss of money in salaries that I did not get.

Mr. E. H. Bloch: And how much did that total, in your mind?

A. Well, I don't know.

Mr. E. H. Bloch: Approximately?

A. A few thousand dollars.

Mr. E. H. Bloch: Now, is it not a fact that you never recovered a single penny of that money?

A. I never recovered a single penny of it.

Mr. E. H. Bloch: And is it not a fact, Mr. Green-

glass, that after you were arrested and after you hired Mr. Rogge, you instructed Mr. Rogge to prosecute a claim against Julius Rosenberg for moneys...?
    A. I did...

Whenever there was testimony that made no sense, it was David Greenglass's, not Julius Rosenberg's. Greenglass said that when the announcement of Gold's arrest came, Rosenberg pressed him and Ruth to go to Mexico. David claimed that Julius brought him $4,000 on June 4, 1950. This sounded impressive. The mastermind Rosenberg was sending his underling Greenglass to Mexico, and providing thousands of dollars for the trip. But the story made no sense. Impossible to reconcile was that while Julius supposedly handed over to David $4,000 in cash, an amount much more than what David claimed was owed to him, David was still so bitter about the $1,000 that he believed Julius owed him that he instructed his attorney to bring suit for it, even though he did not go to Mexico. This was evidence that Rosenberg never gave Greenglass $4,000 or $1,000. Nobody takes four times the amount owed to them, and then sues for a lesser amount originally owed.

When David Greenglass paid O. John Rogge $4,000 in legal fees, the government needed an explanation for David's possession of the $4,000. Saying Rosenberg was the source of that money enabled the government to diffuse the illegal implications of Greenglass's possession of what was at the time a substantial sum of money.

RUTH GREENGLASS

Ruth Greenglass was called as a witness on behalf of the Government. She was questioned by the U.S. Attorney James M. Kilsheimer.

Mr. Kilsheimer: Prior to the time you left New York to go to New Mexico did you have a conversation with the defendants Julius and Ethel Rosenberg?

A. *Yes, I did.*

Mr. Kilsheimer: And where did the conversation take place?

A. *At their home at 10 Monroe Street, Manhattan.*

Mr. Kilsheimer: And about what date did that conversation take place?

A. *It was about the middle of November, 1944...*

Mr. Kilsheimer: Now will you state as best you can recollect...what information did he [Julius Rosenberg] ask you to obtain from your husband if he should be willing to do it?

A. *He wanted a physical description of the project at Los Alamos, the approximate number of people employed, the names of some of the scientists who were working there—something about whether the place was camouflaged, what the security measures were and the relative distance of the project to Albuquerque and Santa Fe. Oh—and he told me—I am sorry—he told me also to tell David to be very circumspect not to indulge in any political conversations and to be very careful not to take any papers or sketches or blueprints, not to be obvious in seeking information, to relate to me only what he retained in his memory...*

Mr. Kilsheimer: Now, did you inform your husband

240

as to the type of information that Julius Rosenberg
had asked you to obtain?

A. Yes, I did...

Mr. Kilsheimer: When did he give you that information?

A. The following day after our conversation.

Mr. Kilsheimer: Now, will you tell us as best you
can recall what information your husband gave you on
that following day?

A. Yes. He said that Los Alamos had formerly
been a riding academy, that it was forty miles from
Santa Fe and about 110 miles from Albuquerque, that
the project itself was on the top of a hill and it was
secluded; you could hardly see it until you were almost on top of it; that there was a guard at the
entrance at all times, and everyone was checked going
in and out. He told me the names of the scientists,
Dr. Urey, Dr. Oppenheimer, Kistiakowski, Niels Bohr...

David Greenglass testified that he gave the information to Ruth the very next day, while he was with
her on a vacation furlough in November, 1944. This
meant that he already had the information and did not
have to go anywhere else to get it, and that the information was prepared and ready to be given to Ruth
when she arrived. And was it necessary to have
Greenglass relate that "Los Alamos" was forty miles
from Santa Fe and about 110 miles from Albuquerque?
And would not every secret project have a guard at
its entrance at all times? And is it not a fact that
Ruth Greenglass manufactured her testimony for the
trial when she said that her husband told her that
Niels Bohr was at Los Alamos in November of 1944,
when her signed statement made long before the trial
did not mention Bohr as one of the scientists whom

her husband named at that time?

Mr. Kilsheimer: Now, after this period you were with your husband of approximately five days, did you return to New York?
A. Yes.
Mr. Kilsheimer: And approximately when did you arrive in New York City?
A. About the middle of the first week in December, 1944.
Mr. Kilsheimer: After you arrived in New York City, did you see the defendant, Julius Rosenberg?
A. Yes. He came to my house on Stanton Street...
Mr. Kilsheimer: Will you state the conversation you had with Julius Rosenberg on that occasion in December, 1944, as best you can recall it?
A. I told him that David had consented to give him the information. He said that he was very pleased, and he asked me to tell him the information that David had sent through me. I repeated what David had told me for him and then he asked me to write it down for him. I wrote it down for him and he waited for the information...
Mr. Kilsheimer: Now, did your husband in fact come to New York shortly after this time?
A. Yes.
Mr. Kilsheimer: Approximately when did he arrive in New York City?
A. On New Year's Day, 1945...
Mr. Kilsheimer: When in relation to the time that your husband came home did Rosenberg come to your house?
A. He came one morning two or three days after David had arrived in New York...Julius said he wanted

David to write down any information for him that he had accumulated since I had been to New Mexico and the technical information that I was not able to bring back...My husband gave Julius the written information and Julius invited us to come to dinner at his house a few days afterwards...

Mr. Kilsheimer: And who was present when you first arrived at the Rosenberg house a few nights after this conversation in the morning?

A. Julius and Ethel Rosenberg, their son, Ann Sidorovich, and my husband and myself...

Mr. Kilsheimer: Now, after Ann Sidorovich left did you have any conversation with the Rosenbergs concerning Ann Sidorovich?

A. Yes...

Mr. Kilsheimer: What was said by whom?

A. Julius Rosenberg said that he had Ann Sidorovich come to his apartment just so that we would be able to recognize her and she know us when she came out to us to get information to bring back to him...

Mr. Kilsheimer: What was said concerning the meeting place?

A. Well, after he suggested that tentative plan, Julius Rosenberg and my husband discussed the best possible meeting place in Albuquerque, and it was decided to meet in a specific Safeway store...

Mr. Kilsheimer: When did your husband leave to go back to New Mexico?

A. It was toward the end of January, I think it was the 20th, 1945.

Mr. Kilsheimer: When did you leave to join your husband out in New Mexico?

A. The last day in February, 1945.

Mr. Kilsheimer: Now, between the time that your husband left, around the 20th of January, 1945, and the time that you left, the end of February, 1945, did you see Julius Rosenberg again?

A. Yes, he came to my house on Stanton Street.

Mr. Kilsheimer: Who was present at the time when he came up to your house?

A. Myself and my sister, Dorothy Abel...

Mr. Kilsheimer: Do you recall what was said on that occasion?

A. Yes. Julius came in and we exchanged some conversation, and after a few minutes he asked my sister, Dorothy, to take a book and go into the bathroom; he said he had something private to discuss with me...

Mr. Kilsheimer: What was the conversation that you had with Rosenberg at that time?

A. Julius told me that in April, the last week in April and the first week in May, I was to go to the store, the Safeway Store that had been designated, and someone would meet me there.

Mr. Kilsheimer: Did he state for what purpose this person would meet you?

A. Yes, to come to get information from David to bring back to him...

Mr. Kilsheimer: Now, did you meet somebody in front of the Safeway Store on that occasion?

A. No...

Mr. Kilsheimer: Did there come a time when somebody did come to see you in Albuquerque?

A. Yes.

Mr. Kilsheimer: When was that?

A. On the first Sunday in June, 1945...

Mr. Kilsheimer: And who is he?

A. Harry Gold...

Mr. Kilsheimer: Will you tell me just what happened on that occasion?

A. Yes. We had just finished breakfast and someone knocked at the door. My husband opened it and
he said he bore greetings from Julius. He came into
the apartment and...he produced half the Jello box
side. Then my husband went to my wallet and got
the other half and they matched them and they fit...

Mr. Kilsheimer: Now, what occurred after the
matching of the two pieces of the Jello box side?

A. Harry Gold asked my husband if he had the
information ready for him, and he said he did not.

Mr. Kilsheimer: Who said he did not?

A. My husband, David. He said he would have to
write it down for him. Then Harry Gold said he
would come back for it later in the afternoon...

Mr. Kilsheimer: Did Harry Gold return in the
afternoon as he said he would?

A. Yes, he did.

Mr. Kilsheimer: What time in the afternoon did he
arrive?

A. It was about 2 or 3 o'clock...

Mr. Kilsheimer: Did Harry Gold give anything to
either you or your husband?

A. Yes, he gave David a white envelope that was
sealed...David opened the envelope and he found $500.

Mr. Kilsheimer: Now, what happened to that $500?

A. David gave the money to me and on the next
day I deposited $400 in the Albuquerque Trust &
Savings Bank and I bought a defense bond for $50 and
the rest I used for household expenses...

Mr. Kilsheimer: Now, I call your attention to
September of 1945; do you recall that in that month
David received a furlough from the Army?

A. Yes.

Mr. Kilsheimer: And what did you and David do on
that furlough—I mean where did you go?

A. *We came to New York and we stayed at my mother-in-law's house, 64 Sheriff Street.*

Mr. Kilsheimer: *Now did you see Julius Rosenberg during that furlough?*

A. *Yes...*

Mr. Kilsheimer: *You went over to the Rosenbergs' house at 10 Monroe Street?*

A. *Yes, we did...*

Mr. Kilsheimer: *Now what occurred in the Rosenbergs apartment on that afternoon in September of 1945?*

A. *David gave Julius the written information. Julius said he was very pleased to get it and he went into another room to read it over, and after he wrote it he said this had to be gotten out immediately and he wanted Ethel to type it right away...And Ethel got out a typewriter and sat down to work on the notes...*

Mr. Kilsheimer: *Now, after the furlough was completed where did you and your husband go?*

A. *We went back to Albuquerque.*

Mr. Kilsheimer: *And for what length of time did you remain in Albuquerque?*

A. *Until the first week of March, after his discharge when we came back to New York...*

Mr. Kilsheimer: *And then when did you move to your apartment on Rivington Street where you went to live?*

A. *I think it was the first week in May 1946.*

Mr. Kilsheimer: *Now, from time to time during the years 1946, 1947 and 1948, did you and your husband visit the Rosenbergs at their apartment?*

A. *Very infrequently...*

Mr. Kilsheimer: *Coming up to the year 1950, do you recall a conversation with Julius Rosenberg concerning whether or not you should leave the country?*

246

A. Yes.

Mr. Kilsheimer: Where was the first conversation, that you recall, on this subject, when you were present?...

A. It was on May 24, 1950, in my house on Rivington Street...

Mr. Kilsheimer: Will you tell us the conversation that was had at that time?

A. Yes. Julius came in with a copy of the Herald-Tribune of that morning and it had a great big picture in it of Harry Gold, and he said, "This is the man who came to you in Albuquerque"; and David and I said it was not, we didn't recognize him; and he said, "You can take my word for it, this is the man who came." He said, "You will be the next to be picked up."

Mr. Kilsheimer: To whom did he say that?

A. To David. He said, "The next arrest will probably take place between June 12th and June 16th; you have to get out of the country before then."

Ruth Greenglass was testifying that Julius Rosenberg told her husband, accurately almost to the exact day, when David Greenglass would be arrested.

Mr. Kilsheimer: What did you say when Rosenberg told you that you would have to leave the country?

A. I said, "We can't go anywhere. We have a 10-day old infant"; and Julius said, "Your baby won't die. Babies are born on the ocean and on trains every day." He said, "My doctor said if you take enough canned milk and boil the water, the baby will be all right."

Mr. Kilsheimer: Did Julius Rosenberg tell you where you should go?

A. Yes.

Mr. Kilsheimer: *Where did he tell you that you should go to?*

A. *To the Soviet Union.*

Mr. Kilsheimer: *Was anything else said concerning arrangements for leaving?*

A. *Yes. He gave my husband a thousand dollars. He said, "Buy everything you need. Don't be too obvious in your spending. You have a month to spend it in, and I will bring you more." He said, "Leave all your household effects. Just take your clothing and what you need for the children and leave."*

Mr. Kilsheimer: *Was anything else said concerning arrangements for leaving?*

A. *Yes. Julius asked me if I could get a certificate from the doctor, stating that we had all been inoculated against smallpox. I said that I would not ask the doctor for a falsified statement. He said, "That is all right, I will take care of it. My doctor will give it to me."...*

Mr. Kilsheimer: *Concerning the thousand dollars which Rosenberg gave you on that day, what did you do with that thousand dollars?*

A. *We put it in a metal closet and we used it to pay household debts and expenses.*

Mr. Kilsheimer: *Was any part of that money put in the bank?*

A. *Yes, $500 deposited in the Manufacturers Trust Company...*

Mr. Kilsheimer: *Did there come a time when you had some pictures taken?*

A. *Yes.*

Mr. Kilsheimer: *When was that as far as you can recollect?*

A. *May 28, 1950.*

Mr. Kilsheimer: For what purpose were those pictures taken?

A. For passports to give to Julius so that he would think we were leaving...

Judge Kaufman: The pictures were taken for passports?

A. Yes.

Judge Kaufman: Did Julius ask you to take those pictures?

A. Yes.

Judge Kaufman: Did he ask you to turn the pictures over to him?

A. He did.

Judge Kaufman: Do you remember how many sets he said he wanted?

A. Yes.

Judge Kaufman: How many sets?

A. He wanted five sets, five photos.

Judge Kaufman: Did he tell you why he wanted the pictures?

A. Yes.

Judge Kaufman: For what purpose?

A. For passports...

Mr. Kilsheimer: How many sets of pictures did you have taken?

A. Six sets.

Mr. Kilsheimer: What did you do with those six sets?

A. We gave five to Julius and I gave the sixth set to the FBI.

Mr. Kilsheimer: When was the subject of your leaving the country again raised between yourselves and Julius Rosenberg?

A. He came on Memorial Day to pick up the pictures from my husband and he told him to get ready to leave.

Mr. Kilsheimer: Then when did you after Memorial Day see Rosenberg again?

A. He came on June 4th to our house.

Mr. Kilsheimer: Now what took place at that time?

A. He gave my husband a package wrapped in brown paper and he said it was $4000, that there would be more money available in Mexico when we got there.

Mr. Kilsheimer: What did you do with the $4000?

A. We put it in the chimney in our fireplace and afterwards my husband gave it to my brother-in-law...

Judge Kaufman: Did you ask him on that occasion anything about what he intended to do? Whether he intended to leave the country?

A. Yes...On May 24th...I asked him what he was doing. He said he was going too, that he would not leave at the same time, and he would meet us in Mexico. We would see him there, and I asked him what Ethel thought about it and he said Ethel didn't like the idea of it herself but she realized it was necessary and they were going to go...

Kaufman's questions once again demonstrated his foreknowledge of Ruth and David Greenglass's testimony, He did not want to take any chances that Ruth would fail to mention that Rosenberg expressed an intention to leave the country. So Kaufman included in his question the phrase "whether he intended to leave the country" in order to remind and instruct as to what her answer should be.

Mr. Kilsheimer: After your husband was arrested did you see Ethel Rosenberg?

A. Yes.

Mr. Kilsheimer: When did you see her?

A. In the middle of July 1950.

Mr. Kilsheimer: And where did you see her on that occasion?

A. She came to my mother-in-law's house to see me.

Mr. Kilsheimer: Will you tell me what occurred on that occasion?

A. Yes. Ethel came with pie for me and gifts for my son, and after we talked in my mother-in-law's house for a few minutes she asked me would I please go out and walk with her. We walked around the block several times and she said her counsel advised her to see me personally and get assurances from me that David would not talk. She said it would only be a matter of a couple of years, and in the long run we would be better off...

Alexander Bloch, Emanuel Bloch's father, then began his cross-examination of Ruth Greenglass.

Mr. A. Bloch: Well, did you ever talk it over with your husband and tell your husband "In the event of your being arrested or my being arrested, we are going to go to the District Attorney and tell him certain things which will lead to somebody else?"

A. I told my husband in 1946...that I wanted to go to the FBI with the story...I had felt that it was wrong. I didn't think that he should have done it to begin with but my husband felt he wanted to and as his wife I went along with him.

Mr. A. Bloch: You thought that way right from the beginning?

A. That's right...

Mr. A. Bloch: When did you first hear that your husband was arrested?

A.   When I was in the hospital on June 16th...

Mr. A. Bloch: Who hired Mr. Rogge?

A.   My brother-in-law, Louis Abel...

Mr. A. Bloch: When were you told about it?

A.   My brother-in-law Louis came to the hospital and told me that my husband had been picked up.   I asked him if he had received any phone calls from David.   He said David had called him during the night and I asked him to go to Mr. Rogge's office.   I told Louis to go right from the hospital there, and he did...

Mr. A. Bloch: Oh, you were the one that sent him to Mr. Rogge?

A.   No, my husband sent him to Mr. Rogge.   He told me my husband's message and I told him to go straight to his office.

Who hired Mr. Rogge or who asked for Mr. Rogge was never clarified. The answers Ruth gave here were not pursued.

Mr. A. Bloch: Did you tell him to hire Mr. Rogge for any particular purpose?

A.   To represent my husband...

Mr. A. Bloch: You told your brother-in-law, in effect, in substance, "You have $4000 of our money. You can turn that over to Mr. Rogge"; is that right?

A.   I told him to go to Mr. Rogge and bring the money he had, yes...

Mr. A. Bloch: Then you went to see Mr. Rogge personally?

A.   No, he came to my house.

Mr. A. Bloch: When?

A.   On June 18th...

Mr. A. Bloch: Did you tell Mr. Rogge that you were innocent?

A. No, I told him the whole truth.

Mr. A. Bloch: You told him just what you told us today, you say?

A. What?

Mr. A. Bloch: You told him the same story that you narrated on the stand before we took a recess?

A. I told him everything I could truthfully remember...

Evidence would later surface, however, that for weeks after her husband's arrest, Ruth vehemently denied her husband's confession, and insisted that he was innocent. It was not until mid-July of 1950 that Ruth, accompanied by O. John Rogge, finally visited U.S. Attorney Saypol and corroborated her husband's story.

Ruth had an infant baby whom imprisonment would keep her from. This powerful lever in the government's hands may have led to Ruth and David Greenglass's decision to manufacture more and more evidence to help convict the Rosenbergs.

Alexander Bloch continued his cross-examination.

Mr. A. Bloch: As a matter of fact, although you are named in the indictment you have not been arrested, have you?

A. No...

Mr. A. Bloch: Now, after you spoke to Mr. Rogge did you have any interview with anyone representing either the FBI or Mr. Saypol's office?

A. Yes.

Mr. A. Bloch: When was that?

A. *The middle of July.*

Mr. A. Bloch: About a month after your husband's arrest?

A. *I think so.*

Mr. A. Bloch: Were you interviewed at all before the middle of July 1950?

A. *I said I was interviewed in the hospital.*

Mr. A. Bloch: The same day your husband was arrested?...

A. *On June 16th.*

Mr. A. Bloch: That is the day you left the hospital?

A. *Yes, that is right...*

Mr. A. Bloch: And who interviewed you?

A. *Two Federal agents...*

Although the defense did not know about it during the trial, it was at this interview, conducted by Special Agents Raymond P. Wirth and Edward R. Tully, that Ruth "denied that Harry Gold visited her or David." Ruth Greenglass's position would change drastically in the weeks that followed.

Mr. A. Bloch: Mrs. Greenglass, I will ask you to direct your mind to the morning of May 24, 1950, when you say Mr. Rosenberg came to your house with the Herald Tribune, wasn't it?

A. *Yes.*

Mr. A. Bloch: And showed you the picture of Gold.

A. *That's right.*

Mr. A. Bloch: And asked you in substance to leave the city immediately?

A. *To leave the country.*

Mr. A. Bloch: Leave the country. And he gave

you $1000?

A. *Yes...*

Mr. A. Bloch: And at the time you received the thousand dollars, you didn't intend to leave the country?...

A. *That's right...*

Mr. A. Bloch: Nevertheless, on the 28th of May 1950 you took passport photographs?

A. *That is right.*

Mr. A. Bloch: Six copies of them, is that right?

A. *Yes.*

Mr. A. Bloch: And at the time these photographs were taken, you knew that you were not leaving the country?

A. *That's right.*

Mr. A. Bloch: Did you talk it over with your husband as to the reason you were taking photographs when you did not intend to leave the country?

A. *Yes.*

Mr. A. Bloch: Was it to deceive Rosenberg?

A. *Yes.*

Mr. A. Bloch: And make him believe that you were going away?

A. *That is right...*

Mr. A. Bloch: Well, what was the object of deceiving him?

A. *Because we didn't want Mr. Rosenberg to think we were going to stay in the country, because we were harmful to him...*

Mr. A. Bloch: Didn't you have in mind at all the $4000 or the $5000 that you were to receive?

A. *That was not the purpose of taking the pictures.*

Mr. A. Bloch: But on the 4th of June 1950, you say Mr. Rosenberg brought you $4000?

A. That's right.

Mr. A. Bloch: You took that $4000?

A. Yes, he gave it to my husband...

Mr. A. Bloch: You had the account, did you not, at that time, in the Manufacturers Trust Company?

A. I did.

Mr. A. Bloch: And none of that $4000 was deposited to that account?

A. Never...

Mr. A. Bloch: Who suggested that the money be turned over to your brother-in-law, Mr. Abel?

A. My husband and I talked it over and we both decided to do that...

Mr. A. Bloch: Were you afraid to keep it in your house?

A. No, I don't think that was it...My husband wanted to tear the money up and flush it. We had no particular love for the $4000; we weren't trying to get money.

Mr. A. Bloch: But you didn't flush it?

A. No, we didn't.

Mr. A. Bloch: And you didn't tear it up?

A. No, because Mr. Abel, when my husband told him what he had in mind, asked him to give him the money, not to do that with the money...

Mr. A. Bloch: Wasn't that money deposited with Mr. Abel so that in the event of your husband's arrest it should not be found in your possession?

A. I don't think we thought of it at that time...

Mr. A. Bloch: Now, didn't something happen in the beginning of 1949 and the end of 1949 that created hostility between you and the Rosenbergs?

A. No, there was no hostility.

Mr. A. Bloch: Did you ever visit the place of business of this machine shop?

A.   Yes. It was near my home.

Mr. A. Bloch: In 1949?

A.   Yes...

Mr. A. Bloch: Did you know that your husband and Mr. Rosenberg had had differences about the business that was being conducted here?

A.   I heard that...I think both my husband and his brother were dissatisfied with the shop...

Mr. A. Bloch: And as a result of that dissatisfaction there were arguments, weren't there?

A.   There weren't arguments, there were discussions over it.

The fact that Ruth and David Greenglass both made concerted efforts to downplay the animosity that existed between themselves and the Rosenbergs indicated that this was an area very disturbing to them and to the prosecution. Logic suggests that the Greenglasses acted in revenge for the financial and social humiliation, feigned or real, they suffered over the years at the hands of the Rosenbergs.

Mr. A. Bloch: Didn't you complain to your mother-in-law and to other members of the family that your husband was being treated as a menial instead of one of the owners of the business?

A.   No, I don't think I put it that way.

Mr. A. Bloch: Well, how would you put it?...

A.   I said I didn't think my husband was being paid commensurate with the work done...

Mr. A. Bloch: Well, was he losing his investment in that business?

A.   We lost everything in that business...

Ruth's statement that they had lost everything was

one of the keys to her and her husband's hatred of the Rosenbergs. Bernard Greenglass, David's brother, also suffered severe financial losses that he attributed to Julius Rosenberg.

Mr. A. Bloch: And don't you know that your husband wanted to be paid the amount of his investment in order to get out of that business?

A. Mr. Bloch, my husband wanted some money for his stock.

Mr. A. Bloch: And he demanded it?

A. He didn't demand it. He asked for it.

Mr. A. Bloch: Very well, but he did not get any money, did he?

A. No, not for the business...

Mr. A. Bloch: Now I am going to ask you a direct question...are you hostile to either Mr. or Mrs. Rosenberg?

A. No.

Mr. A. Bloch: Are you friendly towards them?

A. I have friendly feelings.

Mr. A. Bloch: And do you wish them well?

A. I do...

Mr. A. Bloch: Do you know that your husband asked Mr. Rogge to commence an action against Mr. Rosenberg for the collection of either one thousand or two thousand dollars?

A. He didn't ask him to start an action, Mr. Bloch...I was the one who spoke of it, not my husband.

Mr. A. Bloch: Well, did you tell Mr. Rogge to call up myself and ask or make a demand for the money that your husband claimed Rosenberg owed him?

A. Mr. Bloch, I asked Mr. Rogge...I spoke to Mr. Rogge. I said that David had left the business and

Bernard had left the business and no money had been paid to either one for their share of the common stock, and we wanted to see if we would be paid for it. That is exactly what I asked Mr. Rogge...

Mr. A. Bloch: Well aren't you a bit angry at either Mr. or Mrs. Rosenberg because they did not pay you what you think you were entitled to?...

A. I don't think I am angry. I just can't understand their actions because there was a debt due.

Mr. A. Bloch: You are not angry?

A. No, I am not angry. I don't understand people who do not pay their debts, Mr. Bloch.

Mr. A. Bloch: And you resent it?

A. I don't think I resented it. I couldn't understand why it wasn't being paid for what was rightfully mine...

Ruth Greenglass said that she wished the Rosenbergs well, but the feelings she expressed were anger, resentment, and hostility toward them—she certainly did not wish them well. The balance of her cross-examination was conducted by Emanuel Bloch.

Mr. E. H. Bloch: Now did I understand you correctly to say that one of the points of disagreement between your husband and Bernie, your husband's brother, and Julius Rosenberg while they were in business together at Pitt Machine Products Company was that your husband was not being paid sufficiently?

A. No, I didn't say that...I said I didn't think that my husband was being paid commensurate with the work done...

Mr. E. H. Bloch: When you say you didn't think that he was being paid sufficiently, did you voice that opinion of yours to Julius Rosenberg?

A.   *I voiced it to Julius Rosenberg...I felt that they were all partners.   They shared the common stock.   They had the same number of shares...and I felt that they should share their profits equally but that the salary should be commensurate with the work done...*

Mr. E. H. Bloch: *Isn't it a fact that one of the complaints that was made by Julius Rosenberg against your husband was that he, Julius Rosenberg, was working too hard and that your husband was loafing on the job?*

A.   *That is an untruth.*

Mr. E. H. Bloch: *Whether it is an untruth or not, did he make that complaint?*

A.   *He complained about a great many things... Julius's job was to solicit business.   He could hardly say that my husband was loafing.   Julius was not working on machines.   Only on occasions; he wasn't steadily at the machines in 1946 and 1947...*

Mr. E. H. Bloch: *As a matter of fact, Julius was the one who went out and tried to get business?*

A.   *So he couldn't say that my husband was loafing.   If he got the business David produced it.*

Mr. E. H. Bloch: *Maybe you misunderstand me.   I am not trying to say that your husband may not have had a justifiable grievance.   All we are trying to find out is whether Julius Rosenberg complained that your husband was loafing, that is all.*

A.   *I didn't say my husband had a grievance.   I said Julius complained.   He complained about so many things...*

WITNESSES

Dorothy Abel, Ruth Greenglass's sister, was then called as a witness on behalf of the government. She was questioned by James Kilsheimer.

Mr. Kilsheimer: Did there come a time in the early part of 1945 when you saw Julius Rosenberg at your apartment, at 255 Stanton Street?
A. Yes...
Mr. Kilsheimer: Did Rosenberg come to your apartment?
A. Yes, he did...
Mr. Kilsheimer: Can you tell the Court and jury what occurred on that occasion when Rosenberg came to your apartment?
A. Well, we exchanged pleasantries and then Julie asked me to go, to leave the room, take a book and leave the room...
Judge Kaufman: Well, did he say anything about what he wanted to do?
The Witness: He said he wanted to speak to Ruth privately...
Mr. Kilsheimer: And you went into the bathroom and closed the door; is that right?
A. I did.
Mr. Kilsheimer: Did you from time to time have conversations with Julius and Ethel Rosenberg concerning Russia?
A. Yes, I did...
Mr. Kilsheimer: Does one of these conversations stand out in your mind?
A. I remember a time when...they were talking, Julius and Ethel were speaking to me and...they said

that they, Russia, was the ideal form of government, the Russian form of government. That is all.

Mr. Kilsheimer: Can you fix the time when this conversation took place, as best you can?

A. I think it was in 1944, during the winter time. That is about all I can remember...

Emanuel Bloch then cross-examined Dorothy Abel.

Mr. E. H. Bloch: In the course of this conversation in which you stated that the Rosenbergs told you that the Russian form of Government was the ideal form of Government, did they say anything specifically about the United States form of Government?

A. They didn't think that it compared at all with the Russian form of Government.

Mr. E. H. Bloch: Can you tell us specifically what criticism they made of the United States form of Government?

A. Well, they said that it was a capitalistic form of Government...

Louis Abel, Ruth Greenglass's brother-in-law, was called as a witness for the government, and was also questioned by Kilsheimer.

Mr. Kilsheimer: Now sometime prior to the date when David Greenglass was arrested, did you see David Greenglass?

A. I did.

Mr. Kilsheimer: And where did you see him?

A. In his home.

Mr. Kilsheimer: About how long—about what length of time prior to the time he was arrested?

A. Oh, it must have been about close to a week

before he was taken in.

Mr. Kilsheimer: On that occasion did you have a conversation with David Greenglass?

A. I did...

Mr. Kilsheimer: And as a result of that conversation, what happened?

A. As a result of that conversation, I held some money for David...I took it home and I hid it in a hassock that I have, and I left it there...Well, the—about two in the morning the night after David was arrested, he phoned me and asked me to engage his attorney, Mr. Rogge.

The following morning I went to Mr. Rogge and I explained to him that Dave was in trouble, that he had been picked up by the FBI and—well, I gave him as much information as I knew at the time.

Mr. Rogge went down to see Dave and when he got back he said that David informed me to give him the package, which I did...

Emanuel Bloch then cross-examined Louis Abel.

Mr. E. H. Bloch: Can you tell us exactly the day that you received this package...

A. No, I can't...

Mr. E. H. Bloch: You said it was about a week before his arrest, is that your best recollection?

A. Yes. It might be a little more...

Mr. A. Bloch: Who was present when you received that package?...

A. I believe it was just David—I am not certain...

Mr. A. Bloch: When for the first time did you open it?

A. Well, it must have been a day or so later... that I opened the package.

Mr. A. Bloch: And then you found for the first time that there was money in it?

A. *That is correct.*

Mr. A. Bloch: That is all...

HARRY GOLD

Harry Gold was the next witness called by the government. After being sworn in, he was questioned by U.S. Attorney Myles Lane.

Mr. Lane: What is your occupation?
A. I am a biochemist...
Mr. Lane: Now do you stand convicted of any crime?
A. Yes, I do.
Mr. Lane: Of what crime?
A. I stand convicted of espionage...
Mr. Lane: What was the sentence that was imposed upon you...?
A. I was given a sentence of 30 years in the Federal Penitentiary...
Mr. Lane: Do you know Anatoli Yakovlev?
A. Yes, I do.
Mr. Lane: When for the first time did you meet Anatoli Yakovlev?
A. I met Anatoli Yakovlev in March 1944.
Mr. Lane: Where did you meet him?
A. I met Yakovlev in New York City...I worked with Yakovlev for a period of almost three years. From March of 1944 until late December 1946...
Mr. Lane: What name did you know him by?
A. I knew Yakovlev as John.
Mr. Lane: Now, for how long a period were you engaged in Soviet activities?...
A. I was engaged in espionage work for the Soviet Union from the spring of 1935 up until the time of my arrest...

Mr. A. Bloch: I move to strike out that part of the answer which refers to the Soviet Union, as there is no proof adduced as to who the Soviet Union is, and how he knows it was the Soviet Union...

Judge Kaufman: Are you saying, Mr. Bloch, that you would rather have this witness tell you how he arrives at the conclusion that he was engaged in espionage work for the Soviet Union? Would you rather have that?...

Mr. E. H. Bloch: Now if the Court please, before I respond to that, I want to have an opportunity to consult with co-counsel because there are many considerations involved...

A conference was held by the defense attorneys, after which Bloch addressed the court.

Mr. E. H. Bloch: Counsel for the defendants are unanimous in demanding competent proof on each and every essential element of the crime...

Judge Kaufman: Yes, and I want you to understand that it is being done because you have requested it. If you would have objected to this, I would have sustained your objection to giving these steps...but in view of the fact that you have asked for it, I want the record to be clear that...you wanted to have each and every step which led to that conclusion...

Kaufman had already given the jury the impression that Gold was obviously a spy, and that if the defense attorneys questioned Gold they would only be weakening their already hopeless case. Kaufman was in substance telling the jury that there was already so much evidence to prove the crimes charged that the lawyers were making a mistake by asking for more evidence since it would even more overwhelmingly prove their clients' guilt.

Mr. Kuntz: May I respectfully ask that your Honor's remarks be stricken from the record?...
Judge Kaufman: Oh, no...It won't be stricken...
Mr. Kuntz: May I finish my argument?
Judge Kaufman: Mr. Kuntz, no you may not. It is a lot of gibberish...In view of the particular subject matter that is involved here, I hesitated to have the witness proceed with testimony on the facts until all counsel understood what might come out as a result of it. That is the way the record stands right now...
Mr. E. H. Bloch: May I just, not retort, but make this statement in addition: The indictment charges that these defendants conspired to transmit information to the advantage of a foreign power. Now I am assuming that this line of questions by the prosecution is to elicit that there was a foreign power involved, and I believe that is a substantial fact that must be proved...
Judge Kaufman: All right...

Myles Lane continued questioning Harry Gold.

Mr. Lane: Now...will you give a description of Yakovlev?
A. Yakovlev was about 23 or 30 years of age at the time I knew him. He was about 5 feet 9 inches in height; had a medium build, which tended toward the slender. He had dark or dark brown hair and there was a lock of it that kept falling over his forehead, which he would brush back continually. He had a rather long nose and a fair complexion, dark eyes...
Mr. Lane: Now, did you meet Klaus Fuchs, Dr.

267

Klaus Fuchs, some time in the middle of June 1944?

A. Yes, I did...

Mr. Lane: Now, during this period when you were meeting Dr. Fuchs, were you also meeting Yakovlev at regular intervals?

A. During this period, I had a regularly scheduled series of meetings with Yakovlev. Yakovlev continually advised and instructed me and we talked over together as to how I should continue my work with Dr. Fuchs.

Mr. Lane: Now, did you have any particular modus operandi in your connections, in your work with Yakovlev?

A. Yes, I did.

Mr. Lane: Would you tell the jury, would you relate the details of that?...

A. I worked in the following manner with Yakovlev: My duties were to obtain information from a number of sources in America, and to transfer this information to Yakovlev...

In the midst of Gold's testimony, an interruption occurred and an exchange took place at the bench:

Judge Kaufman: Did you want to put something on the record?

Mr. Kuntz: I suppose you saw the newspapers. It is an unfortunate experience. We were wondering what effect it might have. I didn't know it until I got in the courtroom and Mannie Bloch showed it to me...

Kuntz was referring to a newspaper story about William Perl, a prominent scientist, who had attended City College with Julius Rosenberg. The *New York Times* headline read, "Columbia Teacher Arrested; Linked to Two on Trial as Spies." Kaufman, who signed the bench warrant for Perl's arrest, helped Saypol to time the arrest so that it would occur during the Rosenberg trial. Saypol assured the defense counsels, however, that the indictment had been returned "in the regular course of the administration of justice." Kaufman asked the lawyers to accept Saypol's word. Saypol's assurances and Judge Kaufman's reassurances were all deliberately false. The Circuit Court of Appeals, later scolded Irving Saypol, calling Perl's indictment and his arrest "deliberately timed" and "wholly reprehensible." But the Court would go no further and did not order a new trial.

To protect Kaufman and Saypol, the Court of Appeals said that defense counsel was derelict in not moving for a new trial immediately when Perl was indicted and in not asking Kaufman to caution the jury to disregard Perl's indictment. The Court of Appeals, not unmindful of Kaufman and Saypol's false assurances, added, "if defendants had moved for a new trial, it should have been granted. But they did not so move." Thus the court reasoned that even if defense counsel was deceived, too bad—and if they trusted the words of Kaufman and Saypol—again, too bad.

It was a frightful time. Westbrook Pegler, a noted columnist, wrote on June 29, 1950, "The only sensible and courageous way to deal with Communists in our midst is to make membership in Communist organizations...a capital offense and shoot or otherwise put to death all persons convicted of such," and Pegler meant what he said. America was a mad land.

Judge Kaufman: Well, this is off the record...Will you continue, please?...

Myles Lane resumed questioning Harry Gold:

Mr. Lane: Now, did you have a meeting with Dr. Fuchs in Cambridge, Massachusetts, early in January of 1945?...

A. Yes, I did.

Mr. Lane: Did you have a conversation with Dr. Fuchs at that time?

A. Yes, I did.

Mr. Lane: As a result of that conversation, what did you do?

A. In consequence of the conversation that I had with Dr. Fuchs, I did two things. One the same day that I saw Dr. Fuchs, the same morning that I saw Dr. Fuchs in Cambridge, Massachusetts, I returned from Cambridge to New York City and turned over to Yakovlev a package of papers which Fuchs had given me. About a week later, I wrote a report which I turned over to Yakovlev.

Mr. Lane: When did you turn this report over to Yakovlev?

A. The report was turned over to Yakovlev somewhere around the second week in January...

Mr. Lane: At that time, did you have a conversation with Yakovlev?

A. Yes, I did.

Mr. Lane: What was the conversation?

A. I told Yakovlev that I had received the following information from Fuchs: First, that Fuchs was now stationed at a place called Los Alamos, New Mexico; that this was a large experimental station. It had formerly been a boy's school, a select boys' school. Fuchs told me that a tremendous amount of progress had been made. In addition, he had made mention of a lens, which was being worked on as a part of the atom bomb. Finally, we had set a date, this date to be the first Saturday in June of 1945, and at this date I was to meet Fuchs in Santa Fe, New Mexico...

Mr. Lane: Now in May of 1945, did you have a meeting with Yakovlev?

A. Yes, I did.

Mr. Lane: Will you try to fix the date as best you can of that particular meeting?

A. The exact date of the meeting that I had with Yakovlev in May of 1945 was on the last Saturday in May, and about—pretty late in the afternoon, around four in the afternoon, I would say...

It was interesting to note that Harry Gold, like the Greenglasses, used the weeks of the month as a mneumonic device to recall dates.

Mr. Lane: Now, will you tell the jury what happened on this occasion?

A. I stood at the bar with Yakovlev and we had a drink...Yakovlev told me that he had some matter to discuss with me at length...Yakovlev told me that he wanted me to take on an additional mission besides the one to see Dr. Fuchs. He said that he wanted me to go to Albuquerque, New Mexico. I protested...I told Yakovlev that I did not wish to take on this additional task...Yakovlev told me that I didn't understand that this was an extremely important business, that I just had to go to Albuquerque, in addition to going to Santa Fe, and he said, "That is an order"; and that was all. I agreed to go.

Yakovlev then gave me a sheet of paper; it was onionskin paper and on it was typed the following: first, the name "Greenglass," just "Greenglass." Then a number "High Street;"...The last thing that was on the paper was "Recognition signal. I come from Julius." In addition to this, Yakovlev gave me a piece of cardboard, which appeared to have been cut from a packaged food of some sort. It was cut in an odd shape and Yakovlev told me that the man Greenglass, whom I would meet in Albuquerque, would have the matching piece of cardboard...

Yakovlev told me that I should follow a very devious route on my way to Santa Fe and to Albuquerque. He said that I should first go to Phoenix, Arizona; then to El Paso, and from there to Santa Fe. Yakovlev said that I should do this to minimize any danger of being followed...

Mr. Lane: Now, did you go to Santa Fe in June of 1945?

A. Yes, I did.

Mr. Lane: When did you arrive in Santa Fe?

A. I arrived in Santa Fe on Saturday, the 2nd of June, 1945.

Mr. Lane: And did you meet Dr. Fuchs?

A. Yes, I did...

Mr. Lane: Now, when did you depart from Santa Fe?

A. I left Santa Fe in the very late afternoon.

Mr. Lane: Where did you go?...

A. I went by bus from Santa Fe to Albuquerque...

Mr. Lane: Did you register in any hotel when you were in Albuquerque on this occasion?

A. I stayed that night—I finally managed to obtain a room in a hallway of a rooming house and then on Sunday morning, I registered at the Hotel Hilton...

Mr. Lane: Did you register under your own name?

A. Yes, I did.

Mr. Lane: What name did you use?

A. Harry Gold.

Mr. Lane: Now, what did you do on Sunday? That

is June 3, 1945?

A. *On Sunday about 8:30, I went...to the High Street address...I knocked on a door. It was opened by a young man...I said, "Mr. Greenglass?" He answered in the affirmative. I said, "I come from Julius," and I showed him the piece of cardboard in my hand. He asked me to enter...*

Gold's testimony naming "Julius" seemed routine. But in tape-recorded conversations of his discussions with his attorneys, as well as numerous FBI interviews, Gold reported that he told the Greenglasses that he was sent to them by either Ben or Philip, not Julius. The efforts made by the FBI and the United States Attorney's Office to persuade Gold to say that on visiting the Greenglasses he said to them "I come from Julius" was one of many instances of our government's encouragement and instigation of the use of false testimony.

Gold's statement of August 1, 1950, to Special Agents Norton and Harrington, included the assertion, "I never knew Julius Rosenberg." And when Gold, questioned on that same day about his visit to the Greenglasses at their Albuquerque home, was asked, "What happened when Mrs. Greenglass opened the door?" he answered, "I said that I brought greetings from Ben in Brooklyn." Correcting himself, Gold added what appeared to be lines he had forgotten: "I believe she stated to me that she had recalled a Julius...I understood that Julius was a relative of hers." The special agents questioned him more vigorously: "Can't you state definitely whether she actually said [this] or didn't?" Gold replied, perhaps mockingly, "The word 'believe' was an unfortunate slip. What I intended to say was, 'I recall very definitely during the meeting that Mrs. Greenglass told me she had spoken with a Julius in New York, just prior to her coming to Albuquerque in April 1945.'" But at the close of the interview, Gold still maintained that when he visited the Greenglasses he brought them "Greetings from Ben." His vacillating testimony tormented the FBI.

More work was needed on Harry Gold. An FBI memo stated, "Gold was interviewed in the Tombs [New York City prison] on 12/26/50 in the presence of David Greenglass...concerning the reported salutation, 'Greetings from Ben.' Greenglass proposed that possibly Gold had said, 'Greetings from Julius.'" The FBI report continued, "Gold's spontaneous comment...was that possibly Greenglass was right, that he had mentioned the name of Julius rather than Ben." But the FBI agent said, "Gold, however, is not at all clear on this point."

Harry Gold continued his testimony:

Greenglass then told me that my visit to him on this exact day was a bit of a surprise; he had not expected me right on that day, but that nevertheless he would have the material on the atom bomb ready for me that afternoon.

At this point, Mrs. Greenglass went into the kitchen to prepare some food. Then I gave Mr. Greenglass the envelope which Yakovlev had given me...This envelope was the one that contained $500. Greenglass took the envelope from me. Greenglass told me that he would have the information ready at about 4 o'clock, 3 or 4 o'clock in the afternoon; the exact time I can't recall except that we set it.

At this point, Greenglass told me that there were a number of people at Los Alamos that he thought would make very likely recruits; that is, they were also people who might be willing to furnish information on the atom bomb to the Soviet Union, and he started to give me the names of these people, the names of some of these people. I cut him very short indeed. I told him that such procedure was extremely hazardous, foolhardy, that under no circumstances should he ever try to proposition anyone on his own into trying to get information for the Soviet Union. I told him to be very circumspect in his conduct and to never even drop the slightest hint to anyone that he himself was furnishing information on the atom bomb to the Soviet Union.

Is it reasonable to believe that Gold warned Greenglass not to tell anyone that he was engaged in furnishing the secret process of the atomic bomb to the Russians? Could anyone, much less a master spy, give such obvious advice? And could anyone fail to notice the rehearsed quality of the testimony against the Rosenbergs that comes to us across the years: that both Gold and Ruth Greenglass used the rarely spoken phrase, "to be very circumspect"?

The questioning of Gold continued.

Mr. Lane: Did you return to the home of the Greenglasses on the same day, Sunday, June 3, 1945?
A. Yes, I did.
Mr. Lane: And what time did you return?
A. It was about between 3 and 4 o'clock.
Mr. Lane: And who was present when you returned?
A. Mr. Greenglass was there, and his wife Ruth was there.
Mr. Lane: And did you have a conversation at that time?
A. Yes, I did.

Mr. Lane: Will you tell the jury what that conversation was?

A. Mr. Greenglass gave me an envelope which he said contained the information for which I had come, the information on the atom bomb. I took the envelope. Mr. Greenglass told me that he expected to get a furlough sometime around Christmas, and that he would return to New York at that time. He told me that if I wished to get in touch with him, then I could do so by calling his brother-in-law, Julius, and he gave me the telephone number of Julius in New York City.

Mr. Lane: Do you recall now what that number was?

A. I cannot...

Mr. Lane: And did you return to New York?

A. Yes, I did...

Mr. Lane: Now...when did you arrive back in New York?

A. I arrived in New York on the 5th of June, 1945, in the evening.

Mr. Lane: And did you meet Yakovlev?

A. Yes, I did...

Mr. Lane: On the same day?

A. On the same evening.

Judge Kaufman: What time was it?

The Witness: It was about 10 o'clock at night...

Mr. Lane: What did you do at that meeting?

A. We met and Yakovlev wanted to know if I had seen the both of them..."The doctor and the man." I said that I had. Yakovlev wanted to know had I got information from the both of them and I said that I had. Then I gave Yakovlev the two manila envelopes, the one labeled "Doctor," which had the information I had received from Fuchs in Santa Fe; the one labeled

"Other," which had the information I had received from David Greenglass in Albuquerque, on the 3rd of June 1945.

Mr. Lane: When was your next meeting with Yakovlev?...

The Witness: It was about two weeks after the 5th of June. We are still in June.

Mr. Lane: Did you have a conversation with Yakovlev at that time?

A. Yes, I did.

Mr. Lane: Will you tell the jury whct the conversation was?...

A. Yakovlev told me that the information which I had given him some two weeks previous had been sent immediately to the Soviet Union. He said that the information which I had received from Greenglass was extremely excellent and very valuable. Then Yakovlev listened while I recounted the details of my two meetings, the one with Fuchs in Santa Fe, the one with Greenglass in Albuquerque. I told Yakovlev that Fuchs had related that tremendous progress had been made on the construction of the atom bomb...I told Yakovlev that Fuchs and I had agreed upon a meeting between the two of us in Santa Fe for September of 1945...

Mr. Lane: Now, did you have a meeting with Dr. Fuchs in September 1945?

A. Yes, I did.

Mr. Lane: When and where did this meeting take place?

A. The meeting took place in Santa Fe, New Mexico, on the 19th of September 1945...

Mr. Lane: What was the conversation?

A. The conversation covered the following matters which Fuchs told me: Fuchs had said first that there was no longer open and free and easy cooperation between the British and the Americans at Los Alamos...

The second thing was that Fuchs told me that the first explosion at Alamogordo, New Mexico, in July, had produced a tremendous feeling of awe among the scientists who had been producing it...

The final item I reported to Yakovlev were the details of an arrangement which Fuchs and I had arrived at, which arrangement concerned the means by which someone would get in touch with Fuchs when he returned to England...

Mr. Lane: Do you recall a meeting in November of 1945?...

With Yakovlev?

A. Yes, I do.

Mr. Lane: Will you tell the jury what that conversation was?

A. I told Yakovlev...that we ought to make some plan to get in touch with this brother-in-law, Julius, so that we could get further information from Greenglass. Yakovlev told me to mind my own business. He cut me very short...

Mr. Lane: When was the next time that you saw Yakovlev?

A. The next time that I saw Yakovlev was on the night of the 26th of December 1946...

Mr. Lane: Now, will you tell the jury how you happened to meet Yakovlev in December of 1946?...

A. At about five o'clock in the late afternoon of the 26th of December, the phone rang at the laboratory where I was working in New York City, the laboratory of A. Brothman and Associates. I answered. A voice asked for Harry Gold. I said that I was Harry Gold. The voice said, "Have you been all right?"

Mr. Lane: Did you recognize the voice?...

A. *I recognized it as that of Yakovlev. I said, I told him that I had been fine.* Now, *the phrase used by Yakovlev was a code phrase which was employed to indicate whether there had been any suspicious signs about us, about my being watched, and my answer that I was fine was my code answer which indicated that there was no sign of any surveillance going on.*

Yakovlev told me that he would meet me at the theatre—he didn't specify. He said at the theatre at 8 o'clock that night. And I said—I answered that I would be there.

Mr. Lane: *And what happened?*

A. *By the theatre I knew that Yakovlev meant the Earl Theatre where our last meeting had been scheduled...The man who met me was not Yakovlev...As a result of the meeting I had with the man I met in the lounge of the Earl Theatre, I went to the southwest corner of 42nd Street and Third Avenue, and there later that evening met Yakovlev...Yakovlev asked me if I had anything further from Dr. Fuchs in the interim. I told him I did not...Yakovlev told me that I should begin to plan now for a mission which he had. He said that he wanted me to go to Paris, France, beginning in March of 1947...*

Mr. Lane: *Now, was there any discussion at that time about the name Brothman?*

A. *Yes, there was. Yakovlev began to discuss with me the means by which I should manage to get off from work, in order to make this trip to Paris. I told Yakovlev that once the pressure of work at Abe Brothman and Associates had eased up a bit—and then Yakovlev almost went through the roof of the saloon. He said, "You fool." He said, "You spoiled eleven years of work." He told me that I didn't realize what I had done, and he told me that I should have remembered that some time in the summer of '45 he had told me that Brothman was under suspicion by the United States Government authorities of having engaged in espionage, and that I should have remembered it...Yakovlev then told me that he would not see me in the United States again, and he left me...*

How could Yakovlev be annoyed or even surprised when he learned that Gold worked for Abe Brothman, if Yakovlev called Gold at Brothman's office in December of 1946? Everything about this dialogue was weird. How could Yakovlev be asking if Gold had any information from Fuchs, when he had not been assigned to get information from Fuchs. And why would Yakovlev wait almost a year to ask Gold for this information? Further, how could anyone possibly believe Harry Gold's testimony about how he met Yakovlev at the Earle Theatre, when the story contradicts his earlier statement to the FBI which unequivocally stated the fact that no other person other than Yakovlev met him there? Gold's first statement, recorded on July 10, 1950, said:

> *On June 12, 1950, Gold advised that in the late afternoon of the week between Christmas and New Year's Eve, 1946, he received a telephone call at Brothman's laboratory, where he was then employed, and that he recognized the voice of John, who asked if Gold could see him at 8 or 8:30 that night, and when Gold hesitated, John stated "At the same place as before." Gold stated that that evening he went to the Earle Theatre...He met John inside the theatre near the men's lounge, and John stopped long enough to say, "Third Avenue Bar in an hour."*

It was not until months later, on October 18, that

Gold provided the FBI with a signed statement describing his meeting with Yakovlev at the Earle Theatre in a way that conformed with the testimony he would give at the trial. In this revised statement Gold said that he met another person, Paul, at the Earle Theatre, who told him where to meet Yakovlev. Gold's new statement also specifically provided the date as December 26, 1946. Gold's statement read:

> *I was shown a photograph of an individual whose name is Pavel Ivanovich Fedosimov. I am completely certain he is the person who contacted me in the upstairs lounge of the Earle Theatre in the Bronx...This contact was made about eight p.m. on the evening of December twenty-six nineteen forty six...*
>
> *Upon noticing my astonishment, as I expected "John," this contact said, "I am Paul...You have papers from the Doctor." I replied in the negative and a savage look of disappointment came over the features of this man. The "Doctor" was the code name used by "John" and me for Dr. Klaus Fuchs...*

At the trial Gold provided a further inconsistency when he testified that it was Yakovlev instead of Paul who asked him if he had "anything further from Dr. Fuchs." It seems probable that there were so many inconsistencies because the event never happened. Gold never met Yakovlev at the Earle Theatre, or Third Avenue, or anywhere. Gold never met Yakovlev. Fedosimov appears to have been introduced into the case to stand ready as a substitute indictee in the event the Rosenbergs learned that Yakovlev was not in the United States on December 26, 1946.

Mr. Lane: Now I show you...the picture attached thereto, and tell me if you recognize that individual?

281

A. Yes, I do.
Mr. Lane: Who is it?
A. That is Anatoli Yakovlev...

The trial was adjourned to March 16, 1951.

Harry Gold resumed the stand.
Mr. Lane: The Government, your Honor, has no further questions.
Judge Kaufman: Any cross?
Mr. E. H. Bloch: The defendants Rosenberg have no cross-examination of this witness.
Mr. Phillips: No cross.
Judge Kaufman: The witness is excused.

MORE WITNESSES

George Bernhardt was called as a government witness and questioned by James Kilsheimer:

Mr. Kilsheimer: What is your occupation?
A. I am a physician...
Mr. Kilsheimer: Do you know the defendant Julius Rosenberg?
A. I do...
Mr. Kilsheimer: Can you fix the time when you had a conversation with Julius Rosenberg in the spring of 1950?
A. Yes, I can.
Mr. Kilsheimer: When was it?
A. I think the latter part of May.
Mr. Kilsheimer: Was this conversation face to face in person?
A. No, sir, it was not.
Mr. Kilsheimer: Will you state how you had the conversation?
A. This was a telephone conversation...
Mr. Kilsheimer: Will you state the conversation which you had with Rosenberg at that time?
A. He said, "Doctor, I would like to ask a favor of you. I would like to know what injections one needs to go to Mexico," and I hesitated a little, and he laughed and said, "Don't get scared, it is not for me; it's for a friend of mine." And I then proceeded to give him that information...
Mr. Kilsheimer: Tell us what information you gave him.
A. I told him that he would need typhoid injections and a smallpox vaccination, and I then asked him if

this friend of his was a veteran, telling him that if he was a veteran all he would need would be booster doses instead of going through the entire series of injections, and he said, "Yes, he is a veteran."...

William Danziger was then called as a witness for the Government and questioned by Roy Cohn:

Mr. Cohn: Now, I want to come to the year 1950. Was there a time in 1950 when you left Washington and moved to New York?

A. Yes, there was.

Mr. Cohn: After you moved up to New York in the spring of 1950, did you have occasion to renew your social acquaintance with the defendant Sobell?

A. Yes, I did, I visited at his house in May of 1950...

Mr. Cohn: Did there come a time in June of 1950 when you saw Sobell?

A. Yes...I called him at his home to indicate that I needed an electric drill to do a repair around my home, and he mentioned then that he was getting ready to leave for a vacation in Mexico, and that he was leaving rather shortly and if I wanted the drill, for me to come out and get it...

Mr. Cohn: Did he tell you where he was going?

A. Yes. He said he was going to Mexico—Mexico City...

Mr. Cohn: About what day in June was this, would you say?

A. Oh, the 20th of June...

Mr. Cohn: Did there come a time after that night when you heard from Sobell?

A. Yes, I did. I received a letter from him...

Mr. Cohn: Will you tell us what you remember

concerning that return address?

A. The return address was M. Sowell...

Mr. Cohn: Now, in the entire period of time of your acquaintance with Sobell, did you ever know him to use the name S-o-w-e-l-l?

A. I do not...

Mr. Cohn: Were there any other communications in that envelope to you?

A. Yes, there was a note which said "Please forward the enclosures and I will explain to you when I get back."...

HOTEL HILTON

The following proceedings took place at the bench outside the hearing of the jury.

Mr. Saypol: I now have some testimony which it is possible there may be a stipulation on: The fact of the registration of Harry Gold at the Hotel Hilton on June 3. I have a photostat of the registration card. I also have the original on the way, together with a witness if required. I have testimony as to the bank records...

May I first inquire of counsel whether they will stipulate as to the records or whether they will insist upon strict technical proof?

Mr. E. H. Bloch: I am speaking for myself again: I am certainly not going to insist on strict technical testimony. In other words, Mr. Saypol, let us understand: You want incorporated in the record a concession that Harry Gold stopped at the Hotel Hilton in Albuquerque on June 3, 1945...I certainly have no objection to that introduction.

Mr. Kuntz: We have no objection.

Bloch seemed to think that if he questioned the veracity of records, it could be construed as questioning the integrity of Irving Saypol. But subsequent information turned up by William Reuben in his book *The Atom Spy Hoax* (1955) and by the Schneirs, Walter and Miriam, in their book *Invitation to an Inquest* (1965), and by John Wexley's book *The Judgment of Julius and Ethel Rosenberg* (1955), proved that Saypol, as well as Kaufman and Cohn, was not to be trusted.

Mr. Saypol: I want also to get together the bank records and also that testimony showing the deposits of the various amounts of money as testified to by the witness.

Mr. E. H. Bloch: Well, Mr. Saypol, I certainly am not going to dispute the bank records, but I would like to look at them.

Judge Kaufman: I think he is entitled to look at them.

Mr. E. H. Bloch: Yes, before I make the concession...

Mr. Saypol: If counsel for the defendants are agreeable, I shall proceed to put in evidence a document, rather, a photostat of a document, relating to the witness Harry Gold's presence in Albuquerque on June 3, 1945...So, may I now inquire of the defendants whether there is any objection to the offer in evidence of this photostatic record?...

Judge Kaufman: You have no objection whatsoever to its introduction?...

Mr. E. H. Bloch: No, none whatsoever...

Judge Kaufman: That is the registration of the Hilton Hotel?...

Mr. Saypol: May I proceed to read it to the jury?

Judge Kaufman: Yes...

Walter and Miriam Schneir, authors of *Invitation to an Inquest*, found serious discrepancies in the registration card for Gold's stay at the Hilton Hotel. Though a handwritten entry on the card read June 3, 1945, it was stamped June 4. There were other oddities. Gold claimed that he never used his real name during his years of espionage and he said that he used an alias when he met the Greenglasses. Yet he used his real name when he checked into the Hilton Hotel.

Also, Gold said he arrived in Albuquerque by bus the night of June 2 and slept in a rooming house. He then claimed that before meeting with the Greenglasses, the next morning, a Sunday, June 3, he registered at the Hilton. Since he was scheduled to return to New York that day, it was purposeless to rent another hotel room for that same day. But if the government was provided with a card showing Gold registered at the Hilton on June 3, that is the way the case had to be presented.

Bloch was lulled into stipulating that Gold had been registered at the Hilton on June 3. Bloch also permitted Saypol to submit a photostatic copy of the registration card rather than demanding the original. Years later research by the Schneirs turned up evidence that the card had been tampered with.

Strangely, most of the evidence that could have answered nagging questions like these had been destroyed. Those who destroyed the records explained that it was general procedure to dispose of records after a certain number of years. But the Rosenberg case was not a routine trial subject to routine procedures; it was history, and to destroy historic archives, especially when aspects of the case were still being hotly contested, had to be a deliberate and malicious act.

Hard evidence exists, nonetheless, that Gold's story of being at the Hilton in Albuquerque on June 3, 1945 was a physical impossibility. Disturbing records found by the FBI, but withheld for years, indicated that Gold was in Philadelphia on May 29, 1945. If so, he would not have been able to reach Albuquerque on June 3 after stopping off in Santa Fe on June 2; not by the mode of travel he used. As detailed in a July 21, 1950, memo, this was the conclusion of the FBI when an agent discovered a $50 cash deposit receipt dated May 29, 1945, for Harry Gold's Philadelphia account. But Gold explained to the FBI how it happened: since he was not in Philadelphia at the time, his good friend Morrell Dougherty made the deposit for him "in order to cover an overdraft which Gold had made. Gold stated that it was necessary for Dougherty to make this deposit since Gold had left for Santa Fe a day or two previously."

The government, satisfied with the explanation that Dougherty had made the deposit, looked no further into Gold's bank records. But a search made by the author revealed that Gold was in Philadelphia not only on May 29, but on May 31 as well, making it impossible for him to have been in Albuquerque on June 3. The FBI agent had overlooked a savings account Gold had at the Philadelphia Savings Fund Society. Over time he made substantial deposits in this account and maintained a healthy balance there.

Gold never left Philadelphia—the cover-up was not thorough. Dougherty, having committed himself to explaining the May 29, 1945 deposit of $50 as having been made by him for the purpose of covering Harry Gold's overdraft, could not very well explain the deposit of $150 on May 31, 1945, as being made to cover an overdraft, not when there was a balance of some $1,700 in Gold's account at the time.

Harry Gold's account at the Philadelphia Savings Fund Society follows.

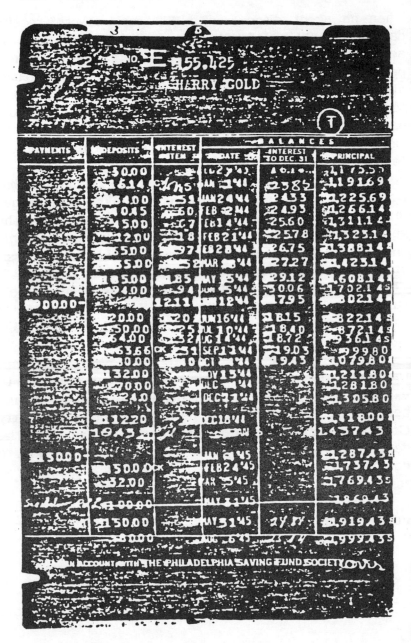

Harry Gold's bank deposits are not the only evidence that the story of his trip to see Greenglass and Fuchs was false; there are also the records of his employer, Pennsylvania Sugar Company. According to them, he did not take a vacation in May or June of 1945. Mrs. Mahoney, who was employed at Penn Sugar as a chemical laboratory assistant from April 1945 until November 1945, told the FBI that she could not recall any trips made by Gold while she worked with him. Since she was at the company for only eight months and worked closely with him the critical months of June and September, it would not have been difficult for her to remember if he took a vacation.

Mahoney's memory and statements were supported by documents at Penn Sugar. The payroll records for 1945 "failed to disclose any vacation taken by Gold during that year," the FBI reported.

The records listed Morrell Dougherty's vacation in July and the vacation of another friend of Gold's, Regina Lookbaugh, in August. Clarence Spratt, the supervisor of the laboratory where Gold worked, also had his vacation in August noted. The FBI interviewed numerous employees at Penn Sugar, and none could recall Gold taking a vacation. Frustrated in these efforts to find evidence that Gold was away in 1945, the FBI concluded: "An unsuccessful attempt to locate a further record of this vacation was made."

JOHN LANSDALE, JR.

Colonel John Lansdale, Jr., a witness called for the government, was questioned by U.S. Attorney Saypol. He testified:

My assignment was while remaining as a member of the general staff organization to be responsible for all phases of the security of the atom bomb project...we were concerned to keep the existence of the project as well as the nature of it secret from all foreign powers, and I do mean all. Secondly, we were concerned to keep it secret within the United States from our own people and from the other branches of the service and divisions of the Government.

Mr. Saypol: Of course, the public, too?

A. Yes, sir...

Colonel Lansdale was a former member of the Military Intelligence Division, War Department, General Staff, who was transferred to the Manhattan Engineering District Corps of Engineers.

Mr. Saypol: As an illustration of the keen determination to keep this secret, can you tell us whether the phrase "atomic bomb" was used in correspondence?

A. Never to my knowledge.

Mr. Saypol: Or in memoranda?

A. Never, and instructions were that it was not to be used...

Mr. Saypol: How long did that practice continue?

A. Until the dropping of the bomb on Hiroshima on August 6th, 1945.

Mr. Saypol: Now let us go back for a moment, if

we may, to the matter of the identity of the scientists who worked on the development of the bomb, both before and after Hiroshima. What was your policy in regard to the identity of scientists?

A. We attempted, in so far as that was practical, to keep their identity secret...particularly two things: No. 1, their concentration in any one location, and, No. 2. the connection of one or two very prominent internationally recognized scientists, such as Neils Bohr, with the project.

Mr. Saypol: Well, what did you do about identifying them?

A. We used fictitious names, particularly when they were traveling. Neils Bohr, for instance, was given the name Nicholas Baker. We soon found it impractical to use names which did not have their own initials...

Mr. Saypol: And so you learned that foreign governments were very much interested in this subject and were working on it?

A. Yes.

Mr. Saypol: Did that apply to the Russian Government, too?

A. We never had any knowledge that the Russians were working on it. However, I should state that...we did ascertain, however, that the Russians were very much interested in what we were doing...

The feelings of the scientists', most of whom were foreign-born, on the subject of secrecy were not discussed at the trial. While they were unquestionably and unanimously opposed to Nazi Germany, their feelings about Russia were in many cases as warm as they were about the United States. A number of the foreign scientists, at least in principle, would have helped Russia if their escape from the Nazis had

293

brought them to that country. Fear of Russia at the time was not a view the scientists shared with the anti-Communist elements of our nation. Scientists such as Hans Bethe, Rudolph Pierles, and J. Robert Oppenheimer, like Klaus Fuchs, all advocated the world's use of atomic energy knowledge. They did not entertain any notions that the United States was morally superior to the Soviet Union. While the vast majority would not secretly provide information to the Russians or any foreign government in disregard of the laws of the nation whose hospitality they were enjoying, many of them understood the thinking of those who would.

Klaus Fuchs was very aggressive in advocating the dissemination of nuclear energy discoveries. So much so that in 1947 he visited the United States on behalf of Great Britain to urge declassification of certain data in the possession of the Atomic Energy Commission. Niels Bohr made a similar appeal in an address to the United Nations in June 1950.

Mr. Saypol: At that time, what official knowledge did you have concerning the identity and background of Niels Bohr?

A. Neils Bohr was a Danish scientist whom I can best describe as being the pioneer and granddaddy, you might say, of nuclear physics. He had an international reputation in the field in which the project was interested...

Mr. Saypol: There did come a time when he arrived at Los Alamos and participated in the research connected with the development of the atomic bomb, is that right?

A. Yes, sir. He went to Los Alamos as a consultant...

Mr. Saypol: Colonel, when did you sever your

connection with the Manhattan District project?

A. I went on terminal leave November 15, I believe, 1945, and at that time severed my connection with the project except for a period of time as a civilian consultant...

Emanuel Bloch then began his cross-examination of Colonel Lansdale.

Mr. E. H. Bloch: Colonel Lansdale, just a few questions. In the course of your official duties as one of the top security officers in military Intelligence, did you come to hear about or know about an employee of the Los Alamos project, known as Dr. Klaus Fuchs?

A. No, sir; at the time I have no present recollection of having known him...

Mr. E. H. Bloch: Well, now, knowing from what you have read can you project your memory backward and tell us whether or not it isn't the fact that there was a Dr. Fuchs working on the project?

Mr. Saypol: I think counsel and the witness are confused. I think the witness thinks that counsel is asking whether he knew Klaus Fuchs, not whether he knew about him...

Bloch's question was not confusing in the least. He asked Colonel Lansdale whether Dr. Fuchs was working on the project, and before Lansdale could answer, Saypol was instructing him to give the answer that the government wanted. Once Lansdale recognized what Saypol required, he responded.

A. Oh, yes. Well, I can answer definitely. I knew about him. We got periodic lists from the British of their people and he was without question one of them...He was a member of the British group at Site Y...

Mr. E. H. Bloch: Have you any independent recollection of when Dr. Klaus Fuchs came to Site Y or the Los Alamos project?

A. No, sir, I do not...

Mr. E. H. Bloch: Well, would it refresh your recollection if we specifically talked about the year 1944? Do you know whether he was there in 1944?

A. All I could do would be to speculate. There was considerable activity during that year and it would be sheer speculation...

Apparently, the government had not been able to establish that Fuchs worked at Los Alamos during the time in question. Lansdale certainly would have known if Fuchs was there in June and September of 1945, when Harry Gold said that he visited him. No business records were offered, just gossip about a British list that was not shown. Fuchs, according to FBI records, did work at Los Alamos at some point, but as far as legal proofs were concerned, no evidence was offered that he was present at the time in question or anytime.

The only witness to testify that Fuchs was at Los Alamos in June and September of 1945 was Gold. The only party to the proceedings who could confirm or reject Gold's contention was the United States government; they were the repository of this information about comings and goings in Los Alamos, and it was their burden and obligation to establish Fuchs's presence. Emanuel Bloch was not asked to and did not stipulate that Fuchs was there. Colonel Lansdale, the witness utilized by the government to verify Fuchs's attendance at Los Alamos, failed to do so. General Leslie R. Groves, the military commander of the atomic research organization at Los Alamos, was not asked to testify. Hence, all of Harry Gold's testimony concerning his receipt of espionage data from Klaus Fuchs should not have been heard in court. The jury was seriously prejudiced by this testimony.

JOHN A. DERRY

John A. Derry was called as a witness for the prosecution. Before the questioning began, Judge Kaufman made an announcement.

Judge Kaufman: Ladies and gentlemen, we are coming to another portion of testimony where I feel compelled to clear the courtroom. As I told you once before, and I repeat, during the course of some cases, particularly a case of this character, while it might be in the interest of the country that we do not hear certain portions of testimony, yet, under our form of jurisprudence the defendants are entitled to absolute confrontation of every witness and every piece of evidence that is offered against them.

So with that in mind, I am going to ask everybody but the press to leave the courtroom.

(All spectators leave the courtroom.)

Judge Kaufman: I might also say, Mr. Stenographer, that with respect to that portion of the testimony that deals with the operation of the atomic bomb, there is to be no transcription made, and your stenographic minutes are to be considered impounded. Of course, if any counsel wants to have it read back for purposes of examination, it may be made available for that purpose...

Mr. Saypol: I should like the record to show that representatives of the Atomic Energy Commission are present in the courtroom, and I take it the Court will allow them to be here?

Judge Kaufman: Yes...

Mr. Saypol: Mr. Derry, you are an electrical

engineer, are you not?

A. *Yes, sir...*

Mr. Saypol: *Did you receive an assignment in December of 1942?*

A. *I did. I was assigned to the Manhattan Engineer District...I was with them in one job or the other until I got out of the Army in August 1946...*

Mr. Saypol: *During the year 1945, did you have occasion to see the actual atomic bomb which was being developed and constructed at the Los Alamos or the Y Project?*

A. *Many times...*

Mr. Saypol: *I take it, you likewise were informed of some of the experiments, many of the experiments incidental to the development of the atomic bomb?*

A. *I was...*

Mr. Saypol: *There has been testimony in this trial by a witness, David Greenglass, regarding the structure of the atomic bomb, and he likewise has identified a cross-section sketch of the bomb, which is Government's Exhibit 8 in evidence. I would like you to listen, Mr. Derry, while the court reporter reads the witness Greenglass' testimony as he gave it here, relating to the bomb...and then I shall ask you some questions.*

Mr. E.H. Bloch: *If the Court please, I object to this method of procedure...I suggest very strongly that before this witness is given Greenglass' testimony, he be asked to describe a cross-section of the bomb...*

Judge Kaufman: *It is overruled...*

Kaufman wanted to make certain that Derry's description of the atomic bomb conformed with Greenglass's previous statement. By having the stenographer repeat Greenglass's testimony for Derry to hear,

Derry could make his testimony conform. Had Derry been asked to describe the atom bomb without Kaufman and Saypol aiding him, his account might differ enough to embarrass the government. Under any circumstances, however, Derry could testify only to the bomb's external appearance. He had no knowledge of the internal structure and scientific principles involved. Still Kaufman, with the press in full attendance, permitted Derry to just endorse the testimony of David Greenglass, after listening to it.

Judge Kaufman: I believe you told us that you knew each and every detail of the construction of that weapon, that was your job?

The Witness: It was my job to know what went into the parts of it.

Derry, who knew some electrical engineering principles and that is about all, was coaxed by Kaufman to boast of knowledge well beyond his capacity.

Judge Kaufman: And you understood the entire subject matter, didn't you?

The Witness: Yes, sir, I did. It was my task that General Groves gave to me.

Mr. Saypol: And you still do understand it?

A. I still do.

Mr. Saypol: Was this information classified at the time?

A. It was classified top secret.

Mr. Saypol: Is it still classified?

A. Yes, sir.

Mr. Saypol: Does this information relate to the national defense of the United States of America?

A. It certainly does...

Mr. Saypol: Does the information that has been read to you, together with the sketch, concern a type of atomic bomb which was actually used by the United States of America?

A. It does. It is the bomb we dropped at Nagasaki, similar to it.

Mr. Saypol: Do you know whether at the time in question, 1945, any foreign government had the knowledge which our scientists possessed regarding the development and structure of that weapon, outside of the British and Canadians?

A. No, I don't know, outside of the British and Canadians.

Mr. Saypol: No nation possessed it?...

A. Yes.

Emanuel Bloch began his cross-examination of Mr. Derry.

Mr. E. H. Bloch: All right. Would you say that Government's Exhibit 8 reflects a sketch of the atomic bomb when it had already been perfected?

A. Substantially...

Mr. E. H. Bloch: Just one further question, Mr. Derry: If you were asked to give a written description elucidating this sketch in Government's Exhibit 8, so that any scientist or any person of intelligence interested might understand what you were talking about and trying to describe, could you compress a description of that within 12 pages?

A. You could give substantially the principle involved...

Years after the trial, lawyers, scientists, and scholars have energetically debated the value of the sketches (reproduced here) that David Greenglass said he gave Harry Gold and Julius Rosenberg. Some questioned Greenglass's education and innate intelligence, doubting his ability to make the sketches, and reasoned that he had to have been coached by qualified scientists. Others said it was entirely possible for him to have produced the sketches. Some said he could, some said he couldn't.

Yet a glance at the sketches shows that they were simple enough. Anyone could have drawn them, but for a scientist to say that they were a reasonable replica of the atom bomb was itself unreasonable. Using similar logic, the author's sketch of a skyscraper follows, appended to Greenglass's sketches. The sketches show how useless they would be to any person who wanted to build an atom bomb or a skyscraper.

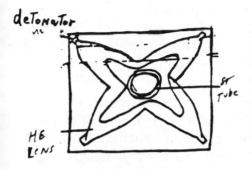

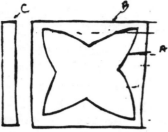

Exhibit 6

High explosive lens mold
Exhibit 2

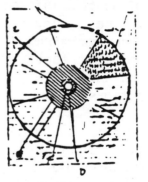

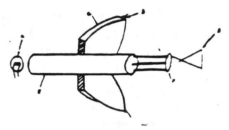

Exhibit 7

Cross section A-Bomb
(not to scale)
Exhibit 8

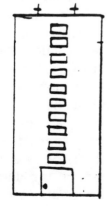

*Author's
Sketch of
Skyscraper*

303

To suppose that the author's sketch of a skyscraper would give any help to a foreign country planning to erect one is not too different from the assumption that Greenglass's sketches were useful in making the atomic bomb.

Greenglass's sketches were as meaningless as the skyscraper sketch. The skyscraper is a work of ages; it involves knowledge of doors and elevators and electricity and bricks. It involves the work of Newton, Galileo, Edison. It involves physics, mathematics, and even chemistry. The atom bomb is of equal complexity.

Backing up Greenglass's sketches, according to the testimony, were twelve pages of written information when twelve thousand would not have been enough. The knowledge required to build an atom bomb did not involve merely one or two ideas, but thousands of ideas and thousands of sketches. That is why there were hundreds of scientists and thousands of employees at Los Alamos.

The Greenglass sketches were of limited use—if not of use only to their originator, Dr. Walter Koski. Even the Atomic Energy Commission did not place much value in Dr. Koski's sketches. How could they when Koski misdescribed his own work, calling it a high-explosive lens mold, when it was not that at all?

The Atomic Energy Commission advised Hoover that the sketch Greenglass called a high explosive lens mold was not that. "It could possibly be described as a sketch of a high explosive lens, rather than a sketch of a high explosive lens mold," the AEC wrote. "We are specifically inviting your attention to the above since we understand that Greenglass was charged in the indictment as having prepared and delivered a sketch of a 'high explosive lens mold.'" Hoover, in his letter to the Attorney General, responded to the Atomic Energy Comission's displeasure in the following manner:

> You will see from the above that there are a number of problems in connection with the technical testimony that will have to be necessarily solved in connection with the prosecution of Greenglass and Rosenberg. We are forwarding the information contained herein to our New York and Albuquerque Offices and are instructing them to discuss this matter with United States Attorneys Grantham and Saypol.

But the faulty description of Greenglass's sketches was never corrected. Hoover and the Government proceeded on the basis that the Rosenberg defense would not discover the errors, and they didn't.

The government experts consisted of Dr. Koski, who could not permit any suggestion that his work was less than indispensable to the bomb, and John Derry, who had little more knowledge about atomic physics than David Greenglass. During the Rosenberg case it was impossible to find a scientist willing to disagree with the experts. Today it is the opposite; a scientist could scarcely be found to seriously state that the Greenglass sketches were of value.

After the sketches were finally released in 1966, Phillip Morrison, a distinguished scientist, said that they were "barren of any meaningful or correct qualitative information." Dr. Henry Linschitz, another world-renowned scientist, characterized Greenglass's material as "garbled" and "naive." He concluded that "the information in question purporting to describe the construction of a plutonium bomb was so incomplete, ambiguous and even incorrect to be of service or value to the Russians." When the London *Sunday Times* interviewed two distinguished American scientists, George Kistiakowsky, professor of chemistry at Harvard, and Victor Weisskopf, professor of physics at Massachusetts Institute of Technology, Kistiakowsky described Greenglass's sketch as "uselessly crude," and Weisskopf described it as "ridiculous, a baby drawing, it doesn't tell you anything."

But in the 1950s, a scientist testifying truthfully in behalf of the Rosenbergs would have found himself out of a job and perhaps indicted as well.

MORTON SOBELL'S FLIGHT

Manuel Giner de Los Rios was called on behalf of the government. He was questioned by U.S. Attorney Roy Cohn and testified through an interpreter.

   Mr. Cohn: Mr. Rios, do you reside in Mexico City?
   A. Yes, sir...
   Mr. Cohn: Will you tell us now where in Mexico City you reside?
   A. No. 153 Calle Octava de Cordoba...
   Mr. Cohn: Now, in July of 1950, were you residing at this address on Cordoba Street in apartment 5?
   A. Yes.
   Mr. Cohn: Did there come a time at the beginning of July when you saw an American at that address?
   A. Yes, sir.
   Mr. Cohn: Do you see that man in court?
   A. Yes, sir, I see him.
   (Defendant Sobell stands)
   Mr. Cohn: May the record indicate that the defendant Sobell has been indentified by the witness...
   Do you know whether or not Sobell had rented an apartment at this address on Cordoba?
   A. Yes, I know he did...
   Mr. Cohn: Did there come a time when Sobell left Mexico City to go to Vera Cruz?
   A. Yes...
   Mr. Cohn: About how long was Sobell gone from Mexico City?
   A. For about 15 days...
   Mr. Cohn: Do you know approximately what date Sobell was deported to the United States by the authorities?

THE TRIAL OF THE ROSENBERGS AND SOBELL

Mr. Kuntz: I object to that, if your Honor please. There is no proof here of any deportation, no proof of any action by the American authorities...

Mr. Cohn: Your Honor, I am going to withdraw the last question...

There was good reason to withdraw the question, since the U.S. Attorney's office had arranged with the Mexican Secret Police to abduct Morton Sobell. On August 16, 1950, Sobell was accused of being a bank robber; he was beaten over the head, knocked unconscious, rushed into a car, and driven 800 miles to the United States. His wife was dragged into another car and similary taken to the U.S. border. On entering the country a card was made out saying that Sobell was "deported from Mexico," when in fact he had been kidnapped. Sobell was portrayed in the newspapers as an A-bomb spy. As the *New York Times* reported on August 19, 1950, "Mr. Saypol said that Sobell had many dealings with Rosenberg in the conspiracy to supply Russia with Atomic secrets."

Saypol, in later emphasizing the "deportation" card in court, said, "Had it not been for that evidence the jury might have inferred that Sobell returned to the United States voluntarily and that he always had intended to do so."

But Sobell had paid his rent in Mexico only for the month of August. On Labor Day his children were due back in school. Furthermore, he had written to his friend Danziger that he would explain certain facts to him when he returned. He apparently intended to return.

Sobell did not testify in his own behalf. He later explained why: "I wanted to testify...I did not do so because my trial attorney insisted that I should not, because the case was so weak that my innocence was already established...that it was so clear that I had nothing to do with any atomic energy conspiracy..."

Sobell did nothing, never delivered secrets to anybody and was never involved with any atomic secrets. Sobell was convicted for flying to Mexico, using aliases which he did, and based on the false testimony of his friend Max Elitcher.

Minerva Bravo Espinosa, called as a witness on behalf of the government, was questioned by Roy Cohn. She testified through an interpreter that Morton Sobell purchased glasses at the Mexico City optical store where she was employed on July 26, 1950 using the name M. Sand.

Glenn Dennis, an employee of Mexican Airlines, confirmed that Sobell used the same alias, Sand, to fly from Vera Cruz to Tampico on July 30, 1950. After Dennis testified, there was a discussion between Judge Kaufman and the lawyers.

Mr. Cohn: May this be marked for identification...Your Honor, the Government now offers in evidence a record from the Immigration and Naturalization Service of the Department of Justice of the United States, duly and properly authenticated concerning the circumstances of the departure of Sobell from Mexico to the United States.

I will show that to counsel (handing).

Mr. Phillips: If your Honor please, that is merely a proof of the existence of a paper but not any proof of the fact...

Judge Kaufman: Well, will you concede that if a representative of the Department of Naturalization and Immigration were called, he would testify that

*that was an entry which was made in the regular
course of business, and that it was the regular course
of business to make such an entry?...*

Mr. Phillips: No...

*Judge Kaufman: I thought that you were anxious
to make concessions...Here is your opportunity to make
one.   Now they have to call a representative of the
Department of Justice...*

*Mr. Phillips: Your Honor please...the witness ought
to be here so we can examine him...*

*Mr. Saypol: In order to keep the trial moving, we
will send a plane down and bring the witness up and
prove it as we have had to prove other things...*

ANATOLI YAKOVLEV

But the Government did not have "to prove other things." Emanuel Bloch did not think it was necessary to question the government on many of its contentions. One of these involved the identity of Anatoli Yakovlev and the date of his departure to the Soviet Union. Phillips thought that the government should prove every element of the charges. Once again, however, Phillips was overwhelmed by the prosecutor, the judge, and the man he least expected to have as an obstacle, his co-counsel Emanuel Bloch.

Mr. Lane: In the interest of saving time I have consulted with defense counsel and we have agreed to a stipulation, if I may read it to the Court and the jury...That Mr. R. B. Walklett, if he were to appear and testify on the witness stand would testify as follows:...

Mr. Phillips: Wait a minute...

Mr. E. H. Bloch: I am sorry, Mr. Lane and I discussed this and we agreed upon it, and I suppose it is true to say—will you take my word that our stipulation here will not harm you in any way?...

The Court: All right, all agreed.

Mr. Lane: R. B. Walklett would testify, and that is a stipulation, were he in the witness box, that he is a representative of the United States Lines...And he will identify the picture on State Department document, Government's Exhibit 15 in evidence, the picture of Yakovlev.

He will further testify that he...had charge of the particular record pertaining to the sailing of Anatoli Yakovlev on SS America on December 27, 1946...and

311

*that on that day Yakovlev and his family, two children
and his wife, sailed for France...*

The defense lawyers' agreement stipulating to the
testimony of R. B. Walklett established that Anatoli
Yakovlev did sail on the *SS America* on December 27,
1946. In this way a major area of disputable evidence
was heard against the Rosenbergs and Morton Sobell
without any opposition. The dubious testimony was
received with the assurances of Emanuel Bloch, who
gave his word that it would not be harmful. He was
wrong; the testimony was harmful.

Lan Adomian, the next witness, was questioned by
U.S. Attorney Myles Lane.

Q. Mr. Adomian, where were you born?
A. Russia.
Q. When?
A. In 1905...
Q. Are you an American citizen?
A. Yes, sir.
Q. When were you naturalized?
A. 1940.
Q. When did you first come to the United States?
A. 1923.
*Q. Were you employed by the Amtorg Trading
Corporation in New York at one time?*
A. Yes.
Q. Will you tell us when?
A. In 1940.
Q. In what capacity?
A. As a translator.
Q. Do you know one Anatoli A. Yakovlev?
A. Yes.
Q. When did you meet him?

A. Around 1944...

Q. How long a period of time did you know him?

A. Off and on for about two years, I would say.

Q. Now did you ever see him in the Soviet Consulate, in New York City?

A. I did.

Q. Do you know what his occupation was?

A. Vice Consul.

Q. Did you have some reason for going to the Soviet Consulate in New York City at that time?

A. Yes, I did...I wanted a visa to go to the Soviet Union for a visit...

Q. When is that last time that you saw Yakovlev?

A. I would say some time in '46.

Q. I show you Government's Exhibit 15 in evidence and I ask you to look at the picture on that exhibit and tell me if you can identify that individual (showing).

A. That looks like a picture of Mr. Yakovlev.

Q. Well, is it Yakovlev?

A. Yes.

Mr. Lane: May the record indicate that the witness has identified the picture on Government's Exhibit 15 as Anatoli Yakovlev.

There will be no further questions, your Honor.

Mr. E. H. Bloch: No questions on behalf of defendants, you Honor.

The Court: All right, no cross.

(Witness excused.)

What the defense attorneys never knew, because they never tried to find out, was that Lan Adomian testified falsely, like many of the other government witnesses. Adomian, who had changed his name from Jacob Weinroth, was a musician, according to FBI records. He never worked for the Amtorg Trading Corporation, as the FBI concluded after carefully scrutinizing his work and school records.

The manner in which Adomian was presented as a witness almost made it appear that he was a co-worker or a business associate of Yakovlev. This was not the case; he was a reluctant witness impressed to testify.

On August 9, 1950, a government memo asking for authority to interview Adomian said:

> *Lan Adomian, a musical composer, was born John Jacob Weinroth April 29, 1905, at Mogilev, Russia. He entered the United States at New York City on November 1, 1923. He traveled to Spain in February, 1938, to join the Spanish Army, and he returned to the United States in December, 1938...*
>
> *Adomian has been under investigation by the Bureau since May, 1946, because he was known to be in close and friendly contact with certain officials of the Soviet Consulate in New York, particularly Anatoli Yakovlev, who now has been identified as an important Soviet agent interested in atomic energy espionage.*

Adomian was interviewed by the FBI well before he testified at the trial. At the time of the interview, when a picture of Yakovlev was displayed to him, "Adomian refused to identify the photograph as anyone he ever knew." The FBI report noted that inasmuch as the "entire interview depended upon Adomian's willingness to discuss his contacts with Yakovlev, further interview was postponed...to allow Adomian time to confer with his attorney." The government knew, however, that sooner or later he would say whatever they wished, because they had a powerful hold over him. The FBI had evidence that before Adomian became a United States citizen in 1940 he had evaded immigration authorities and had been an illegal stowaway aboard a vessel that had taken him to Europe in 1938 to join the Lincoln Brigade. Adomian's status as a U.S. citizen was in jeopardy of being lost. By the time of the trial, he was ready to identify photographs of Yakovlev.

Without Anatoli Yakovlev there was no case against the Rosenbergs and Sobell; no evidence that anything, much less atomic bomb information, was given to Russia. His identity and the question of whether Harry Gold ever knew him or had any contact with him were mysteries that continuously vexed the FBI. A report dated May 5, 1951, just weeks after the testimony concerning Yakovlev was presented to the jury, stated:

> *Confidential informant advised that in November 1946 A. A. Yakovlev was in Russia awaiting shipment to France as vice-consul...*

While it could be claimed that Yakovlev may have flown back to the United States in November or December 1946, enabling him to board the *SS America* on December 27 and return to France, the facts are that Yakovlev did not return to the United States nor did he sail on the *SS America*. How embarrassing that Yakovlev was already in Russia on his way to Paris while Gold was supposedly talking to him in the Bronx. But as long as the Rosenbergs didn't know it, they could go quietly to their deaths.

On April 1, 1951, just four days before the Rosenbergs were sentenced, a photograph of Anatoli Yakovlev appeared in the *New York Times*. A confidential informant of known reliability stated that the photograph in the newspaper "was not the person known...as Anatoli Yakovlev" who he described as extremely thin-faced, with light-blue eyes and ash-blond hair. The confidential informant's description was very different from the description Harry Gold gave of a man with a medium build, dark eyes, and dark-brown hair. The informer of known reliability went further: he could not identify the additional photographs purporting to be Yakovlev that were shown to him.

The FBI succeeded, however, in finding another confidential informant, but of unknown reliability. That informant identified a photograph of Anatoli Yakovlev as being the person known as Anatoli Yakovlev, vice-consul of the Soviet Consulate.

So far there was one version that had Anatoli Yakovlev in France at a time when he was supposed to have met Harry Gold and another placing him in New York City. There was a photo of Yakovlev identified by an informer of unknown reliability, while an informer of known reliability could not identify it. There was one description of Yakovlev as having light-blue eyes and ash-blond hair, while another said he had dark eyes and dark hair. And all the while the Rosenbergs had no idea that the FBI had this contradictory information.

Furthermore, a letter from J. Edgar Hoover dated January 5, 1951, in reference to Anatoli Yakovlev said that "a search of the name and alias file of the Identification Division has failed to reflect a fingerprint record for the above named fugitive."

Now, the manner in which Yakovlev was identified by Harry Gold was also questionable. Gold was shown photographs of Yakovlev that were at least seven years old; these were the same photographs that were identified by Lan Adomian. Whomever Gold and Adomian identified was not Anatoli Yakovlev. Even Gold's identification of Yakovlev was very tentative. The FBI noted that on May 27, 1950, when he was first shown photographs, he "picked out photograph of Anatoli Antonovich Yakovlev as possibly being John." It took several days for him to make a positive identification.

Gold often qualified his identifications of suspects by phrases such as "it is possibly him" or "it looks like him," and he was often wrong. His claim that John De Graaf was his Soviet espionage contact Paul Peterson was one of many examples from the FBI files of Harry Gold's mistakes.

The FBI reports concerning Anatoli Yakovlev were so blacked out that little could be determined from them. But in a 1944 report the FBI forgot to black out the sentence reading, "They have no children." The person whom the government, with Harry Gold's help, was attempting to establish as Anatoli Yakovlev had at least two children, twins, born in New York City, who were three years old in 1944. Victoria and Pavel Yakovlev were born on June 23, 1941, at Beth Israel Zion Hospital in Brooklyn.

There were other absurdities concerning the government's manufacture of Yakovlev's identity. Supposedly the FBI had him under a constant surveillance directed by Edward Scheidt, the FBI agent in charge who also conducted the investigation of Max Elitcher. According to the FBI reports, the surveillance was daily and constant to the day of his departure from the United States on December 27, 1946. But if so, why didn't the agents follow him to the Earle Theatre on December 26, 1946, the day before he left the United States so they could observe him chatting with Harry Gold? And why, if they had been watching him so carefully for so many years, did they fail to find him even once with Gold, who said he met with Yakovlev at least twenty times? The Government was in a quandary. If Yakovlev did in fact meet Gold, how could the government admit to knowing of Gold's existence before 1947, when they went to such lengths to establish that the first time they heard of him was on May 29, 1947?

Yakovlev was an area of much concern to the FBI. The problem of his existence kept turning up, even years after the Rosenbergs had been executed. On May 11, 1956, a woman named Helen Wilcox notified the FBI that she had seen Yakovlev's wife at Hunter College in February of that year. Wilcox, a former teacher at Amtorg Trading Corporation, knew the Yakovlevs well from her association with them at Amtorg. Mrs. Yakovlev's presence in the United States long after she and her husband were supposed to have gone back to Russia could prove an embarrassment. The issue was resolved by a special agent of the FBI named Roetting, who concluded that Wilcox was simply wrong.

Another FBI report stated, "On February 26, 1960 Mrs. Luba Petrova Harrington advised SA Richard F. McCarthy...after viewing a photograph of Yakovlev that to her knowledge she had never seen or heard of the individual shown to her in the photograph. Harrington advised that a number of years ago she knew Yakovlev, but that this person had been a Russian emigre and was deceased."

Anatoli Yakovlev was a name. Anatoli Yakovlev had a personal biography. Anatoli Yakovlev had a physical description. They did not match up in the same Anatoli Yakovlev. The Anatoli Yakovlev presented by our government was not the Anatoli Yakovlev whom Gold had identified.

ELIZABETH BENTLEY

Elizabeth Bentley was then called as a witness on behalf of the government.

Mr. Saypol: Miss Bentley, what has been your education?

A. I have an A. B. degree from Vassar College and a Master's degree from Columbia University, and I had a year's study in Italy.

Mr. Saypol: When did you graduate from Columbia?

A. I received my degree in January 1935...

Mr. Saypol: Will you tell us now when you joined the Communist Party, Miss Bentley?

A. Yes, in March 1935...

Mr. Saypol: In the fall of 1938, was it, you first met Mr. Golos?

A. Yes. In October, 1938.

Mr. Saypol: Until when did you continue your activities in the Communist Party in association with Mr. Golos?

A. Until his death on November 25, 1943.

Mr. Saypol: That is for a period of approximately five years?

A. Yes, that is correct...

Mr. Saypol: Now, what did you do in connection with Mr. Golos and members of the Party in that five-year period? What were your activities?

A. I continued myself to collect information which was to be passed on to Mr. Golos...

Mr. Saypol: Was his office at Communist Party headquarters here in New York or elsewhere?

A.   *His office was a business, and it was a cover for his activities. He ran World Tourist...*

Mr. Saypol: *What was World Tourist?*

A.   *World Tourist was a travel agency which was set up originally in 1927 by the Communist Party...*

Mr. Saypol: *At this time, Miss Bentley, had you learned what was the relation of the Communist Party of the United States to the Communist International?*

A.   *It was part of the Communist International and subject to its jurisdiction as such...*

Mr. Saypol: *Then what did you do...pursuant to directions from either of them or any of them?*

A.   *I would say the bulk of the work was collecting information from Communists employed in the United States Government and passing it on to Mr. Golos or other Communist superiors for transmission to Moscow.*

Mr. Saypol: *Well, what connection did the Communist Party membership of you and Golos have with the destination of this material to Russia?*

A.   *The Communist Party being part of the Communist International only served the interests of Moscow, whether it be propaganda or espionage or sabotage...*

Irving Saypol regarded Elizabeth Bentley's testimony as indispensable to the prosecution of Abraham Brothman, Miriam Moskowitz, William Remington, and now Julius Rosenberg, Ethel Rosenberg, and Morton Sobell. Roy Cohn also relied heavily on her. More than a year after the Rosenbergs were convicted, he confided to an FBI agent:

> *Bentley's testimony in the Rosenberg case was the only testimony that linked up the*

ELIZABETH BENTLEY

*Communist Party and Communist espionage...The
Circuit Court took many pages to comment on
the testimony of Bentley, which definitely tied
in the Communist Party with Communist
espionage.*

The government prosecutors considered it essential
to connect Bentley with Julius in some way. Elitcher's
perjured statements which took him weeks to concoct,
claimed that Julius Rosenberg mentioned Bentley's
name to him. This opening enabled the government to
utilize her now routinely provided testimony that
American Communists were directed by Moscow. Her
statements were tailored to fit the provisions of the
newly passed McCarran act, which declared, in essence, that Communists in the United States were
loyal to the Soviet Union and thus were agents of a
foreign government. Bentley's testimony served the
government well in its overall purpose in the
Rosenberg trial: to once and for all destroy the
Communist Party in America.

Judge Kaufman: May I ask a few questions?
Mr. Saypol: Indeed.
*Judge Kaufman: Based upon your membership in
the Communist Party, based upon your work for the
Communist Party and your activities in behalf of the
Soviet Union, can you say that there was a close
relationship, indeed almost an adhesive relationship
between the Communist Party of the United States
and the Communist International?*
A. Yes, quite definitely...
*Judge Kaufman: Would you say further from your
experience that any member of the Communist Party
of the United States who did not adhere to the Party
line as dictated by the Communist International would*

321

be expelled from the Communist Party of the United States?

A. Yes, they would be.

Judge Kaufman: And were so expelled when they did not adhere?

A. Yes, they were.

Kaufman repeatedly stressed the evils of Communism. Indeed, he and Saypol acted like joint prosecutors, taking turns in questioning witnesses.

Judge Kaufman: Do you want to take it from there?

Mr. Saypol: Yes, if I may. I think your Honor has—well, I wanted to make an observation but I do not think it is necessary. Your Honor has relieved me of a considerable burden...

Judge Kaufman: I think I forgot to ask, were the headquarters of the National or of the Communist International—was that in Moscow?

The Witness: That was in Moscow, yes...

Mr. Saypol: In the course of your Communist Party activities with Golos, were there occasions when you accompanied him to meetings or to the vicinity of meetings that he was holding with some of his contacts?

A. Yes, quite a few occasions. We would possibly be on our way to dinner and going to some other place, and I would drive along in his automobile with him.

Mr. Saypol: Do you recall when there was any occasion like that when you accompanied him to the vicinity of Knickerbocker Village?

A. Yes, I do remember.

Mr. Saypol: About when was that?

A. *I should say it was in 1942, probably in the early fall, possibly, of 1942; might have been late fall.*

Mr. Saypol: *Will you describe what occurred?*

A. *Yes. Mr. Golos said that he had to stop by to pick some material up from a contact, an engineer...*

Judge Kaufman: *Miss Bentley, during this period of time that you talk about, we will say '41, '42, '43, '44, were you personally receiving any material relating to the National defense of a secret nature?*

The Witness: *Yes, I handled all the American Communists who were working in the United States Government, and I was getting it from agencies like the OSS and the Treasury.*

Judge Kaufman: *You were?*

The Witness: *Yes.*

Judge Kaufman: *And this material was then transmitted to Russia?*

The Witness: *That is correct...*

Mr. Saypol: *Subsequent to this occasion when you went to the vicinity of Greenwich Village with Golos and saw this man, did you have a telephone call from somebody who described himself as "Julius"?*

A. *Yes, I did...*

Mr. Saypol: *Can you tell us when you had a conversation such as I described?*

A. *Do you mean the first telephone conversation or the last?*

Mr. Saypol: *You can give us either. How long did they continue?*

A. *They continued up until almost November 1943, at intermittent intervals...*

Judge Kaufman: *When did they begin?*

The Witness: *I would place it in the fall of 1942.*

Judge Kaufman: *Now, do you want to say something, Mr. Bloch?*

Mr. E. H. Bloch: Yes, I would like to move that the answer be stricken out...

Judge Kaufman: She hasn't given the conversation yet.

Mr. E. H. Bloch: Yes, but Mr. Saypol, in the form of the question to which I have objected, has already gotten to the jury something about this.

Judge Kaufman: All right, it will be for the jury to determine, not for you, nor for me, it will be for the jury to determine from all the evidence whether or not the "Julius" she is referring to is the defendant Julius Rosenberg on trial...

Mr. Saypol: From your conversations with Julius and with Golos, did you come to learn in what vicinity Julius resided?...

A. Yes...he lived in Knickerbocker Village...

In fact, Elizabeth Bentley had already tentatively identified another person as being Julius. In 1946, according to an FBI memo, while she was visiting at World Tourists, Inc., she was introduced to a Jules Korchien, and she observed that "Korchien bore a resemblance to the engineer whom she knew as 'Julius,' a known contact of Jacob M. Golos in 1942 and 1943..."

Judge Kaufman: Might I say this: These conversations, that you referred to, with someone who called himself Julius, might I characterize the part that you played in those conversations, that you carried messages from this person called Julius to Golos, and back to Julius from Golos?

The Witness: My part was that I took messages from Julius to Golos and told Golos that he wanted to meet him, and so on. I was a go-between...

Emanuel Bloch then cross-examined Elizabeth Bentley.

Mr. E. H. Bloch: Miss Bentley, when did you say you first went to the FBI?

A. *In the latter part of August, 1945.*

Mr. E. H. Bloch: Where did you contact the FBI at that time?

A. *In New Haven, Connecticut.*

Mr. E. H. Bloch: Did you go to the FBI and inquire about a certain captain?...

A. *Yes...*

Mr. E. H. Bloch: He had taken you out socially?

A. *Yes, rather, on and off, yes...*

Mr. E. H. Bloch: And from the first time you went to the FBI in New Haven, in 1945, until some time in 1947, you continued your activities as a member of the Communist Party under the instructions of the FBI; is that not right?

A. *I continued contacting the Communists, yes...*

Mr. E. H. Bloch: Now you have referred to the man by the name of Jacob Golos...

A. *John was the name he used with his undercover contacts. His real name was Jacob Nathan Golos...*

Mr. E. H. Bloch: What name did you call him?

A. *You mean personally?*

Mr. E. H. Bloch: Yes.

A. *I called him Yasha.*

Mr. E. H. Bloch: You were pretty friendly with him, weren't you?

A. *I think I have said this in other trials; I was in love with Mr. Golos...*

Mr. E. H. Bloch: And you lived with him, did you not?...

*A.   I didn't live with Mr. Golos on the same prem-
ises, if that is what you are getting at...*

Mr. E. H. Bloch: But you had relations with him?

A.   Yes, I have told you that once before...

*Mr. E. H. Bloch: Did you know that Golos was
married at the time you started to have relations with
him?*

*A.   Mr. Golos was never legally married to any
woman in his life.   Any other woman had the same
relationship I had.   He did not believe in bourgeois
marriage.   He was a Communist...*

In her book Elizabeth Bentley gave many details of
Jacob Golos's troubled life in Russia, and of the great
love she shared with him before his death in November 1943. But the truth was that she obtained most of
the details of his life from Caroline Klein, the woman
who was actually his girlfriend, after he died. In a
statement to the FBI made long after Golos's death,
it was reported:

> *Informant Gregory advised that when she
> first knew Golos he was residing at the home
> of Caroline Klein, 106 West 13th Street, New
> York City...Informant Gregory advised that
> subsequent to Golos's death Caroline Klein had
> attempted to contact her on numerous
> occasions and as a matter of fact she saw her
> a few times after Golos's death but gradually
> disassociated herself with this individual. She
> remarked that it was quite apparent that
> Caroline Klein was in love with Golos...On
> December 19, 1945...the informant had a
> rather long conversation with Caroline Klein
> and as a result obtained some information
> concerning Golos's background which she had
> previously not been aware of, and also
> obtained other information concerning Golos,
> World Tourists, Inc., and Golos's wife, which*

informant stated probably would be of some value to this investigation...

Bloch continued cross-examination, focusing on Bentley's contacts with the man she called Julius:

Mr. E. H. Bloch: Did you recognize the voice of the man who you say called you up and said, "This is Julius"?

A. What do you mean recognize?...I have heard the man over a telephone, that is all...What does he mean?

Judge Kaufman: Did you ever meet a person, did you ever meet anybody in person, whose voice you heard, and you can now say is the voice of the man who identified himself as Julius on the telephone?

A. No, I have never met anyone whose voice I heard, whom I could identify as Julius.

Mr. E. H. Bloch: Can you tell us more specifically when these calls came in?

A. Yes, they always came after midnight, in the wee small hours. I remember it because I got waked out of bed.

Mr. E. H. Bloch: You were living at that time in Mr. Golos's apartment?

A. I have just informed you, I think twice, that I did not live with Mr. Golos. I lived at 58 Barrow Street, by myself...

Judge Kaufman: The question was whether Mr. Golos was with you at 58 Barrow Street at the time when any of these calls came in.

A. Yes, on one occasion he was.

Mr. E. H. Bloch: And on that one occasion, did you answer the phone?

A. I always answered the phone.

Mr. E. H. Bloch: Did you always ask the people who called you their names?

A. If I didn't get the voice right off, but this particular party always started his conversation by saying "This is Julius"...

Mr. E. H. Bloch: Miss Bentley, have you written a book recently?

A. Yes, I have written a book.

Mr. E. H. Bloch: On what subject?

A. Well, the title may get changed again. I can't tell you exactly what the title is going to be yet.

Mr. E. H. Bloch: I didn't ask you about the title. I asked you on what subject?

A. The subject of how a person can become a Communist, and how they can be disillusioned and get out again...

Mr. E. H. Bloch: And has that book been published yet?

A. No, it has not been published.

Mr. E. H. Bloch: Have you completed your draft and submitted your draft to the publisher?

A. The draft has been completed. It has not yet been finally OKed...

Mr. E. H. Bloch: Did you receive any money from the publisher for that book?

A. I received an advance from the publisher, as many authors do, yes...

Mr. E. H. Bloch: Have you also lectured on the subject of communism?

A. Yes, I have.

Mr. E. H. Bloch: And have you received fees for lecturing on communism?

A. Sometimes I do; sometimes I don't. It depends on the groups I address...

Mr. E. H. Bloch: Did you, in any of the written

material that you sent to your publisher in connection with your autobiography dealing with your work in the Communist Party, ever write down anything about this telephone conversation that you related where somebody called up a few times asking for Mr. Golos and stating on the wire, "This is Julius"?

A. Yes.

Mr. E. H. Bloch: When?

A. I haven't the least idea when that particular part of the book was written, but that was put into the book very definitely. Whether it is still in or whether it has been cut out I don't know.

Mr. E. H. Bloch: I would like you, please, Miss Bentley, to test your recollection as best you can and tell us, if you can, the first time you say you submitted evidence of this telephone conversation that we are talking about to your publishers.

A. I haven't the least idea. I was dealing with a book haphazard. I can't tell you on that...

The passage from her book where Bentley wrote of Julius's calls asking for Golos read:

> *Meanwhile, Yasha had taken on Communist agents whom he handled himself and about whose existence I knew nothing—or very little. In the fall of 1942 he announced that he had acquired a Communist cell of engineers...The leader of this group, he said, was named Julius...Julius has since been identified as Julius Rosenberg, sentenced to death in April 1951 for atom-bomb espionage activities.*

Because Julius Rosenberg was sentenced after Bentley had testified at his trial, the passage about Julius had to have been a later insert in the book.

Saypol then questioned Bentley.

Mr. Saypol: Now, Mr. Bloch has asked you some questions about these telephone calls from Julius and the fact of their incorporation in your book. Do I understand correctly your purpose in including reference in that book was to illustrate the method of maintaining contacts between couriers and agents in this system?...

A. That was partly it. The other reason was to show the incredible things that Communists will go through in order to carry out their jobs because it meant that when I was called at 2 in the morning, I often had to go out and go many blocks in the cold to get a pay telephone to call Mr. Golos.

Mr. Saypol: Do I understand from that that sometimes when you received calls of this type, whenever the occasion required it, you would in turn go immediately to a public telephone to get in touch with Mr. Golos?

A. That is correct. It was considered unsafe for me to call out of my own telephone...

But since Golos's phone was more likely to be monitored than Bentley's, it made no sense for her to use a public phone to call him. Golos was the one who, according to the FBI, was under investigation. The story of Elizabeth Bentley's "receiving" calls from a coin box at 2 A.M. and then leaving her house to call Golos from a coin box so that he could call "Julius" for the purpose of avoiding detection was patently incredible.

Mr. E. H. Bloch: I would like to ask a few more questions...I am going to promise the Court that I am not going to be long.

Judge Kaufman: Before you get into that, let me make sure that I have understood Miss Bentley's answers to what I consider the main issue and main purpose of her testimony.

Judge Kaufman then began to question her.

Judge Kaufman: You said, did you not, Miss Bentley, that you had knowledge of the instructions and the teachings of the Communist Party officials to the members of the Party?

A. Yes, that's right.

Judge Kaufman: And you had personal knowledge of that between the years of—what?

A. Personal knowledge between the years I was working with the Party, which would be between '35 and '47.

Judge Kaufman: Very well. Now with particular reference to the instructions concerning help or aid to Russia, did I understand your testimony that the Communist Party officials instructed the members of the Party orally and in writing in a general way, to do everything possible to aid Russia?

A. That's correct, yes.

Judge Kaufman: Very well.

Mr. E. H. Bloch: When was the first time that you told the FBI [agents] about this telephone conversation—"This is Julius"—I do not want to go into all the details. You know what I am referring to?

A. I gave the entire story, including Julius and the telephone calls and all, to the FBI when I went into them at various successive meetings. We couldn't get it all done at once. It would have been, I guess, in the fall of 1945, along in there.

Mr. E. H. Bloch: Did you give it to them in the fall of 1945 this specific telephone conversation?

A. It must have been because the basic material that I had to give them was in that period, so it must have been included in there...

Mr. E. H. Bloch: Have you ever been paid by the Government of the United States for any of the evidence that you have disclosed to it?

A. No.

Mr. E. H. Bloch: Not one penny?

A. No, not one penny...

Exactly when Bentley began to receive money from the government for her testimony has never been established. By mid-1952, however, it is a matter of record that she was being paid. This was verified by the FBI themselves. One of their memos provided the surrounding circumstances as to how the government went about paying her for her testimony. It was written by Special Agent G. Spencer on May 7, 1952, and was prepared for U.S. Attorney Roy Cohn. It related that she complained of a severe beating she received from the caretaker of her Connecticut home. The man had frightened her so much that she moved to a New York City hotel. Spencer noted that Bentley was

> *afraid of calling the local police in view of the fact that she would undoubtedly receive such bad publicity that her credibility as a witness would probably be nullified and likewise she would probably lose any hope of conducting any further lectures, to which she looks forward for a great part of her livelihood...*

Assistant U.S. Attorney Roy Cohn was greatly concerned over the harm that such publicity could do.

Cohn was so worried about controlling Bentley, Spencer reported, that he met with her frequently and took a personal interest in her circumstances. On May 13 Spencer summarized what Cohn had told him after a meeting with her.

> *Cohn after the interview advised the writer that this was the most serious problem he had faced since coming into the United States Attorney's office...*
> *Cohn stated that he realizes that Bentley is acting like a spoiled child and that of course her requests are very much out of line. He stated, however, that he wanted to strongly urge that the writer impress on the Bureau the need for her testimony...*
> *Throughout the conference Bentley referred to the fact that she hasn't any money; that it is costing her $10 a day to live at the Prince George Hotel; that undoubtedly her Doctor bill will be rather substantial; and then went into sort of a tirade about Louis Budenz and Whittaker Chambers, indicating that Budenz had become wealthy as a result of his testimony and his writings and that Chambers was about to make a small fortune out of his writings...*

On May 11, 1952, Cohn recommended that the FBI authorize payments to Bentley of $50 per week for three weeks. The FBI staff, however, was opposed to giving her money. On July 11 an FBI report stated, "The agents who are familiar with Miss Bentley and who have been in contact with her over the years have gained the definite impression that Miss Bentley is improvident."

Her mental state seemed to be growing worse, for on August 29 Bentley was arrested for hit and run driving. Roy Cohn contacted Commissioner Edward Hicky of the Connecticut State Police and asked the commissioner to keep the matter quiet.

On September 23 another FBI report prepared by Special Agent Lester O. Gallagher discussed a trip in which he accompanied Bentley from Madison, Connecticut, to New York City on September 17.

> *Throughout the trip from Madison, Bentley was rambling and incoherent in her speech, making unreasonable accusations against the state of Connecticut, the Connecticut State Police...engaged in some back-seat driving, weeping, sleeping, and fingering a small crucifix, and chain-smoking. Upon arrival at the Prince George Hotel, she demanded that the agents enter the hotel with her...*
>
> *It is believed by the writer that while some of Miss Bentley's condition can be explained by overuse of alcoholic beverages, it is nevertheless felt that even when not under the influence of liquor she is becoming mentally unstable...It is felt that if this condition continues, her credibility as a witness in the various cases we have pending which involve her will be seriously affected...*

On September 23 Bentley demanded $1,000 from Roy Cohn, claiming that he had promised it to her. According to an FBI memo:

> *She indicated that if the lump sum payments referred to above were not forthcoming in the immediate future, she would feel disinclined to cooperate in future interviews or make further appearances as a witness...However, it was pointed out to her that if this attitude persisted, further payments of a weekly stipend of $50 would undoubtedly be discontinued. At that point she agreed to furnish the requested information...*
>
> *As a result of Bentley's demands, on September 25 Cohn contacted Special Agent Lester O. Gallagher and asked him if the*

> *Bureau could make arrangements for a lump*
> *sum payment of $200 to Miss Bentley, together*
> *with an advance of about $600 on the $50*
> *weekly payments she had been receiving.*

In view of Elizabeth Bentley's demanding nature, as well as Roy Cohn's ambition and unscrupulousness, it is difficult to believe that she received "not one penny" for her testimony at the Rosenberg trial

In early 1955 Harvey Matusow, the former government informer, the FBI noted, told the Senate Internal Security Subcommittee that Bentley was a paid informer whose livelihood depended on providing false testimony.

> *He indicated he learned this at dinner with*
> *her on his birthday...He said that during the*
> *dinner Bentley cried and told him she had to*
> *find information about which to testify in*
> *order to live.*

Elizabeth Bentley denied the charges and denied having dinner with Matusow on October 3, 1952, the day he said he had dinner with her. But the FBI found abundant evidence to verify that Matusow had met Bentley. It is a wonder that they questioned Matusow's claims, since their own experience with Bentley confirmed them. Nonetheless, the FBI conducted a massive investigation to discredit Matusow's testimony. A March 15, 1955, FBI memo said:

> *Matusow's allegations are a serious attack*
> *on the Government's whole security program.*
> *In attacking Elizabeth Bentley, Matusow*
> *appears to have selected a person whose*
> *reliability has never seriously been challenged.*
> *It is therefore of vital importance that this*
> *entire matter receive the most thorough*
> *investigative attention possible.*

The statement echoed the fears of J. Edgar Hoover and the elite members of his office, as well as Irving Saypol, Roy Cohn, Myles Lane, Irving Kaufman, and all those whose success in their careers depended on the continued acceptability of Elizabeth Bentley as a government witness. She, for her part, was well aware of her power, making increasingly costly demands upon the government, accompanied by threats of reprisal if they did not fulfill her whims.

A June 27, 1955, FBI memo reported that "on June 24, 1955, Bentley contacted representatives of New Haven office...that she was going to issue a press release 'to blow the lid off the administration'" if the government did not notify Sacred Heart, the Louisiana school where she was then teaching, that she owed no taxes to the government. The FBI went to great lengths to appease Bentley, even meeting with officials of the school. Despite FBI overtures, Sacred Heart was not anxious to have Bentley continue as a teacher there, and did not renew her contract.

One of the most interesting exchanges in the FBI papers was the correspondence between Elizabeth Bentley and J. Edgar Hoover some six years after the Rosenbergs were executed. The letters, though short, were measured with undercurrents.

Bentley wrote as if she expected that her letters would be read by others. Not wanting anyone to get any ideas that she and the Director had ever had contact with each other, she wrote first as if to a stranger. But in reality, it appears that she was re-minding Hoover between the lines of what she was capable of doing if she were not handled properly. On August 10, 1959, Bentley wrote:

ELIZABETH BENTLEY

Dear Mr. Hoover,
I have not had the pleasure of making your acquaintance, but I have heard a great deal about you during the days when as a civilian, I was working for the Federal Bureau of Investigations. It is for this reason that I am turning to you now...
There are still some unenlightened people who still believe that I am not a loyal American. This is a great handicap, especially since I am at present in search of a position...Would it therefore be possible for you to give me a letter which would for once and all allay doubts in the minds of school superintendents and principals and in the minds of the general public as well?
I do hate to bother you when I know you are very busy...

Hoover answered on August 13.

Dear Miss Bentley,
Your cooperation with this Bureau is a matter of public record. You will recall that I made the following statement November 17, 1953 before the subcommittee of the Senate Committee of the Judiciary:
"All information furnished by Miss Bentley, which was susceptible to check, has proven to be correct..."
I trust this will answer your request.

Bentley wrote back:

I should like to thank you very much for your letter of August 13...
The way to defeat Communism is to build good citizens in the coming generation. If we can salvage even a few of these outcasts from society, we have, I think, helped to contribute to a better America.
Thank you for your thoughtfulness.

At the Rosenberg trial, Emanuel Bloch continued

his questioning of Elizabeth Bentley. The questions he put to her about whether she knew Harry Gold were far more disturbing to the government than Bloch may have realized.

Mr. E. H. Bloch: *Did you testify in the trial of William Remington?*

A. *I did.*

Mr. E. H. Bloch: *And did you testify in the trial of Abe Brothman?*

A. *I did.*

Mr. E. H. Bloch: *Do you remember testifying at that trial that you succeeded a man—or you preceded a man by the name of Harry Gold?*

A. *I don't think I could possibly have testified that because I didn't know Harry Gold. I think what I did was describe the process by which I handed Abe Brothman over to another contact, who it seems to have turned out to be Harry Gold.*

Mr. E. H. Bloch: *Do you know whether Harry Gold was a Communist?*

A. *I am sorry, I don't know Mr. Gold. I didn't read his testimony or I wasn't in court when he testified. I know very little about him.*

Mr. E. H. Bloch: *Didn't you talk to Mr. Gold, Harry Gold?*

A. *I have never met him, I do not know anything about Harry Gold. I never met him. I never talked to Mr. Golos about him. I didn't know that he was existing...I would even doubt it seriously if Mr. Golos himself knew who Mr. Gold's identity was...*

Mr. Saypol: *I want to serve warning—just a moment, if your Honor please. I want your Honor to notice that I refrained entirely in my direct examination from this subject.*

Judge Kaufman: All right.

Mr. Saypol: But if counsel opens the door, I will have to go entirely into the circumstances—

Judge Kaufman: I think counsel is closing the door right now.

Mr. Saypol: Your Honor knows what I mean...

While warning Bloch of the dire results to his clients if he dared to enter into the Golos-Gold-Bentley connection, the prosecutor and the judge were actually demonstrating their own fear of what an interrogation on this subject could have produced. Bentley knew Gold and, with the knowledge of the FBI, provided false testimony in the Brothman-Moskowitz trial as well as the Rosenberg-Sobell trial.

Elizabeth Bentley's testimony was concluded, and James S. Huggins, a government official, next testified that he wrote that Morton Sobell was "deported from Mexico," though he did not know it for a fact. Harold Phillips, Morton Sobell's lawyer, then petitioned Judge Kaufman to recognize that there were two conspiracy charges; one involving the atom bomb, which had nothing to do with Morton Sobell, and the other relating to Sobell's attempt to obtain information from Elitcher. Kaufman considered both episodes to be branches of the same conspiracy and denied Phillips's request to treat them separately.

JULIUS ROSENBERG

The prosecution finished calling witnesses, and the defense took over. Julius Rosenberg was called to the witness stand. The early part of his testimony described his work and educational background. In September 1940, Julius Rosenberg, who had received a degree in engineering from City College the previous year, was hired by the U.S. Army Signal Corps as a junior engineer. In March 1945, however, he was fired from his job and branded a Communist. Rosenberg managed to find work with Emerson Radio until December 1945 when he was laid off. Then, in early 1946, he was approached by his wife's brother, Bernard, and asked to participate in starting a war surplus business. David Greenglass, who had returned from the Army, also joined the business. The new firm was called the Pitt Machine Products company.

Emanuel Bloch then moved on to the heart of the case.

Mr. E. H. Bloch: Now, Mr. Rosenberg, are you aware of the charge that the Government has leveled against you?

A. I am...

Mr. E. H. Bloch: What are you being charged with?

A. Conspiracy to commit espionage to aid a foreign government...

Mr. E. H. Bloch: Did you know of the existence of the Los Alamos Project in December, 1944?

A. I did not...

Mr. E. H. Bloch: Did you, at any time during Dave

Greenglass' furlough in New York in January 1945, describe to him an atom bomb?

A. I did not...

Mr. E. H. Bloch: Now, tell me, Mr. Rosenberg, you received an engineering degree, did you not?

A. That is correct.

Mr. E. H. Bloch: Did you, in the course of your studies looking toward getting that degree, ever take courses in nuclear physics?

A. I did not.

Mr. E. H. Bloch: Or any advanced physics?

A. I did not...

Mr. E. H. Bloch: What was your field as an engineer?

A. My field as an electrical engineer was the production of electronic communications equipment, radio receivers and transmitters, and radio telephones...

Mr. E. H. Bloch: Did you ever know any Russian by the name of John?

A. No, sir, I did not.

Mr. E. H. Bloch: Did you know any Russian who was connected with the Soviet Embassy or any of the Soviet Consulates or any official of the Russian Government at any time in your life?

A. I did not...

Judge Kaufman: Excuse me. Did you know anybody at all in the Russian Consulate office?

The Witness: I did not, sir...

Mr. E. H. Bloch: Now, did you, while Dave Greenglass was on his furlough here, ever introduce Dave Greenglass to a man on First Avenue, I believe, somewhere between 42nd and 59th Street...and then you went with this man and Dave left; did any such incident ever occur?

A. That incident never occurred, sir.

Mr. E. H. Bloch: Now, I would like to direct your attention to the time when you invited Dave Greenglass and Ruth Greenglass to your house for dinner; that did occur, did it not, on Dave's first furlough?

A. Yes, it did.

Mr. E. H. Bloch: And could you tell us now from your recollection whether or not there was a woman by the name of Ann Sidorovich present?

A. I could not, sir.

Mr. E. H. Bloch: Do you know Ann Sidorovich?

A. Yes, I do...

Mr. E. H. Bloch: Now, did you ever invite Ann Sidorovich to your house to meet the Greenglasses for the purpose of effecting an introduction between Ann Sidorovich and the Greenglasses so that Ann Sidorovich could go out to the Southwest or the West and exchange some information with the Greenglasses?

A. I didn't do any such thing...

Mr. E. H. Bloch: Did you ever have any discussion with Ann Sidorovich or her husband at any time with respect to getting any information relating to the national defense in this country?

A. I did not.

Judge Kaufman: Did you ever discuss with Ann Sidorovich the respective preferences of economic systems between Russia and the United States?

A. Well, your Honor, if you will let me answer that question in my own way, I want to explain that question.

Judge Kaufman: Go ahead...

A. I am not an expert on matters on different economic systems, but in my normal social intercourse with my friends, we discussed matters like that. And I believe there are merits in both systems, I mean from

342

what I have been able to read and ascertain.

Judge Kaufman: I am not talking about your belief today. I am talking about your belief at that time, in January 1945...

A. Well, that is what I am talking about. At that time, what I believed at that time I still believe today. In the first place, I heartily approve our system of justice as performed in this country, Anglo-Saxon jurisprudence. I am in favor, heartily in favor or our Constitution and Bill of Rights and I owe my allegiance to my country at all times.

Mr. E. H. Bloch: Do you owe allegiance to any other country?

A. No, I do not.

Mr. E. H. Bloch: Have you any divided allegiance?

A. I do not.

Mr. E. H. Bloch: Would you fight for this country?

A. Yes, I will.

Judge Kaufman: Did you approve the communistic systems of Russia over the capitalistic systems in this country?

The Witness: I am not an expert in these things...

Mr. E. H. Bloch: Did you ever make any comparisons in the sense that the Court has asked you, about whether you preferred one system over another?

A. No, I did not. I would like to state that my personal opinions are that the people of every country should decide by themselves what kind of government they want...

Mr. E. H. Bloch: Do you believe in the overthrow of government by force and violence?

A. I do not.

Mr. E. H. Bloch: Do you believe—do you believe in anybody committing acts of espionage against his own country?

A. I do not believe that...

Judge Kaufman: Well, did you ever belong to any group that discussed the system of Russia?

The Witness: Well, your Honor, if you are referring to political groups—is that what you are referring to?

Judge Kaufman: Any group.

The Witness: Well, your Honor, I feel at this time that I refuse to answer a question that might tend to incriminate me...

Judge Kaufman: Well now, I won't direct you at this point to answer; I will wait for the cross-examination...

Mr. E. H. Bloch: Now, let us come to this night when the Greenglasses were in your house: Did you ever have any transaction with the Greenglasses in which a Jello box was involved?

A. No, I did not...

Mr. E. H. Bloch: Have you any independent recollection of what specific subject you discussed that night with Dave and Ruth?

A. Well, we were talking about the effort all the different allies were making in the war and we noted that the Russians were carrying at that particular time the heaviest load of the German Army...

Judge Kaufman: Did you express any opinion that the Russians were not getting the cooperation from the Allies that they were entitled to?

A. No, I expressed the opinion, not as an expert, but as an individual, that there should be a second front at that time. I don't remember if it was at that time.

Judge Kaufman: What I am asking you is, did you express the opinion that...the Russians were not getting the cooperation from the Allies that they were entitled to.

A. No, I didn't express that opinion, sir...

Mr. E. H. Bloch: Did you ever talk to Harry Gold in your life?

A. No, I did not.

Mr. E. H. Bloch: Did you see Harry Gold or did you see any Russian or did you see any person with respect to arranging a meeting between Harry Gold and the Greenglasses in New Mexico in June 1945?

A. I did not.

Mr. E. H. Bloch: Or at any other time?

A. I did not...

Mr. E. H. Bloch: I want to ask you something: Did you ever know a man by the name of John Golos?

A. No, I did not.

Mr. E. H. Bloch: Did you ever know a woman by the name of Elizabeth Bentley?

A. No, I did not...

Mr. E. H. Bloch: Now, let us come back to September 1945. Did Dave Greenglass and Ruth Greenglass ever come over to your house and deliver to you, whether at your request or without your request, any information about an atom bomb?

A. No, they did not...

Mr. E. H. Bloch: Well, did you ever receive a sketch of a cross-section of the Atom Bomb from Dave Greenglass at the time he was here on his second furlough in 1945?

A. No, I did not...

Mr. E. H. Bloch: Did your wife ever type up at your request any matter as a result of your having received any of that 12-page descriptive matter?

A. She did not type any such thing...

Judge Kaufman: Is your wife a typist?

A. Yes, she is.

Judge Kaufman: Do you have a typewriter at home?

A. That is right...

Mr. E. H. Bloch: Now, let us come back to September 1945. Did you ever take any material that was ever transmitted to you by Dave or Ruth Greenglass and turn it over to the Russians or anybody else?

A. No, I did not...

Judge Kaufman: Did you know any Russians at that time? By Russians, I mean people who were Russian citizens.

A. You mean citizens of Russia?

Judge Kaufman: That is correct.

A. No, I didn't.

Judge Kaufman: Didn't know any at all?

A. None at all...

Kaufman questioned Rosenberg in a prosecutorial manner. Kaufman would caustically intervene in this fashion whenever it appeared that Rosenberg sounded sincere and was making a favorable impression upon the jury.

Mr. E. H. Bloch: There has been testimony here...that in 1950, in May, you gave Dave Greenglass or Ruth Greenglass $1000 in cash. Did you ever advance that sum or give that sum to them?

A. I did not...

Mr. E. H. Bloch: Did there come a time when Dave Greenglass left the Pitt Machine Products Company?

Judge Kaufman: Before you answer that question: Did you have any discussion with Greenglass about his going to Mexico?

A. I didn't have any discussion with Greenglass about going to Mexico, but one time the word Mexico was mentioned. If you want me to discuss that...

Judge Kaufman: Just tell me when.

A. In the middle of May...

Judge Kaufman: Tell us how that came about.

Mr. E. H. Bloch: Just pardon me, if the Court please. I know that the Court's question is absolutely proper and relevant. What I was doing here is going along chronologically...Now, did there come a time when Dave Greenglass left the Pitt Machine Company?

A. Yes, there did.

Mr. E. H. Bloch: And what year was that?

A. In 1949...

Mr. E. H. Bloch: Did you remain in the business?

A. I did...

Mr. E. H. Bloch: Were you negotiating to get an assignment of Dave Greenglass' stock in 1949 after he left?

A. Yes, I was.

Mr. E. H. Bloch: And was there a discussion about price?

A. There certainly was...

Mr. E. H. Bloch: And did you continue to have discussions with him about that right from January 1950 up to May 1950?

A. I had continuous discussions with him.

Mr. E. H. Bloch: Did you finally agree with him on a price of $1000?

A. Yes, I did...

Mr. E. H. Bloch: Now, did you see Dave later that month?

A. Yes, I did.

Mr. E. H. Bloch: Tell us the circumstances.

A. Well, about the middle of May, I can't tell the exact date, David came to my shop one morning. He came into my office...

He said..."Julie, you have got to get me $2000. I

need it at once."

I said, "Look, Dave...I just don't have the money."...

So he said, "Well, if you can't help me like that, maybe you can do something else for me."

I said, "What is it? If I can help you, I will."

He said, "Will you go to your doctor and ask him if he would make out a certificate for a smallpox vaccination?"...

And I said, "It is highly irregular, but I will ask my doctor if he will do that."

And he said, "Don't tell him who it is for, and also, incidentally, while you are talking to him, ask him if he knows what kind of injections are required to go into Mexico."

Kaufman again intervened.

Judge Kaufman: Now, up to that time, you had been having some heated arguments, as you call it, heated arguments with David, and I take it you were not particularly friendly with him then, were you?

A. Well, I would say this: that I was not antagonistic to him. He was my wife's brother.

Judge Kaufman: But you were not friendly. That friendship had been strained?

A. Yes, there was strain.

Judge Kaufman: Can you think of any reason why on this occasion he would come to you and confess to you, and ask you to help him out instead of going to somebody else?

A. I have no idea why he came to me...

Mr. E. H. Bloch: Now, there has been testimony here by Dave Greenglass and Ruth Greenglass that on May 23rd or May 24th, 1950, you came over to their *house and...you told Dave that he ought to get out of the country, and you gave him $1000 in cash; did you ever give him that money?*

A. I didn't give that money.

Judge Kaufman: Nor did you give him the $4000, as he testified?

A. No, I did not, sir...

Mr. E. H. Bloch: Well, did you, at any time, get any money from anybody, in these denominations of a thousand and $4000?

A. No, I did not...

Mr. E. H. Bloch: Did you see Dave Greenglass a few days after you had spoken to the doctor about the Mexican vaccination?

A. Yes, I did.

Mr. E. H. Bloch: Tell us the circumstances of that.

A. Well...a couple of days after that, on my way to work, I stopped in and told him the doctor had said he wouldn't give him the vaccination, the vaccination certificate, and he said he would take care of it himself. That is all that happened at that time.

Mr. E. H. Bloch: Now, where did this conversation take place?

A. It took place in his house...

Mr. E. H. Bloch: Did you have any further conversations with Dave Greenglass after you told him that the doctor, your doctor, would not give a phony certificate?

A. Yes, I did...

Rosenberg explained that Greenglass called him about a week later and asked him to come over to his house, but when Rosenberg arrived, Greenglass would not let him in. Rosenberg said that Greenglass called him again a day or two later and asked him to come

349

over, which he did.

Mr. E. H. Bloch: Did you then go out of the house with Davey?

A. I did.

Mr. E. H. Bloch: Tell us what happened...

A. I said to Dave at this point, "You look very agitated. Calm yourself, take it easy. What's troubling you?" And he said, "Julie, I am in a terrible jam...I must have a couple of thousand dollars in cash...I just got to have that money, and if you don't get me that money, you are going to be sorry."...and I left him at that time, and I made up my mind at that point that I wouldn't have anything to do with him, and I was very agitated.

Mr. E. H. Bloch: Did you give him any money?

A. I did not give him any money...

Judge Kaufman: And you can't think of any reason whatsoever, can you, why Dave Greenglass would, of all people he knew, his brother, all the other members of his family, single you out, as he did apparently, and as you say he did, and say that you would be sorry unless you gave him the money?

The Witness: Well, he knew that I owed—he had an idea that I owed him money from the business, and I guess that is what he figured he wanted to get the money from me.

David Greenglass, who turned on his brother-in-law Julius and his sister Ethel and accused them of being Communist spies, may have justified his actions on the basis that they could have enabled him and his wife to flee the country and escape prosecution if they had only paid him what he thought was money that belonged to him. Both David and Ruth Greenglass may have felt that the Rosenbergs were only getting what they deserved for not paying their debts.

Mr. E. H. Bloch: Did you ever get a citation or a certificate or any document or any oral congratulations from the Russian government or any agent of the Russian government or any citizen of the Russian government for services that you had rendered on behalf of the Russian government?

A. I got nothing of the sort.

Mr. E. H. Bloch: Did you ever render any services for the Russian government?

A. I did not...

Mr. E. H. Bloch: Did you ever receive a watch from the Russian government or anybody authorized by the Russian government or any agent or representative of the Russian government, or any Russian?

A. I didn't receive any watch from any Russian or anybody...

Mr. E. H. Bloch: All right. Now then, Dave and Ruth Greenglass testified that you said to them that you received a console table from the Russian Government; do you remember that?

A. Yes, I heard that testimony.

Mr. E. H. Bloch: Did you ever make such a statement?

A. I did not.

Mr. E. H. Bloch: Did you ever receive a console table from the Russian government?

A. I did not...

Mr. E. H. Bloch: You purchased a console table from R.H. Macy?

A. That is correct...

Mr. E. H. Bloch: Now, can you be as specific as you possibly can about the date of that purchase?

A. Well, I can't remember exactly the date, but it was somewhere between 1944 and 1945 that I personally purchased the console table.

Mr. E. H. Bloch: How much did you say you paid for it?

A. Somewhere in the neighborhood of $21...

Mr. E. H. Bloch: Now, was the table that you purchased at Macy's the same console table that was in your home at the time the FBI finally came around to arrest you?

A. Yes, it was...

Mr. E. H. Bloch: Let me ask you: did that console table have any special apparatus for photographing material?

A. No, it did not.

Mr. E. H. Bloch: Now, Mr. Rosenberg, do you know your co-defendant, Morton Sobell?

A. Yes, I do...

Mr. E. H. Bloch: Now, did you meet him after you graduated?

A. When we lived in Washington, D.C., in 1940, for a couple of months we bumped into each other at a swimming pool. At the same time I met him, I saw Max Elitcher and Elitcher's brother at that pool. It was an accidental meeting...

Mr. E. H. Bloch: Did Morton Sobell and his wife Helen Sobell ever visit you at your home?

A. Yes, they did...

Mr. E. H. Bloch: What year?

A. It was either '47 or '48; and they both came over, and we just visited socially.

Mr. E. H. Bloch: Were there any other people present at the time, that you can remember?

A. Yes, there were other people present.

Mr. E. H. Bloch: Do you remember the names of

352

any people who were present, outside the Sobells, now?

A. I could recall only one name at this time.

Mr. E. H. Bloch: What is her name?

A. A Miss Vivian Glassman...

Mr. E. H. Bloch: Did Sobell ever deliver to you any information relating to the national defense of the United States?

A. He did not.

Mr. E. H. Bloch: Did Sobell ever disclose to you anything concerning information or material that he had obtained by reason of his position with the General Electric Company in Schenectady, New York?

A. He did not...

Judge Kaufman: You heard Mr. Elitcher testify that you came to see him in June of 1944 in Washington, D.C...And when you went to see him on this occasion in '43 or '44, you heard him say that you had mentioned Mr. Sobell's name during the course of that conversation. Do you remember that?

A. I heard what he testified to.

Judge Kaufman: Now, did you go to see him pursuant to Mr. Sobell's instructions or advice, or anything like that?

A. I did not...

Judge Kaufman often used the judicial device of questioning Julius Rosenberg instead of permitting his attorney Emanuel Bloch to question him, when it was expected that Rosenberg would deny the allegations brought against him. Judge Kaufman by this method displayed for the jurors his doubts of Rosenberg's veracity.

Mr. E. H. Bloch: Did Mr. Sobell ever bring to you

*any microfilm can or microfilm or any material what-
soever?*
A. He did not.
Mr. E. H. Bloch: I think that is all...

Irving Saypol, the United States attorney, then
began cross-examination.

*Mr. Saypol: Mr. Rosenberg, tell us a little bit
about your associates when you were at City College.
Who were they?...Was there a man or a boy by the
name of Perl or Mutterperl?*
A. Your Honor, I read in the newspapers about—
*Judge Kaufman: You had better not say anything
you think may hurt you...*

Kaufman's insincere warning to Rosenberg was the
means he used to communicate to the jurors the implication that Saypol had made a telling point and that
Rosenberg had to be in great fear of the balance of
cross-examination of him on this subject.

Actually, Rosenberg had nothing of substance to
fear in being questioned about Perl. His only concern
was to avoid questions concerning his, Perl's, or other
acquaintances' membership at one time or another in
the Communist Party. Rosenberg's chivalry and honor
in refusing to hurt anyone else was repeatedly used
against him, as was his frequent pleading of the fifth
amendment.

*The Witness: I read in the newspapers about a man
being arrested for perjury...My name was mentioned,
and I feel that I refuse to answer any questions that
might tend to incriminate me...*
Judge Kaufman: You mean, you assert your consti-

354

tutional privilege against self-incrimination.

The Witness: That's right...

Mr. Saypol: Now, you remember while testifying before, in response to your lawyer's questions as to conversations at your home sometime in January of 1945 with the Greenglasses, you testified about the comparative systems of justice in this country and in Russia. Do you recall that?

A. I didn't testify that we had a conversation at my house about the comparative systems of justice. I was asked my opinions on it...

Mr. Saypol: So you did talk about it, didn't you?

A. I don't remember if it was that specific conversation at that time or another time, but I talked about these things...

Judge Kaufman: Was that one of the topics that was discussed at the family gatherings?

A. It was one of the topics we discussed...

Judge Kaufman: Did I understand you to say here, or if you didn't, I ask you the question; Did you in 1944 or 1945 state, and I believe you stated on direct but I am not quite sure, that you had thought Russia was carrying the brunt of the war at that point?

A. That is right, sir...

Mr. Saypol: And Russia, as an antagonist and a participant in the war, you felt was entitled to more help than the allies were giving to her?

A. I didn't say that, Mr. Saypol.

Judge Kaufman: He is asking you whether or not you felt that.

The Witness: No. I felt that Russia should get as much help as possible to help them defeat the Nazis.

Judge Kaufman: Well now, did you feel that if Great Britain shared in all our secrets that Russia should at the same time also share those secrets in

1944 and 1945?

A. *My opinion was that matters such as that were up to the Governments, the British, American and the Russian Governments.*

Judge Kaufman: You mean the ultimate decision?

A. *Yes.*

Judge Kaufman: Well, what was your opinion at that time?

A. *My opinion was that if we had a common enemy, we should get together commonly...*

Mr. Saypol: Well, what did you know about the subject to express an opinion? Did you talk about it with others?

A. *I read it in the newspapers.*

Mr. Saypol: Did you talk about it in groups?

A. *Socially, when people came over to the house.*

Mr. Saypol: Did you talk about it perhaps in any Communist unit that you might have belonged to?

A. *I refuse to answer that question on the ground that it may incriminate me...*

Judge Kaufman: I want the jury to understand that they are to draw no inference from the witness' refusal to answer on his assertion of privilege. Proceed...

Rosenberg would answer any question relating to the charges of espionage without even a hint of reluctance. But his refusal to answer questions exposing him to relatively minor consequences concerning his Communist affiliations were repeatedly presented by Saypol and Kaufman as evidence of his guilt in respect to the major charges he faced.

Mr. Saypol: Is it not a fact that on March 28, 1945, you were summoned and in the presence of another officer of the Army, Captain Henderson, advised...of the action that was being taken against you to separate you from the service because of information reaching the office that you were a Communist Party member?...

Mr. E. H. Bloch: If Mr. Saypol wants a concession, I will concede right now that this witness was removed from Government service upon charges that he was a member of the Communist Party...

No matter how he tried, Bloch could not stop Saypol from hammering at the point that Rosenberg was a Communist. Even when Bloch led Rosenberg to admit to facts that implied his Communist Party membership, Saypol wanted the questions repeated over and over again.

Saypol had another edge; he knew in advance how Rosenberg would respond to his questions. Throughout the trial, while waiting to testify, Rosenberg's cellmate and closest friend was Jerome Tartakow, a criminal and government informer. Tartakow was interviewed regularly by the FBI. In one of these interviews, dated March 22, 1951, Tartakow informed Agent Cammarota that

> *Rosenberg stated that there are two questions he would refuse to answer in court on the grounds that they would tend to incriminate him. The first was as to whether or not he is a member of the Communist Party. The second was as to whether or not he knows William Perl.*

Since he had this information before he questioned Julius Rosenberg, U.S. Attorney Saypol knew that Rosenberg would refuse to answer whether or not he was a Communist Party member no matter how many times the question was asked of him.

But when it came to the question of whether Rosenberg obtained information on the atomic bomb from David Greenglass or transferred it to Anatoli Yakovlev, or whether Rosenberg had anything to do with giving the secret of the atomic bomb to the Russians, Tartakow said his impression was that Rosenberg had nothing to do with the atom bomb conspiracy, since he had told him that "the whole thing does not exist," Saypol made certain this information was kept from the jury. Indeed, Tartakow's reports provided an unambiguous statement of Julius Rosenberg's innocence of the charges. Special Agent Cammarota reported on March 19, 1951:

> *Rosenberg swears to Tartakow...that he is not acquainted with Anatoli Yakovlev. In this connection it is noted that Tartakow advised that he feels Rosenberg is telling the truth. According to Rosenberg, he has never seen or met Yakovlev.*

COMMUNIST PARTY MEMBER 12179

The questioning of Julius Rosenberg continued.

Mr. Saypol: Were you a member of the Communist Party?

A. I refuse to answer on the ground that it might incriminate me...

Mr. Saypol: Is it not a fact that in February 1944, you transferred from Branch 16-B of the Industrial Division of the Communist Party to the Eastern Club of the First Assembly District under Transfer No. 12179?

A. I refuse to answer.

Mr. Saypol: Is that one of the charges Captain Henderson read to you?

A. That is...

Mr. Saypol: Now, at that time, in response to these charges, did you file an answer, Mr. Rosenberg?

A. I did.

Mr. Saypol: And do you remember having, on April 3, 1945, made the following statement in a communication to the Commanding Officer of the Newark Signal Corps..."I am not now, and never have been a communist member...Either the charge is based on a case of mistaken identity or a complete falsehood. In any event, it certainly has not the slightest basis in fact."

Did you make that answer to those charges, yes or no?

A. I refuse to answer a question on the contents of that letter.

Mr. Saypol: I ask you whether you made that answer to those charges as I have read them to you?

Mr. E. H. Bloch: May I advise the client, your Honor, that he should answer that question yes or no.

Judge Kaufman: Very well.

A. Yes, I sent the letter in answer to those charges.

Mr. Saypol: Was that answer true at the time you made it?

A. I refuse to answer...

Rosenberg, still hopeful that he would be found innocent of the espionage conspiracy charges he now faced, was defending himself against possible re-indictment on perjury charges of the kind that resulted in the convictions of Abraham Brothman and William Remington. A mere honest answer to Saypol's questions could be very dangerous to Julius Rosenberg.

The information that led up to Rosenberg's dismissal from the Signal Corps was improperly presented and reviewed. FBI reports, inter-office memoranda, and communications with the U.S. Attorney's office indicated that the government agencies before, during, and after the trial were aware that they did not possess provable evidence that Julius Rosenberg was a member of the Communist Party.

On June 8, 1944 an FBI report stated that a confidential informant "who had access to the headquarters of the New York County Committee of the Communist Party" provided them with information about transfers of individuals within the Party from one branch to another. The report referred to a "slip of paper on which these transfers [were] noted." The report stated that a Julius Rosenberg, 10 Monroe Street, New York City, was one of the transferees.

On October 6, 1944, the FBI sent a letter to Colonel S. V. Constant in the Security and Intelligence Division of the War Department advising him of what had been reported to them about Julius Rosenberg. On March 9, 1945, Milton Ladd of the FBI noted that "apparently as a result of that information the Army has suspended Rosenberg and his attorney has filed a complaint with the War Department."

But a problem surfaced in connection with this suspension. The FBI did not have a copy of the letter, nor the "slip of paper" with the information that prompted the Army to dismiss Rosenberg, and the Army had no copy of it either. The Army had suspended Julius Rosenberg based on the FBI's October 6, 1944, letter, which merely summarized the charges brought against Rosenberg without providing the "slip of paper" as evidence. Ladd instructed his agents to find the source information contained in the letter as well as the letter itself.

A telephone call to Ladd on March 10, 1945, from one of his assistants appeared merely to tell Ladd not to worry. The assistant told Ladd, "We are entirely clear in the matter; that based on our letter to them, the Army conducted a complete investigation and it was as a result of their investigation that they took any action."

The source information was apparently never found. A review of the file more than five years later, on August 18, 1950, noted that on March 26, 1945, the Army was still looking for the source information. The FBI report on this review described how the Signal Corps responded to their dilemma. Major General Claton Bissell, the Assistant Chief of Staff decided that the Army's problems were caused by the stupidity of Captain John W. Henderson who, after informing Rosenberg of the reasons for his "removal from the War Department" allowed him to make a verbatim copy of the charges read to him. General Bissell, it was reported, expressed the opinion that "by making the above mentioned revelation to Rosenberg," Captain Henderson "had seriously compromised the source of the FBI's information and had jeopardized the relationship between the Bureau and the War Department." Bissell recommended that Henderson be relieved of his duties as intelligence officer.

An August 18, 1950, government report addressed directly to J. Edgar Hoover stated:

> *The above information is being furnished for your consideration inasmuch as it is conceivable that in the course of a trial Rosenberg's attorneys might attempt to embarrass the Bureau as well as weaken the government's case by introducing this matter into evidence.*

As far back as 1945 Julius Rosenberg had managed to incur the hatred of the FBI. He embarrassed the Bureau and its director by showing them to be incompetent and dishonest. Captain Henderson provided Rosenberg with nothing more than he was entitled to, and the rebuke of this officer was simply a face-saving device.

Here are excerpts from the government's charges and Julius Rosenberg's April 3, 1945, response to them:

> *Those charges allege first:*
> *That you are a Communist member. It is alleged that you transferred from Branch 16-B Industrial Division of Communist Party to the Eastern Club of the 1st Assembly District, NY, under Transfer No. 12179, in February, 1944.*
> *[Julius Rosenberg responded:]*
> *I am not now, and never have been a Communist member. I know nothing about communist branches, divisions, clubs, or*

transfers... Either the charge is based on a case of mistaken identity or is a complete falsehood. In any event, it certainly has not the slightest basis in fact...

It is further charged:
Your instructor at the school is reported to have been a Director of the Abraham Lincoln Brigade and a member of the Loyalist Air Forces in the Spanish Civil War. It is further reported that he signed a Communist Party Election Petition in 1939...
[Julius Rosenberg responded:]
Certainly, the law does not operate to remove from Federal employment any individual who ever took a course from a man who was a Communist...

It is further charged that:
It is reported that your wife resided in an apartment owned by one ▮▮▮▮, *who was reported to have been active in student organizations affiliated with the Communist Party...*
[Julius Rosenberg responded:]
This is so preposterous a charge that I will not even bother to answer it. Does the law operate to remove from Federal employment anyone who is the tenant of a Communist?

It is further charged that:
It is reported that your wife also signed a Communist Party petition during the same period.
[Julius Rosenberg responded:]
My wife does not recall the circumstances surrounding her signing of any communist Party petition...Again, I wish to call to your attention that I am being removed here not by my wife, my landlord, my employer, or my teacher.

It is further charged that:
This officer has also received evidence indicating that you were a member of the

Communist Party in 1940 in New York State.
  [Julius Rosenberg responded:]

I can make no refutation of the charge in its present form since there is no specification set forth in the charge. I can only deny that I was a member of the Communist Party in 1940, or at any other time...

In the early part of 1941 I was investigated by the Civil Service Commission on the charge of alleged membership in the Communist Party. After a thorough investigation, the evidence produced was merely that I was a member of the Federation of Architects, Engineers, Chemists and Technicians...The charges were dropped and the issue terminated by a letter dated July 18, 1941...

In conclusion I urgently request an early review of your decision to rectify the mistake in the interest of justice and fair play.

Respectfully yours,

Julius Rosenberg

Rosenberg lost his job though there was no documentary evidence that he was a member of the Communist Party. Proof of the injustice done to him was revealed nearly ten years later, on February 4, 1954. At that time the FBI submitted replies to questions posed by an unidentified *New York Times* reporter who was gathering material for a book. Question 6 read, "When did the Bureau discover that Julius Rosenberg was a member of [the Communist] Party?" The FBI answered, "The Bureau first became aware that Julius Rosenberg was a member of the Communist Party through information supplied by an anonymous source on March 15, 1944." Question 7 read, "Was he an important member of the Party at that time?" The FBI responded, in part, "It would appear from the information known that he was not an important member of the Communist Party." Question 8 read,

364

"Did Ethel Rosenberg's name ever turn up as a member of the Party?" The FBI answered, "A review of the New York files failed to reflect any documentary evidence of membership of Ethel in the Communist Party." The FBI's summary at the end of the questionnaire demonstrated that the Bureau was still blaming the Army Signal Corps for Julius Rosenberg's dismissal:

> *In answer to questions 6, 7, and 8, it is recommended that no direct statements be made that the Bureau has positive information concerning the membership of Julius. NY takes this position because of the nature of the source of information, and secondly because of the possible embarrassment to the Bureau in the event that in his book* ▮▮▮▮ *would credit proof of membership to the Bureau.*

The following Monday morning, when Rosenberg returned to the witness stand, Saypol decided to discontinue questioning him concerning his membership in the Communist Party. Saypol announced, "This issue ultimately should be resolved by the jury, as to the guilt or innocence based on the indictment rather than on the collateral, or I should say, the related but not primary issue of membership in the Communist Party. I will withdraw my request at this time, and I do also in the interest of expedition." His cross-examination continued:

Mr. Saypol: You testified on direct examination that on one occasion when the Sobells visited your home at 10 Monroe Street, there was present a woman by the name of Vivian Glassman?
A. That is correct...
Mr. Saypol: How long have you known her?

A. *I don't know the exact length of time, but she was introduced to my wife and myself by Joel Barr, a classmate of ours...*

VIVIAN GLASSMAN

If ever there was a mysterious personality in the Rosenberg drama, it was Vivian Glassman. Though she was ignored throughout the years as a minor figure in the Rosenberg trial, analysis of her movements finds her at the heart of almost every investigation. When Joel Barr, a primary espionage suspect, sailed away from the United States never to return, Vivian Glassman, who was scheduled to leave with him and had a ticket purchased in her name, decided at the last moment to stand on the dock and wave goodbye to her friend and lover.

From what could be learned about Glassman, she was a very attractive woman. She was also a very intelligent woman, an apprentice psychologist studying for her master's at Columbia.

In 1950 Ruth and David Greenglass told the FBI that Julius Rosenberg used a New York City apartment in the vicinity of 12th Street and Avenue A for espionage purposes. The FBI responded to this information, reporting:

> On July 22, 1950, the entire vicinity of 12th Street and Avenue A, New York City, was canvassed by Agents of the New York Office in an attempt to ascertain the location of this apartment which David and Ruth Greenglass alleged that Rosenberg had used in connection with his espionage endeavors.
> Mr. and Mrs. Frank Tusky, Superintendents for 131 East Seventh Street, New York City, and who reside at 113 Avenue A, New York City, were interviewed by Special Agents William R. Yates and Daniel B. Fleming on July 22, 1950. Both Mr. And Mrs. Frank Tusky positively identified pictures of Julius

Rosenberg as a tenant who occupied Apartment 4A, 131 East Seventh Street, New York City, for approximately six to eight months in 1946...

Mrs. Tusky stated that Apartment 4A was then taken over by a married couple...Mrs. Tusky stated that the second couple resided in this apartment for only a couple of months.

Mrs. Tusky advised that one day tenants in the building told her that the second couple had moved out...and that two girls were now residing in the apartment...Mrs. Tusky stated that one of the girls, a Red Cross worker, was named Glass or Glassman and continues to reside in the apartment...

Indeed there she was again, Vivian Glassman, living at 131 East 7th Street in apartment 4A. Apparently, Glassman was so frequently visited there by Julius Rosenberg that the superintendent, Frank Tusky, mistakenly thought he was a tenant. Glassman, when questioned by the FBI, explained that Rosenberg indeed visited her often—to chat and drink coffee.

At the trial Saypol questioned Rosenberg about Vivian Glassman

Mr. Saypol: How often did you see her in 1950?

A. I would say she has been over to our house a number of times...

Mr. Saypol: What did you talk to her about the last time you saw her?

A. Well, she is a social worker and my oldest boy has been very emotionally disturbed for quite a number of years, and she used to work at the Jewish Board of Guardians, and I discussed the problem of my oldest boy with her...

Mr. Saypol: What else did you talk to Vivian Glassman about?

A. I had nothing else to talk to her about but that.

Mr. Saypol: Did you ever give her any money?

A. No, sir; never did.

Mr. Saypol: Did you ever send her on a trip to Cleveland?

A. No, sir; never did...

Mr. Saypol: Is this the first time you heard any suggestion that you gave her some money?

A. That is correct.

Mr. Saypol: Isn't it the fact that you gave her $2000 to take out to somebody in Cleveland?

A. That is not the fact, Mr. Saypol...

Saypol continued cross-examining in this vein, though he never called Vivian Glassman as a witness. He had no need to, since the damage to Julius Rosenberg was already accomplished merely by posing the questions.

The story of Vivian Glassman's visit to William Perl's Cleveland apartment, the circumstances that led up to the visit, and even the events that followed it, were the most bizarre and mysterious of the many escapades of that very adventurous woman. An FBI memo, dated July 28, 1950, containing Perl's statement given to them two days earlier, read:

> *Last Sunday, July 23, 1950, at about noon...a woman appeared through the curtain which shields the alcove from the stair leading to the street. This woman identified herself as, and I recognized her as, Vivian Glassman of New York City...I asked her what she wanted... She sat down on the couch in the apartment, motioned me to sit next to her and indicated that I was to read what she was writing. She wrote approximately as follows: That she had*

been instructed to talk to me by writing rather than talking. That she had been approached by a stranger in New York City and told to go to Cleveland to see an aeronautical engineer; that she was to give him money and instructions which she had memorized as to how he and a friend were to leave the country. In this connection I remember the word Mexico... As nearly as I can remember she also wrote to the effect that she knew Julius Rosenberg...I told her in effect that I did not know what she was talking about; that I hoped that she had a clear conscience and was not getting mixed up in anything; that I thought this whole thing was some kind of trap and I asked her to leave...I was quite upset by her visit and destroyed the papers on which she had been writing.

The FBI reacted quickly. Their response was reported in an August 5, 1950, memo, which read:

A surveillance of subject was conducted on the evening of July twenty-seven, but subject's apartment is located on the top floor of a large apartment house and surveilling agents were therefore unable to observe the visit of the aforesaid stranger in the apartment of subject on this date.

Now this was a very odd FBI report. Why would they be expecting a stranger to visit Vivian Glassman on July 27? Glassman did not tell Perl or anybody that the stranger was returning that day or any day. Even more curious, Glassman told the FBI that the stranger actually did visit her on July 27, though the agents failed to detect him.

When Vivian Glassman was interviewed on August 3, she readily admitted her visit to William Perl at the behest of a stranger who gave her $2,000 to pass on to him. Her story was similar to Perl's, differing only in that she denied writing down Julius Rosenberg's name. This denial seemed reasonable enough, since if Perl had kept the paper, and it contained Glassman's handwriting on it, she would have been left totally unprotected and her credibility forever placed in question. Glassman told the FBI agents that on the evening of July 27, the stranger reappeared, was told by her of her trip to Perl, and was given back the $2,000 which Perl had rejected.

What followed appeared to be a massive campaign of harassment to force Glassman to appear before a grand jury. An FBI memo dated September 7, 1950, reported that she refused to testify on August 11 and again on August 14, despite the intensifying threats of U.S. Attornies Irving Saypol and Myles Lane:

> Lane told Glassman that on the following day he was going to ask Judge Davis to cite her for contempt for failure to answer questions before the Grand Jury, and that if she did not decide to cooperate with the Government and so testify, she should bring additional clothing with her on August 15, 1950, as she was going to jail...
>
> On August 15, 1950 the subject again appeared before the Grand Jury and refused to answer any questions...
>
> On August 28, 1950 Assistant United States Attorney Lane advised that he had decided against instituting contempt proceedings against the subject...he was going to rely upon voluntary cooperation of the subject through the influence upon her of her attorney...
>
> Lane advised the subject that he wishes her to tell the story of the July 21, 1950 contact to the Grand Jury on Monday, September 11, 1950. No appointment was made and the subject was not given a subpoena by Assistant United States Attorney Lane for her appearance on this date...

371

Time and time again the prosecutors did not follow through on their threats and the logic of the evidence demonstrates that the interchanges between Glassman and the U.S. Attorney's office were orchestrated. They were designed to portray a woman steadfastly clinging to her constitutional right to remain silent, when in fact it was the government who insisted she remain silent. The exchanges continued well into 1951, when on March 17 an FBI report prepared by Edward Scheidt, referring to U.S. Attorney John M. Foley's questioning of Glassman on the identity of the man who visited her on July 21, 1950, said:

> *She was adamant to all questions during the interview. When subsequently escorted to building elevator by agent upon conclusion of interview, she remarked, "You people probably do know the identity of the person who came to my apartment that night. He was probably one of your agents."*

Threatened with indictment if she did not tell who visited her on July 21, 1951, Glassman more than implied that she thought the FBI knew who it was. Her conclusion seemed reasonable. Why did the FBI assume that anyone visited her? Why didn't they doubt her story and consider her a major figure in the espionage conspiracy who took her own $2,000 to William Perl? Why did it have to be a stranger? Why would a stranger give her $2,000 to go to Cleveland and then have the nerve to return to retrieve the money without calling first to see if it was delivered? Wouldn't the stranger be afraid that government agents would watch for his return? Wouldn't only a person without a worry, like an FBI agent, be brave enough to pay the return visit on July 27? Why, after Perl told the

372

FBI that Glassman had visited him, were agents posted at her home on the very day that Glassman said the unknown man came and left without being observed? Why did the agents claim that they had difficulty observing the visit because the building was large— when in fact the building was small and had perhaps eight tenants?

And can anyone believe that the FBI found the apartment at 131 East 7th Street by canvassing the area, based on a tip from David Greenglass that Rosenberg had an apartment in the vicinity of 12th Street and Avenue A, a quarter-mile away? Can anyone believe that among the hundreds of apartment houses and multiple thousands of tenants, FBI agents would visit just the building where Vivian Glassman happened to live, on the same day that she left New York to visit William Perl in Cleveland; and on the same day they began this search? Could anyone visualize the sight of FBI agents moving to the right of the staircase so that the "Soviet espionage agent" could pass them on the left side of the staircase on his way to Glassman's apartment while the FBI visited her super and other tenants in the building? And can anyone picture this very similar scene happening again a few days later on July 27, 1950?

It seems more likely that David Greenglass told the FBI exactly where to go. Why he sent them to Vivian Glassman, and why the FBI made it appear that a massive investigation was necessary to locate the 131 East 7th Street apartment are not questions the author can answer. Nor can the author understand the curious notes in the FBI files that contained David Greenglass's statement that back in 1948, he had already begun to secretly follow Julius Rosenberg.

THE DAYTONS AND SARANTS

Irving Saypol continued questioning Julius Rosenberg.

Mr. Saypol: *Do you know a man by the name of Alfred Sarant?*

A. *Yes, I do.*

Mr. Saypol: *When did you see him last?*

A. *Possibly the early part of 1950 or the later part of 1949...*

Mr. Saypol: *Where did you first meet him?*

A. *I met him when he was introduced to me by his friend, Joel Barr. I met him in an apartment they were sharing in Greenwich Village.*

Mr. Saypol: *Where was that?*

A. *I don't recall the exact name of the street. I begins with an M. It is either—*

Mr. Saypol: *65 Morton Street, isn't it?*

A. *Morton. That is the place, Morton Street...*

Mr. Saypol: *How often had you been at Sarant's home on Morton Street?*

A. *On a number of occasions...*

Mr. Saypol: *Alone or with your wife?*

A. *I believe on one occasion my wife went with me.*

Mr. Saypol: *Were you over there with Sobell?*

A. *No, sir.*

Mr. Saypol: *Were you over there with Elitcher?*

A. *No, sir...*

Mr. Saypol: *Do you know a girl or lady by the name of Carol Dayton?*

A. *I don't recall the name.*

Mr. Saypol: *Never heard of it before?*

A. *I may have, I may not have.*

No study of the Rosenberg trial can be complete without the story of the Sarants, the Daytons, and the apartment at 65 Morton Street in Greenwich Village where clandestine microfilming was said to have been done. What did the Morton Street apartment have to do with the charges against the Rosenbergs and Morton Sobell? Absolutely nothing. But since there was no true evidence other than the false testimony of David Greenglass and Max Elitcher, supported by the false testimony of Harry Gold and Elizabeth Bentley, the sideshow on Morton Street became a welcome distraction for the government to dwell upon.

It was in 1943 that Alfred Sarant rented apartment 6-I at 65 Morton Street. Sarant, an engineer, was deeply interested in physics and worked in a physics lab at Cornell University. There he developed a relationship with Hans Bethe, the world-renowned scientist. Until he married in 1945, Sarant shared his Morton Street apartment with Joel Barr. Then his wife Louise moved in with him, and they lived there until September 1946. At that time they moved to Ithaca, New York, and sublet the apartment to Joel Barr and later to William Perl.

In Ithaca the Sarants became acquainted with Bruce Dayton and his wife Carol, who had moved there a few months before them. Dayton, a scientist who had worked on top-secret government projects, now worked in Cornell's nuclear physics laboratory. Before coming to Cornell, Dayton was at the California Institute of Technology from August 1944 to October 1945. He worked there under Henry DeWolff Smyth, the author of the *Smyth Report* on the atomic bomb.

Thus if anyone knew about the atom bomb and its

secrets, it was Bruce Dayton. A September 22, 1953, FBI report said, "Dayton was the only man in the purported espionage ring with the competence to understand atomic physics. He was a well-known physicist with outstanding qualifications and contacts in the world of science."

In 1947 the Daytons built a home in Ithaca, and the following year the Sarants built on an adjacent lot. The couples had become very close, and the Sarants lived with the Daytons while they waited for their house to be completed.

Two days after Julius Rosenberg was arrested, Sarant was visited by FBI agents. They described him as very accommodating, but the results of their interviews with him were not particularly remarkable. In fact, Sarant stated unequivocally, according to a memo dated July 20, 1950, that "Rosenberg did not at...any time ask him for any information for transmittal to Russia." Sarant also told the FBI that he had not seen or heard from Vivian Glassman since he moved to Ithaca. Vivian Glassman? Yes, Vivian Glassman. While Glassman was living at 131 East 7th Street for two months in 1948, July and August, she also paid rent to Sarant for the Morton Street apartment. Her explanation: she was considering renting the apartment and thought that by paying rent she could hold it until she made a final decision. She finally decided against it.

The interviews with Sarant continued. The last occurred on July 28, 1950, after which he could no longer be found. He had run away, taking with him Bruce Dayton's wife Carol, who left behind two young children. While it looked as if Sarant had fled as a result of the FBI's harassment, there was evidence that he had something of the sort planned well before the FBI interviews began. Agents learned that on May 2, 1950, he gave his wife full power of attorney for all his possessions. The government was uncertain as to what course it should take. An FBI memo said that on August 6, 1950, Assistant U.S. Attorney Myles Lane

> *informed the Department the case against Sarant was weak at this time, and that he did not intend to authorize filing a complaint unless the Department so directed. Mr. Lane also stated that he did not intend to serve Sarant with a Grand Jury subpoena since it would serve no purpose because Sarant probably would not talk against himself.*

With Sarant gone, the FBI focused on Bruce Dayton, who denied that he had ever been to the apartment at 65 Morton Street, and that he had ever known William Perl. But the superintendent of the Morton Street building, Floyd Elwyn, Jr., positively identified Dayton as the man he had seen moving furniture with Perl in January 1950. Two other members of Elwyn's family supported his identification of Dayton. And the Elwyns were not the only ones to recognize Dayton as a visitor to the Morton Street premises. On June 12, 1951, Gary Pickard, who had also attended Cornell, said that he met both Bruce Dayton and William Perl at 65 Morton Street in late January 1950.

Evidence was mounting against Dayton, not evidence to show that he was involved in espionage, but evidence that would at least substantiate a charge of perjury against him. But then Dayton made a clever strategic move, reported in an FBI memo on April 24, 1951. He retained the law firm of Paul, Weiss, Rifkind, Wharton & Garrison to represent him. One of the partners, former Federal judge Simon Rifkind, was

Judge Kaufman's closest friend and benefactor. Serious investigation of Bruce Dayton seemed to evaporate overnight, and this may have been one of the reasons.

There could have been other reasons why the investigation of Bruce Dayton was aborted, and why U.S. Attorney Myles Lane showed great reluctance to prosecute Alfred Sarant. What was worrisome to the government was the undesirable direction an investigation of Dayton and Sarant could take. Hans Bethe and Wolfgang Smyth, two of the most highly regarded atomic energy scientists in the world, were friends of Dayton and Sarant. Like most of the scientists doing important work for the government, they may not have been been morally opposed to giving the results of their studies to the Russians. Still, the U.S. government was not anxious to find out if any of them actually did pass on secrets.

It would have been very dangerous to prod more deeply. But whereas an investigation of Bruce Dayton and Alfred Sarant would have been most unwelcome, destruction of inconsequential people like Julius Rosenberg and his wife Ethel would accomplish the government's objective. It would give enough warning of what could happen in the future to any scientist who had ideas about helping the Russians.

THE COMPLETION OF ROSENBERG'S TESTIMONY

The questioning of Julius Rosenberg continued.

Mr. Saypol: Let us have a little talk about this console table. Is your best recollection that you bought that at Macy's in 1944 or 1945?

A. That is about the best I can recall, sir...

Judge Kaufman: Was it delivered, or did you take it with you?

The Witness: It was delivered. It was too big for me to take with me.

Mr. Saypol: Do you know, Mr. Rosenberg, that we have asked Macy's to find that check and they can't find it?...

The Witness: Your Honor, I have requested my attorneys to find that receipt...Now, I feel that if somebody looks through all the numbers through those years, they will find one for Julius Rosenberg, and it is worth finding if it is such an important issue...

The console, table and whether or not the Russians bought it for him to hold photographic apparatus, was an important issue. It was one of the few instances where Rosenberg could dispute his accusers and documentary evidence could establish whether he was telling the truth or not. All the other testimony presented by the prosecution witnesses came down to their word against his. Now an issue was before the Court that could be determined for its truth or falsity by factual evidence. Julius Rosenberg insisted that he purchased the console table at Macy's for approximately $21.

Mr. Saypol: Don't you know, Mr. Rosenberg, that

you couldn't buy a console table in Macy's, if they
had it, in 1944 and 1945, for less than $85?
A. I am sorry, sir. I bought that table for that
amount. That was a display piece, Mr. Saypol, and I
believe it was marked down...

In fact, it was later determined that Rosenberg
told the truth. He bought the table in 1944 for $19.97
plus tax, which amounted to approximately $21.

Mr. Saypol: Now, Mr. Rosenberg, do you remember
having testified about an incident with Ruth Green-
glass in February, 1945, when she asked you to come
to her apartment?
A. Yes.
Mr. Saypol: Will you tell me...
Mr. Phillips: Excuse me——how about the usual
morning recess?
Judge Kaufman: Is there something about this
subject that suggests a recess to you?...

Kaufman's theatrics were designed to make the
jury believe that the defense was in some manner
worried about the question posed. Rosenberg responded
to the question, explaining how Ruth Greenglass told
him back in February 1945 of her concern about her
husband's thefts of materials from the Army. He advised her to warn him to stop doing it. Irving Saypol
then questioned Rosenberg's morality by asking, "Do
you say the idea of stealing is right or wrong?" to
which Rosenberg replied, "It is wrong."

Ironically, Saypol in later years, after he had
become a New York State judge, was accused of
criminal misconduct. The charge was that in his capacity as a judge, he helped arrange for his son Roger to

obtain fees in a real estate matter that his son was not entitled to. Phony names were used to conceal his and his son's role. Saypol's political affiliations helped him survive criminal indictment, though there were tape recordings that proved he was illegally involved.

Mr. Saypol: In other words, you, knowing that at one time you had been told this man had larcenous ideas, nevertheless you went into business with him?

A. Well, Mr. Saypol, David Greenglass talked about a lot of things. He used to boast about things. I don't know if he really did a thing like that, or just talked about it.

Judge Kaufman: Well, didn't you question him before you went into business with him a little more thoroughly and before you put your money into that business to find out whether or not he had more than ideas about these things?

A. It was only mentioned to me once by his wife. I had no proof that he did anything like that. I actually didn't know whether he would carry out his thought into action...

Judge Kaufman: And the question I put to you is whether or not before you invested your money in a business with this man you did anything by way of questioning him more thoroughly concerning his ideas of stealing things from the Army?

A. No, I didn't question him at that time because I didn't know if he actually did them...

Judge Kaufman: Were you trying to protect him at that time?

A. Well, I didn't know what he was accused of, your Honor. I had a suspicion he was accused of stealing some uranium at that time.

Judge Kaufman: Well, in connection with that, were

you interested in protecting him?

A. I wasn't interested in doing him any harm at that particular point.

Judge Kaufman: Were you interested in protecting him, I asked you.

A. Well, I felt that when a man is in trouble, the one thing his family should do is stick by the man, regardless of the trouble he is in...

Judge Kaufman: You said you believed it has something to do with stealing uranium.

A. I had an idea...

Mr. Saypol: You know concerning the fact that David Greenglass had been questioned in February by an agent of the FBI regarding the theft of uranium, didn't you?

A. That is correct...

Irving Saypol not only contradicted David Greenglass's testimony; he was testifying for him. Without being sworn, Saypol was stating for the jury to hear that Greenglass had been questioned by FBI agents regarding thefts of uranium, when Greenglass had already testified that he was not questioned on this subject. Emanuel Bloch did not object, perhaps thinking that Saypol's remarks benefited the Rosenbergs.

Saypol continued questioning Rosenberg.

Mr. Saypol: Do you remember the occasion in 1950 when David Greenglass saw you and said he wanted $2,000, or a medical certificate...Did you suspect why he wanted it?

A. I suspected he was in some trouble...

Mr. Saypol: Did you suspect that he wanted to flee the country?

A. I didn't know exactly what he wanted to do but

I suspected it...

Judge Kaufman: *Did you know at that time that he probably wanted the certificate to flee from the United States?*

A. *Sir, I didn't know what he wanted to do. he wouldn't tell me what he wanted to do.*

Judge Kaufman: *What did you think?*

A. *I didn't know why he wanted the certificate.*

Judge Kaufman: *I mean, did the thought occur to you?*

A. *I didn't know what his purpose was. I tried to arrive at his purpose by questioning him.*

Judge Kaufman: *I know you say you don't know, but I am asking you, did the thought occur to you that he wanted it to flee the United States?*

A. *I didn't know; I didn't know what he wanted it for...*

Mr. Saypol: *Did you tell him the doctor said he did not want to give him a phony certificate? Is that what you told him?*

A. *I said the doctor would not give him a certificate. That is all I told him...*

Mr. Saypol: *Now, what was the experience that you had with him a few days after you reported back to him about the doctor?...*

A. *He asked me for $2000. He said I have got to get it for him...he said to me, "If you don't give me the money, you are going to be very sorry." And I saw that he was getting mad, and I was afraid that he might do me bodily harm, and I decided to cut the conversation at that point...*

Mr. Saypol: *Now in June did you tell your wife about that?*

A. *I certainly did...I said, "I don't think we should have anything to do with Davey after he tried to blackmail me like that."...*

Judge Kaufman: Blackmail you? Where did he try to blackmail you?

A. Well, he threatened me to get money. I considered it blackmailing me.

Judge Kaufman: What did he say he would do if you didn't give it to him? You said he said you would be sorry.

A. Yes. I consider it blackmail when someone says that.

Judge Kaufman: Did he say what he would do to you?

A. No, he didn't.

Judge Kaufman: Did he say he would go to the authorities and tell them you were in a conspiracy with him to steal the atomic bomb secret?

A. No.

Judge Kaufman: Do you think that was what he had in mind?

A. How could I know what he had in mind?...

Mr. Saypol: So we are now down to June 16th when the agents came to see you early in the morning, is that right?

A. That's correct...

Mr. Saypol: You said to the agents that you would cooperate with them?

A. Correct...

Mr. Saypol: Did the agents ask you on June 16, 1950 whether you had talked to Ruth before she went to New Mexico and whether you had suggested to her that she get information from David relating to the Project that was out there?

A. They asked me that question and I told them I did not say anything of the sort...

Mr. Saypol: Did the agents ask you as to whether

384

arrangements had been made for her to be contacted in Albuquerque by the Soviet agents and what means was to be used?

A. They asked me that question.

Mr. Saypol: And what did you do?

A. I told them I did not do anything of the sort, I did not make arrangements. I can't recall exactly all the questions and answers...

Mr. Saypol: Did they ask you concerning this meeting with a man in an automobile up around 42nd or 59th Street?

A. I believe they did ask me about it.

Mr. Saypol: And did you deny it?

A. I did deny it.

Mr. Saypol: And did you then ask the agents whether David had accused you of doing these things?

A. That's correct...

Mr. Saypol: Are you a member of the Communist Party today?

Mr. E. H. Bloch: I object to the question upon the ground it is incompetent, irrelevant and immaterial.

Judge Kaufman: Well, let's see.

A. I refuse to answer that question...

Judge Kaufman: You mean, on the ground that to do so will tend to incriminate you?

The Witness: That's right; will tend to incriminate me.

Mr. Saypol: Were you a member of the party in 1944 and '45?

A. I still refuse to answer the question...

Mr. Saypol: Did you, in the month of June, 1950, or in the month of May, 1950, have any passport photographs taken of yourself?

A. No, I did not.

Mr. Saypol: Did you go to a photographer's shop

at 99 Park Row and have any photographs taken of
yourself?

A. I have been in many photographers' shops and
had photos taken...

Mr. Saypol: Do you remember telling the man at
99 Park Row that you had to go to France to settle
an estate?

A. I didn't tell him anything of the sort...

Mr. Saypol: When did you find out that Sobell was
in Mexico?

A. When did I find out?

Mr. Saypol: You heard my question, didn't you?

A. Yes.

Mr. Saypol: Was it a hard one?

A. Yes, I heard that Sobell was in Mexico through
the newspapers.

Mr. Saypol: What did you have to do with sending
Sobell away?

A. Nothing.

Mr. Kuntz: I object to that, if your Honor please.
There is no testimony here that he had anything to do
with sending Sobell or anybody else away.

Judge Kaufman: You are excited, Mr. Kuntz.

Mr. Kuntz: I mean, to ask a question that way, I
can convict anybody by that kind of question.

Judge Kaufman: The jury will please disregard that
statement by Mr. Kuntz, supposedly in behalf of his
own client.

Mr. E. H. Bloch: If the Court, please—

Judge Kaufman: Your objection is overruled. Did
you have anything to do with sending Sobell away to
Mexico?

A. I certainly did not, sir.

Mr. Kuntz: That was not the question, Judge.

Judge Kaufman: All right, I...asked the question, so

the other question has gone by the board.

Mr. Phillips: But, your Honor made no ruling on the objection of Mr. Kuntz to Mr. Saypol's question.

Mr. Kuntz: I am satisfied with his answer.

Mr. Phillips: I would like to have a ruling that it was an improper question.

Mr. Kuntz: I am satisfied with it.

Judge Kaufman: Are co-counsel fighting with each other there?...Please be seated, Mr. Phillips. We have heard enough of that...

Kuntz by now was terrified of Kaufman and did not wish to challenge him in any way. It took Phillips just a little longer to learn that Kaufman was not someone to test.

Kuntz began his examination of Julius Rosenberg.

Mr. Kuntz: Mr. Rosenberg, I don't know whether this has been covered yet, but I would like to cover it. There was some testimony by Elitcher, that some time in July, 1948, he got into Sobell's car; that Sobell had a can, I think he described it, it looked as if it might have 35 millimeter film; that he went to Catherine Slip; that he left the car and that in the course of that trip he said he had to deliver that to you. Now, I want to know whether in July 1948 or any time from the beginning of the world to today did Sobell ever give you a can with any film in it?

A. No, he did not...

Mr. Kuntz: Did you ever tell Sobell anything about Bentley or anybody else who is mentioned in this trial?

A. No, sir; I did not...

Mr. E. H. Bloch: Did you ever tell Dave Greenglass that you stole a proximity fuse?

A. I never told him anything of the sort, Mr. Bloch.

Mr. E. H. Bloch: Did you ever steal a proximity fuse?

A. I did not, sir...

After Julius Rosenberg completed his testimony, John Gibbons, an employee of the *Herald Tribune* was called as a witness by Emanuel Bloch to verify a photograph of Harry Gold that appeared in the newspaper on May 24, 1950. After Gibbons testified, Thomas V. Kelly of R. H. Macy & Company was called as a witness. Kelly testified that while purchase records of the console table bought at Macy's were no longer available, there were delivery records of the transaction that could still be located.

ETHEL ROSENBERG

Ethel Rosenberg presented her testimony next. As a teen-ager she had been a good enough singer and actress to support herself on the prize money she won in talent contests. While singing and acting, she worked as a clerk for National Shipping, where on August 31, 1935, at the age of nineteen, she led 150 other women in a strike that shut down the company for a full day. Having lost her job because of union activities, she was out of work when she met Julius Rosenberg at a party given by the International Seaman's Union. She was 21; he was 18.

Ethel Rosenberg was called as a witness in her own behalf and questioned by Alexander Bloch. She testified as follows:

Mr. A. Bloch: When...were you born?

A. September 28, 1915...

Mr. A. Bloch: How many children have you?

A. I have two children.

Mr. A. Bloch: What are their ages?

A. Well, Michael was eight March 10th...And Robert will be four May 14th...

Mr. A. Bloch: Where are your children now?

A. They are at a temporary shelter in the Bronx.

Mr. A. Bloch: Have you seen them since you were arrested?

A. No, I have not...

Mr. A. Bloch: Mrs. Rosenberg, I call your attention to the testimony given by your sister-in-law Ruth, that on the occasion in November, 1944, when she was about to visit her husband in Albuquerque, she had a conference at your home, and at that conference you and your husband persuaded her against her will or inclination to enlist her husband in espionage work, and I ask you whether on that occasion you persuaded or attempted to persuade your sister-in-law to enlist her husband in espionage work?

A. I did not...

Judge Kaufman: Did you know that your brother was working on the atomic bomb project?

A. No.

Judge Kaufman: When did you find out about that for the first time?

A. Oh, when he came out of the Army.

Judge Kaufman: You mean in 1946?

A. Yes.

Judge Kaufman: Did you know that he was working on a secret project while he was in the Army?

A. Well, he told us that when he came in on furlough.

Judge Kaufman: When?

A. At my mother's house.

Judge Kaufman: In January 1945 or in November 1944?

A. I don't know the exact date of the furlough, but the first time...

Mr. A. Bloch: Tell me, did you ever know a man by the name of Yakovlev?

A. No, I never did.

Mr. A. Bloch: Did you ever know a man by the name of Golos?

A. No, sir; I never did.

Mr. A. Bloch: Did you ever know a woman named Bentley, who was on the stand here?

A. No, I never did...

Mr. A. Bloch: Did you know a man by the name of Harry Gold?

A. No, I did not.

Mr. A. Bloch: Did you know a man by the name of Fuchs, Dr. Fuchs?

A. Not until I saw his name in the newspaper.

Mr. A. Bloch: And the same thing with Gold, you never knew of him until you read about it in the newspapers?

A. That is right...

Mr. A. Bloch: Did you ever know any Russian at all?

A. No, I never did.

Judge Kaufman: You didn't know any Russian?

A. No, I didn't know any Russian...

Judge Kaufman: Well, I think her husband said he didn't know any Russians either.

In effect, Kaufman was telling the jury that just as Ethel's husband denied knowing any Russians, the judge expected the jurors to recognize that she was doing the same.

Mr. A. Bloch: Did your husband ever mention to you the fact that he was in touch with Russians?

A. No, he never mentioned any such thing.

Mr. A. Bloch: Did your husband at any time ever mention to you that he was engaged in any spying or espionage work or transmitting information received from various sources or from any source to the Russians?

A. He wasn't doing any such thing. He couldn't possibly have mentioned it to me...

Irving Saypol cross-examined.

Mr. Saypol: Did you ever go with your husband to

have any passport photographs taken?

A. No...

Mr. Saypol: Did you have any pictures taken for any purpose whatsoever in May or June 1950?

A. We may have; we may have.

Mr. Saypol: Do you remember where?

A. No, all I remember was some commercial photographer...

Judge Kaufman: How did you happen to get to that particular photographer? Who recommended that particular photographer?

A. Nobody ever recommended any particular commercial photographer to us...We happen to be what you would call "snapshot hounds,"...

Mr. Saypol: Now then, did you learn sometime in 1950 that the FBI was asking questions about Davey stealing uranium?

A. Yes, I did hear about that...I spoke of the incident to my husband, we were discussing the fact that the FBI had been to see my brother about lost uranium...

Mr. Saypol: When you heard that the FBI was questioning or had questioned him about the theft of uranium, did you say anything to your husband or did he say anything to you concerning the fact that that might have to do with the atomic bomb?

A. No, not that I can recall...

Mr. Saypol: Did it occur to you that perhaps you ought to talk to Davey about it?

A. Well, it might have occurred to me, but I felt that whatever I might have to say on the subject, whatever it might be, would fall on deaf ears by that time.

Mr. Saypol: Why?

A. Because our relationship, my husband's and my

brother's and mine, and my sister-in-law, had been slowly deteriorating...

Mr. Saypol: But in any event, there came a time when you did decide you wanted to do something to help Davey?

A. There never was a case of my having to decide that I wanted to help Davey; I had always helped Davey in the past, and I continued to feel the same way about anything involving Davey...

Mr. Saypol: Did you talk at that time about the possibility that perhaps Davey was going to implicate you in this?

A. Well, we did recall that the FBI had mentioned, had spoken to my husband in terms of my brother having implicated us, but frankly we didn't believe them...

Mr. Saypol: Now, you came before the grand jury on August 7th; do you remember that?

A. Yes, about that time.

Mr. Saypol: And everything you told the grand jury was the truth?

A. Right...

Mr. Saypol: Do you remember having been asked this question before the grand jury and giving this answer:

> Q. Did you discuss this case with your brother, David Greenglass?
> A. I refuse to answer on the ground that this might tend to incriminate me.

Was that the question asked, and did you give that answer?

A. Yes...

Mr. Saypol: How would that incriminate you, if you are innocent?

A. As long as I had any idea that there might be some chance for me to be incriminated, I had the right to use that privilege.

Ethel was simply availing herself of her constitutionally guaranteed right to remain silent. And indeed, she needed this protection, since no matter how truthful her answers might be, if they differed from a favored Government witness's, she could become the perjurer. Whatever David Greenglass could say, no matter how false, would incriminate her rather than him if it differed from what she said.

Mr. Saypol: Do you remember having been asked this question, and having given this answer:

> *Q. Do you recall a furlough visit that your brother made to New York in the late fall or first part of January, 1944, 1945?*
> *A. I decline to answer on the ground that this might tend to incriminate me...*

Judge Kaufman: You did answer that question here in court, didn't you? You did remember that furlough visit?
A. Yes.
Judge Kaufman: So that you had no objection here upon any grounds, whether it is incrimination or anything else, to answering that question?
A. That's right.
Judge Kaufman: However, before the grand jury, you did assert you privilege, did you not?
A. Yes...
Mr. Saypol: Did your lawyer tell you that you had a right to refuse to answer any and all questions before the grand jury?...

A. He advised me as to my rights, but he also advised me it was entirely up to me to decide, on the basis of what the question was, whether or not I thought any answer might incriminate me, and I so used that right...

Judge Kaufman: Has something transpired, between the time you were questioned before the grand jury and the date of this trial, which makes you feel that your answers at this time, at the trial, to those particular questions, are not incriminating, and if so, what is it?

The Witness: I am afraid I don't get that...

Judge Kaufman: I have given the witness every opportunity to explain, indeed I have sought an explanation if she could give it to me as to anything that occurred that caused this change...

Kaufman was relaying to the jurors, rhetorically, a message that assumed that there was a mutual level of impatience that had finally been reached by himself and the jurors, concerning Ethel Rosenberg's deceitful testimony, that she stubbornly would not correct though he had given her every opportunity to.

Mr. Saypol: You testified here today in response to questions from your counsel that the first time you saw Harry Gold was in this courtroom, is that so?

A. That is right...

Mr. Saypol: Do you remember being asked this question and giving this answer:

> *Q. You don't deny that you met Harry Gold?*
> *A. I...decline to answer on the ground that it might tend to incriminate me...*

Do you remember that question and answer?
A. Yes, I do...
Mr. Saypol: Was that truthful?
*A. When one uses the right of self-incrimination,
one does not mean that the answer is yes and one
does not mean that the answer is no. I made no
denial. I made no assertion that I did know him. I
simply refused to answer on the ground that that
answer might incriminate me.*

Ethel Rosenberg did not know what could be incriminating when she testified before the grand jury.
If the government had presented evidence that she
had met Harry Gold, no matter how false that evidence might have been, it would have been grounds
for a perjury indictment against her. If Gold had
decided to say he met her, her truthful answers might
well have resulted in her being charged with perjury.
During these inquisitional times, witnesses brought
before the grand jury were in such fear that they
pleaded the fifth amendment haphazardly, sometimes
without reason. Concerning Harry Gold, it had long
been established beyond question that Ethel never met
him. Both Saypol and Kaufman knew this. Nobody,
including Gold, ever said she met him, nor was it ever
charged that she did.

*Judge Kaufman: But you did answer it here in
court, isn't that true?*
A. That is right.
*Judge Kaufman: And your answer here was that you
never met him until he took the witness stand?*
A. That is correct.
*Judge Kaufman: So that you didn't assert any
privilege with respect to that here in this courtroom?*

A. No...

Mr. Saypol: Now, you came back before the grand jury on August 11th, didn't you?

A. Sometime after the first time...

Mr. Saypol: Were you asked...before the grand jury?...

> *Q. Do you know Anatoli Yakovlev?*
> *A. I decline to answer on the ground that this might tend to incriminate me.*

Were you asked that question and did you give that answer?

A. Now that you read it, I suppose they did ask me that, and I did answer that.

Mr. Saypol: And yet you had never met Yakovlev in your life?

A. That is right.

Mr. Saypol: Would you care to explain how you might be incriminated on the basis of that question and answer?

A. It is not necessary to explain the use of self-incrimination...

Judge Kaufman: I want the jury to understand...The witness has answered the question here in court, and on previous occasions had asserted privilege. As I said before, there is no inference to be drawn from the assertion of privilege against self-incrimination, but it is something the jury may weigh and consider on the question of the truthfulness of the witness and on credibility...

Kaufman seriously hurt Ethel by saying that while she could assert the privilege against self-incrimination, the jury could consider her use of the privilege as a test of her credibility. So despite the fact that she never met Gold or Yakovlev, and despite the fact that nobody ever claimed she did, the jury was left with the impression that it was up to them to decide whether she knew or did not know them. Judge Kaufman subverted the meaning and purpose of the Fifth Amendment and its civil rights guarantees.

Mr. Saypol: You profess a love for your brother, don't you?

A. You mean I once had a love for my brother.

Mr. Saypol: You mean that that has changed?

A. I would be pretty unnatural if it hadn't changed...

Mr. E. H. Bloch: Defendants Julius Rosenberg and Ethel Rosenberg rest...

BENJAMIN SCHNEIDER

Evelyn Cox, Ethel Rosenberg's maid, and Helen Pagano, O. John Rogge's secretary, then testified, after which Benjamin Schneider was called by the Government.

Mr. Saypol: When was the first time, Mr. Schneider, that you had any knowledge, any notice, any conversation with any human being regarding the fact of your being a witness here?
A. Yesterday.
Mr. Saypol: What time?
A. About 11:30.
Mr. Saypol: At that time, were you visited by some agents from the Federal Bureau of Investigation?
A. Yes, sir.
Mr. Saypol: And was it the very first time?
A. Yes, sir.
Mr. Saypol: What is your business?
A. A photographer, sir.
Mr. Saypol: Where is your place of business?
A. 99 Park Row...
Mr. Saypol: Last May or June or some time in the spring or summer, were you visited by a family consisting of a husband and wife and two children, at your place of business?...
A. Yes, sir...
Mr. Saypol: Do you see the two adults here who visited you at that time?
A. Yes.
Mr. Saypol: Will you point them out, please? Where is the man and where is the woman?
A. (Pointing) That is the man.

Mr. Saypol: You mean the man standing up?

A. Yes.

Mr. Saypol: Is that the woman (indicating defend-ant Ethel Rosenberg) standing?

A. That is the woman.

Mr. Saypol: Did they have some talk with you?

A. The man did...They ordered three dozen photo-graphs, passport size.

Mr. Saypol: Do you get an order like that every day?

A. No, I do not...

Mr. Saypol: Did they pay you?

A. Yes, they did.

Mr. Saypol: Did you take pictures of the children, too?

A. Yes.

Mr. Saypol: Passport pictures?

A. Yes, passport size.

Mr. Saypol: Did you have any conversation with the man or the woman, that you have just identified, regarding the use to which they wanted to put the photographs?

A. Yes. As he was leaving, he was telling me they were going to France; there was some property left; they were going to take care of it; the wife—that is, his wife, was left some property...

Mr. Saypol: And is that the last time you saw him before today?

A. That's right.

But as it turned out, Schneider had just committed perjury with the full knowledge of the U.S. Attorney Irving Saypol. Evidence of the fraud was revealed in *The Atom Bomb Spies*, a book written by a *New York Post* reporter, Oliver Pilat, published in 1952. Pilat, who worked closely with the prosecutor's office in researching material, without realizing how compromising the statement was, wrote:

> *While Julius was still on the stand, an FBI agent brought into the courtroom a photographer...He [the photographer] wanted to look at Rosenberg to be sure...*

When Emanuel Bloch read Pilat's book, he immediately recognized this as perjury. The photographer had taken the stand and sworn that he was seeing Rosenberg for the first time since he took the passport photos, when in fact he had seen Rosenberg the day before. Saypol had the photographer see Rosenberg first in order to be sure that he would identify him later. This came out after the trial was over and became one of the many instances of injustice that were unsuccessfully appealed to the higher courts.

Bloch continued his questioning of Schneider.

Mr. E. H. Bloch: Who was the gentleman from the Government who came in to see you yesterday? Do you see him in court?

Judge Kaufman: Look down over there...

Mr. Saypol: Will Mr. Bloch allow me to say that he is not here?

By interjecting his comment, Saypol prevented the photographer from identifying the wrong government official. If Schneider had done so, it would have cast doubt on his previous identification of Rosenberg. Saypol had so little confidence in his witness that he resorted to cheating.

Judge Kaufman: The defense rests?

401

Mr. E. H. Bloch: Defense rests.

Judge Kaufman: All right. Now I had hoped to be able to send it to the jury tomorrow...Will counsel please stay here. I will hear motions.

MOTIONS AND SUMMATIONS

Mr. E. H. Bloch: If the Court please, on behalf of the defendants, Julius and Ethel Rosenberg, they move to dismiss the indictment and for a judgment of acquittal...

Judge Kaufman: Motion denied.

Alexander Bloch with visible timidity then made his next motion, excusing himself profusely before he did.

Mr. A. Bloch: I am doing it reluctantly, but I feel it my duty to make it.

I move for a mistrial upon the ground that the frequent questioning by the Court, not intending harm, of course, of witnesses, especially of the defendants, had a tendency of unduly influencing the jury to the prejudice of the defendants and depriving them of their constitutional right to a fair and impartial trial.

Judge Kaufman: You never took an objection on that ground while I was questioning, Mr. Bloch...and there was plenty of time to take your objection at that time...I think it is purely an afterthought...

Mr. A. Bloch: Not at all. It is done in good faith.

Judge Kaufman: Well, I question it.

Mr. E. H. Bloch: May I say to the Court, as a statement of a lawyer, that we discussed this question very seriously, as to whether or not to make this specific motion at the end of the prosecution's case, and we refrained from making it, because we, ourselves, were not satisfied at that time that the motion would have had any real validity.

Judge Kaufman: Yes.

Mr. E. H. Bloch: But you can understand, your Honor—and I want to say this for the Court, and I, for one, and I think all my co-counsel feel, that you have been extremely courteous to us and you have afforded us lawyers every privilege that a lawyer should expect in a criminal case, but if our conscience would bother us, your Honor, if we didn't make this motion, I hope that your Honor will understand that it is made in the utmost good faith and without in any way trying to impugn the Court.

Judge Kaufman: Very well, the motion is denied.

Mr. A. Bloch: I may add that my statement is that it was unintentional on your part...

Both Emanuel and Alexander Bloch were so afraid of Kaufman that one must wonder whether or not they were appealing to him not to institute disbarment proceedings against them at the trial's conclusion, an eventual consequence they could not rule out. Other lawyers who had represented Communists had been so treated.

Mr. Phillips: I now make a motion on the ground that the indictment as drawn is so vague and indefinite as not to afford our defendant an opportunity to be apprised of the nature and character of the charge and of the facts underlying the charge...

Judge Kaufman: Denied. You need not labor the point...

Mr. Phillips: I tell you now that until the opening by Mr. Saypol, I was not aware that there would be [an] attempt to join our client, Morton Sobell, with anything relating to the giving away of atomic energy secrets, underlying the structure of the atom bomb...

MOTIONS AND SUMMATIONS

Emanuel Bloch presented his summation:

Mr. E. H. Bloch: May it please the Court, ladies and gentlemen of the jury...I would like to say to the Court on behalf of all defense counsel that we feel that you have treated us with the utmost courtesy, that you have extended to us the privileges that we expect as lawyers despite any disagreements we may have had with the Court on questions of law, we feel that the trial has been conducted and we hope we have contributed our share, with that dignity and that decorum that befits an American trial.

Unfortunately many of Bloch's comments exonerating and excusing the conduct of Judge Irving Kaufman and the prosecutor Irving Saypol were very damaging on appeal. The appeals court often used these concessions as the basis for denying valid legal arguments later raised concerning Kaufman's conduct.

Bloch continued the summation.

I would like to also say to the members of Mr. Saypol's staff that we are appreciative of the courtesies extended to us, and even though Mr. Saypol and I have engaged in a certain amount of repartee, it doesn't mean anything; it happens in every trial; and we feel, as we come here in the closing stages of this case, that as much has been done both by the prosecution and by the defense to present to you the respective sides of this controversy...

Here is one question for you to decide, just one: Did these defendants agree and confederate with each other and with others to transmit information relating to the national defense of the United States to the Soviet Union with that intent or reason to believe that that information so transmitted would be advantageous to the Soviet Union...

You have to determine for yourself whether or not the Greenglasses were telling the truth or whether the Rosenbergs were telling the truth...

Now, let us take Dave Greenglass...Is he a self-confessed spy? Is there any doubt in any of your minds that Dave Greenglass is a self-confessed espionage agent?...

Ruth Greenglass admitted here that she was in this conspiracy. Is there any doubt about that?...

Not only are the Greenglasses self-confessed spies, but they were mercenary spies. They spied for money...

There is a man by the name of Harry Gold...a self-confessed spy who has been sentenced to thirty years in prison, a very bright man, an intelligent man, a nervous man; remember that; a pathetic figure. But you know, hope is abandoned with him...That is why I didn't cross-examine him. I didn't ask him one question because there is no doubt in my mind that he impressed you as well as impressed everybody that he was telling the absolute truth, the absolute truth...

Emanuel Bloch's endorsement of Harry Gold's honesty was incomprehensible. He knew that Gold was a liar, making the homage he paid him an act of incompetence that damaged the Rosenbergs as well as Morton Sobell. While Bloch may have been a decent man, and while this case may have caused his untimely death, and while whatever he could have done, considering the hysteria of the times, would have resulted in failure under any circumstances, Bloch's performance as a lawyer was unacceptable. He did not test Gold's credibility, though it could have been tested, and he never tried to impeach Gold's testimony by showing his previous inconsistent statements, of which there were many.

The problem was that calling Gold a liar was tantamount to calling the government, the FBI, Saypol, and Judge Kaufman liars, and Bloch was not willing to do that. Instead he said of Gold, "I didn't ask him one question because there is no doubt in my mind that he impressed you as well as he impressed everybody that he was telling the truth." Continuing his summation, Bloch stated:

He said that he was in cahoots with a Russian, John; and that he was sent by John out to Albuquerque to see Dr. Fuchs and to see Dave Greenglass. He saw Dr. Fuchs and he saw Dave Greenglass, and he gave Greenglass $500 and he got information from Dave Greenglass.

Now, Gold, I think, we can infer was a pretty important guy in this conspiracy. Did Gold tell you that he ever met Rosenberg? Did Gold tell you that he ever spoke to Rosenberg? Did Gold tell you that he ever had any traffic or transactions with Rosenberg? He did not. He did not because he did not. Strange, isn't it? Gold, one of the top conspirators, never saw Rosenberg, never met him, never had any transactions with him...

Then Bentley testified, Miss Bentley. You know, there are ministers of the cloth who are deeply religious men, and then there are people who have intruded themselves in the religious field because it is a good thing; they are professional religionists; they make a little money on it. Bentley is a professional anti-Communist. She makes money on it. I am sure the Government doesn't pay her any money...she lectures.

This is her business; her business is testifying...

Though Emanuel Bloch had always been a civil rights lawyer so aggressive in defense of his clients that in one case he was barred from the courtroom because of his "discourtesy and contempt for the Court"; the Emanuel Bloch who represented the Rosenbergs was not the same man; he was a frightened man, who could not afford to alienate Judge Irving Kaufman or U.S. Attorney Irving Saypol. Hence his unsolicited comment that the government did not pay Elizabeth Bentley was beyond his knowledge and should not have been said.

Bloch did cry "foul," but much too late. According to an FBI report of December 11, 1952, he said that "the New York newspapers had condemned and convicted the Rosenbergs before their trial and that stories of their guilt had been fed to the papers by FBI Chief J. Edgar Hoover...and United States Attorney Irving Saypol." The FBI report also stated that on the day of the Rosenbergs' execution, Bloch said, "I am ashamed I am an American today," and at their funeral he called their execution murder.

After Bloch began speaking out, harassment of him began in earnest. An October 7, 1953, FBI memo reported:

> *Mr. Frank C. Gordon, chief attorney, Grievance Committee...stated that in view of Mr. Bloch's attacks against officers of the US Government, the Court, and his criticism of the Administration of Justice, he is most anxious to see Mr. Bloch disbarred...*
>
> *Mr. Gordon stated that he had been informed confidentially by Judge Irving Kaufman...that there was a rumor to the effect that Bloch had something to do with the*

opening of a bank account for the Committee to Defend the Rosenbergs.

Mr. Gordon further stated that Judge Kaufman had told him while discussing this matter that in connection with statements made by the Rosenbergs that were critical of the Court, it would appear that some kind of table could be drawn up which would show...that the statements contained in the press release purportedly made by the Rosenbergs were in fact made by Bloch.

An interoffice FBI letter declared:

It is believed that if the Bar Association could be successful in pressing charges against Bloch it will be an example to the legal profession, and lawyers who espouse the Communist line will not in the future be able with impunity to make unfounded attacks against the Director...and other responsible public offi- cers, as well as the courts of the United States.

Bloch died on or about February 1, 1954, approximately eight months after the Rosenbergs were executed. *L'Humanité* reported on February 6 that while he lay dead in his apartment in New York City, the FBI ransacked it under the pretext of searching for "valuables." At the trial, Bloch's summation continued:

Now I want to come to Elitcher. Elitcher is a pathetic character...

Take this fact into consideration...here is a man who claims he was wooed for four years and saw Rosenberg and Sobell at different times and didn't give them one solitary piece of information...

After Emanuel Bloch completed his summation for Julius and Ethel Rosenberg, Edward Kuntz presented his for his client Morton Sobell.

Mr. Kuntz: Now...I am not going to be charitable like Manny Bloch. I have tried cases a little longer than he has. I am through being charitable when the life of a man depends on my actions and my words...But I am not going to be as charitable as Manny Bloch with this Elitcher.

Why should I be charitable? When I cross-examined him, I asked him, "Elitcher, aren't you a liar?" and he said, "Yes."

"Aren't you a perjurer?" He said, "Yes."

How could I be charitable with a liar and perjurer?...

Elitcher was not a psychotic liar; he was a miserable liar, a man who will involve, who will kill another man to save his own miserable skin...

And I am going to point my finger at this man (indicating Mr. Saypol)...He happens to be a lawyer with a government job now...And what I see what is going on with some of our government officials, please excuse me if I don't put a halo around him...I have been living in this country too long to see what is going on...

And listen to this question, listen to it and tell me if this is poison or it isn't poison, if a man's life hangs on this or it doesn't. Just listen. This is a question asked of Elitcher:..."In the time that you worked with Sobell at Reeves Instrument Company...did you ever see Sobell take any papers or documents?"...

Now, let us see what the answer is. This is Elitcher's answer, not mine: "Well, in the course of his duties I did, as far as I know, I saw him take—he had a briefcase and he did take things out of Reeves Instrument...he did have a briefcase and he took mate-

rial out, but what it was, or what the material was, I do not know." And that is his answer.

Is that poison or isn't it?

Is that a poisonous question by Saypol, the man who is working for us, for me? Yes, for me.

I don't like that kind of stuff. I want to tell you that I am more concerned with the safety of our country than he is, because I tell you, ladies and gentlemen, you injure the liberty or life of one citizen and you wipe the foundation out of our country. We don't do things like that. We don't like them done. I don't like them done.

Of course he took documents. The man had an important job; going out to Roosevelt Air Field. His job was communication, as Elitcher said...

Is there one single solitary word that Sobell was involved with atom bomb secrets or the atom bomb dealings? Is there? Did Greenglass mention him?...

I don't care why he went to Tampico under an assumed name, and I don't care why he went to Vera Cruz. It is none of our business.

To get some idea of what Morton Sobell would have testified to had he known that he could not rely on his presumption of innocence and other constitutional guarantees, we can turn to an affidavit he presented to the Court of Appeals on September 23, 1953, more than two years after he was sentenced. It read, in part:

> I wanted to testify on my own behalf at my trial. I did not do so because my trial attorneys insisted that I should not, because (1) of the fact that the case that the prosecution had put in against me was so weak that my innocence was clearly established; and

411

(2) that it was so clear that I had nothing to do with any atomic espionage conspiracy...I now know I should have insisted on telling my story.

I am completely innocent of the charges made against me. The fantastic tale Max Elitcher told about a wild midnight ride to Julius Rosenberg's apartment is untrue, and I had thought this to be plain, particularly since he admitted at the trial that he did not concoct it until after several interviews with FBI agents...

The only other testimony concerning me at the trial related to a trip to Mexico which I made with my family, which had nothing to do with espionage, and which only after the trial did I realize was given significance by court and jury out of all proportion to what the facts actually showed. It was only after the trial that I realized how this testimony was misconstrued and misused, and to make the record clear, I want to tell the whole story now.

My wife, daughter, infant son and I left New York in late June, 1950 for Mexico City. This was no suddenly developed plan...we had been planning and dreaming of such a trip for several years...

Although we naturally made no public announcement of our plans, there was no secret about it either. I wrote my employer for an indefinite leave of absence, applied for and obtained necessary visas from the Mexican consul in New York (which the prosecution must have known but denied to the Court), and bought round-trip tickets at the American Airlines ticket office...

There was one aspect to the trip, however, which differentiated it from a routine vacation. I was not alone, in mid-1950, in having become apprehensive over signs of political intimidation and repression in this country...Although a scientist, I was not oblivious to political developments, and in fact, in common with many other scientists,

412

saw a danger to my future in the oppressive
atmosphere in which we had to work...All this,
coupled with my dissatisfaction with my job
anyway, and the fact that we had saved up
some money meant that when we left, we just
didn't know whether we would come back or
not...

Then, in the midst of our uncertainties, the
newspapers suddenly published the news of
Julius Rosenberg's arrest as an alleged
"atom-spy." To me, the charge was absurd...I
felt that he was being persecuted for political
reasons and that the charge was calculated to
intimidate and silence political dissent in the
United States...But this led me to make the
mistake of feeling that a dictatorship was
already taking over my country.

Then, and only then, was it that I left the
family in the Mexico City apartment and
traveled around Mexico—to Vera Cruz and
Tampico—even using false names, and inquiring
about passage to Europe or South America for
all of us...

I went back to Mexico City, and my wife
and I talked it over once again. We realized
that our ties to home were too strong...

So my wife and I decided to come back to
New York...We made plans for our return.
There is tangible, documentary proof of this,
too, for we then secured vaccinations in
Mexico City—which we had not needed to get
there, but which we did need to return to the
United States.

But then came the unheard-of attack which
deprived us of the chance to return
voluntarily. My apartment was invaded by
armed men who represented themselves as
Mexican police...The United States Attorney at
my trial as much as admitted that the FBI had
engineered the whole affair. I cannot
understand to this day, how this lawless act,
apparently calculated to prevent me from
returning voluntarily—for I was never informed
of so much as even that I was wanted for
questioning—has remained unrebuked.

413

To return to the trial, Kuntz concluded his summation for Sobell, and Irving Saypol then gave the Government's summation.

Mr. Saypol: You will remember that one of the defendants made blanket negatives, blanket answers, in denial as to whether she knew Harry Gold, as to whether she had ever talked to David Greenglass about his work at Los Alamos, as to whether she or her husband ever talked about atomic bombs, and yet I showed you that in the grand jury, on the advice of her counsel, she refused to answer those questions on the ground that to answer them would be self-incriminating...

Saypol thus implied that Ethel Rosenberg knew Harry Gold even though Gold had said he didn't know her, and even though there had been no allegation that she knew him. The way the trial was conducted, the mood of the times, and especially Judge Kaufman's conduct could easily have left the jury with the impression that Ethel Rosenberg knew Harry Gold. Saypol's effort to connect Ethel with Gold during trial and in his summation was a legal impropriety so severe that standing alone it should have called for reversal of her conviction and the institution of disciplinary proceedings against Saypol.

Saypol continued:

Rosenberg's Communist espionage superior in the early 1940s was Jacob Golos, a member of the Communist Control Commission in this country, one of the top Soviet espionage agents. During the time prior to Golos's death, when Golos was Rosenberg's Communist

espionage superior, Rosenberg became known to Eliza-
beth Bentley, who had gone from membership in the
Communist Party to a position of importance in Go-
los's espionage apparatus...

We know of Golos's clandestine meeting in which
he received information from Julius, the engineer who
lived in Knickerbocker Village. We know this from the
telephone calls Miss Bentley received from this engi-
neer, from Knickerbocker Village, Julius, as an inter-
mediary, arranging clandestine meetings between Julius
and Golos, his Communist espionage superior. But most
important of all, we know of Rosenberg's dealings
with Bentley from statements made by Rosenberg
himself to Max Elitcher and David Greenglass.

We know of these other henchmen of Rosenberg in
this plot by him, by Sobell, by the Soviet Union and
its representatives and by other traitorous Americans
to deliver the safeguards to our security into the
hands of a power that would wipe us off the face of
the earth and destroy its peace.

We don't know all the details, because the only
living people who can supply the details are the de-
fendants. Rosenberg and his wife have added the su-
preme touch to their betrayal of this country by tak-
ing the stand before you, by taking advantage of
every legal opportunity that is afforded defendants,
and then, by lying and lying and lying here, brazenly,
in an attempt to deceive you, to lie their way out of
what they did.

I have said that there is much about this that we
have not disclosed...

With this statement Saypol used the same method
employed by the French military to persuade the appellate courts of France to deny Captain Dreyfus's

appeals. Information that the military claimed was too sensitive to be made public (and that was later found to be false) led the French magistrates to deny Dreyfus's appeals lest their own loyalty be questioned. Now in the Rosenberg trial, the prosecutor was implying to the jury that there was so much more evidence against the Rosenbergs that could not be revealed for security reasons.

Saypol continued:

We know that Julius Rosenberg and Ethel Rosenberg infected Ruth and David Greenglass with the poison of Communist ideology. We know that Julius Rosenberg and Ethel Rosenberg were engaged in a continuing campaign to enlist recruits for the Soviet cause through the Communist Party. And we know that in 1944, Julius and Ethel Rosenberg carried their campaign one step further and persuaded David Greenglass to steal atomic bomb secrets for the Rosenbergs to be turned over to the Soviet Union...

The difference between the Greenglasses and the Rosenbergs? The Greenglasses have told the truth. They have tried to make amends for the hurt which has been done to our nation and to the world...

The veracity of David and Ruth Greenglass and of Harry Gold is established by documentary evidence and cannot be contradicted...

Saypol claimed that the Rosenbergs stole the secret of the atom bomb and Ethel typed it up. He characterized ordinary photographs of the Rosenbergs as passport pictures to suggest that they were planning flight to avoid prosecution. With Kaufman's approval, he related information about Julius Rosenberg for the jury to hear that was not supported by the evidence. He gave an indisputably false account of Rosenberg's activities with Jacob Golos. Saypol also called Ann Sidorovich an "espionage courier" and "Soviet agent" when there was no evidence to justify his slanders.

Saypol continued:

You heard the Rosenbergs testify...You heard them tell about the $21 console table...How strange, on the one hand, the testimony from the Greenglasses that that was a present from the Soviets, the testimony from the Rosenbergs that they paid $21 for it in 1944 and 1945, when furniture was scarce, at Macy's;...

What is the evidence of Sobell's participation here? The evidence is that Sobell had been an associate of Rosenberg since City College days. They were joined by the common bond of communism and devotion to the Soviet Union. The evidence is that Sobell acted with Rosenberg in this conspiracy to commit espionage for the Soviet Union by delivering material to Rosenberg and by fulfilling Rosenberg's orders to recruit Max Elitcher and others into this Soviet espionage ring...

From beginning to end, Saypol's summation was predicated upon fraud. He knew that the testimony of David Greenglass and Harry Gold was perjured. He and Roy Cohn, with the help of Judge Irving Kaufman, manufactured the entire case against the Rosenbergs. When he was first arrested and for weeks after, Gold did not even know what he was supposed to testify to. His statements were supplied to him during the unfolding months. In order to convict the Rosenbergs, Harry Gold and David Greenglass's testimonies had to be made to conform. That is why they were lodged

417

together in jail and kept together for months.

Julius Rosenberg passionately denounced these government tactics two weeks before his execution, when he scolded James V. Bennett, the director of the Federal Bureau of Prisons: "You yourself, Mr. Bennett...know that Greenglass and Gold were together in the tombs for nine months, discussing the case, studying notes from a big, loose-leaf book, rehearsing testimony, talking to FBI agents, the prosecution and their attorney." Indeed, Assistant U.S. Attorney Roy Cohn coached Greenglass personally for months.

Judge Kaufman then addressed the jury.

The defendants are accused of having conspired to commit espionage. Espionage, reduced to essentials, means spying on the United States to aid a foreign power. Because of the development of highly destructive weapons and their highly guarded possession by nations existing in a state of tension with one another, the enforcement of the espionage laws takes on a new significance. Our national well-being requires that we guard against spying on the secrets of our defense, whether such spying is carried on through agents of foreign powers or through our own nationals who prefer to help a foreign power.

This does not mean that the mere allegation or use of the word "espionage" should justify convicting innocent persons; however, irrational sympathies must not shield proven traitors...

I believe it is my duty as a Judge to help you crystallize in your minds the respective contentions and evidence in the case, and I shall therefore review briefly these contentions of the prosecution and of the defendants.

MOTIONS AND SUMMATIONS

The prosecution claims that the defendants on trial conspired together with each other...and with others, such as Anatoli A. Yakovlev, David Greenglass, Ruth Greenglass, and Harry Gold, to communicate, deliver and transmit to the Union of Soviet Socialist Republics, and representatives and agents thereof, documents and information relating to the national defense of the United States, with intent and reason to believe that it would be used to the advantage of the Union of Soviet Socialist Republics...that the representative of the Union of Soviet Socialist Republics for the purpose of receiving the secret information was Anatoli A. Yakovlev, who was a Vice-Consul for the Union of Soviet Socialist Republics at its legation in New York City and who left the country in December, 1946...

The prosecution further claims...that Harry Gold as courier collected the information regarding the atomic bomb from various persons in this country, including Dr. Klaus Fuchs and David Greenglass; that David and Ruth Greenglass were drawn into this conspiracy by Julius and Ethel Rosenberg's urgings...They further contend that secret information regarding the atom bomb project was transmitted by the Greenglasses to Julius Rosenberg; that the information was typed from written reports by Ethel Rosenberg, microfilmed by Julius Rosenberg, and then transmitted to the Russians...

Judge Kaufman reviewed the government's contentions, focusing on the evidence the prosecution presented of David Greenglass's introduction by Julius Rosenberg to a Russian; Harry Gold's identifying himself to David Greenglass by saying, "I come from Julius"; the gifts the Rosenbergs received from the Russians; Morton Sobell's flight; and the Rosenbergs'

419

attempts to persuade the Greenglasses to flee the country. Kaufman continued:

The Government contends that you have a right to infer that there existed a link between Julius Rosenberg and Yakovlev in that Julius Rosenberg in some way transmitted the recognition signal, that is, the Jello box-side to Yakovlev...

It is contended by the Government that the defendants intended to benefit Russia and that their membership in the Communist Party and adherence to its principles showed a preference for the Soviet form of government...

Now, on the other hand, the defendants' version of this case is as different as night is from day. The two versions are not reconcilable. You must determine which one you will believe. The defendants Julius and Ethel Rosenberg categorically deny that they or any of them ever conspired among themselves or with anyone else to obtain secret information pertaining to the national defense of the United States, intending to transmit the information to the Union of Soviet Socialist Republics...

Counsel for Sobell contend that Sobell was not a member of the conspiracy, that Elitcher is a perjurer who should not be believed, and that the Government has failed to prove Sobell guilty beyond a reasonable doubt as required...

No matter how careful a judge may be to avoid it, there is always the possibility that the jury or some particular juror may get an impression that the judge has some opinion with reference to the guilt or innocence of the defendants, or that he thinks that some particular phase of the case is more important than another, or that some particular witness is more credible than another or that a certain inference of fact should or should not be made and so on. If you have formed any such impression, you must put it out of your mind and utterly disregard it. Nothing I have said during the trial nor in these instructions was intended to give any such impression...

Many commentators who have studied the trial have accepted these self-serving statements as confirmation that Judge Kaufman did conduct a fair trial with no bias toward either side.

Kaufman went on to say:

I charge you further that no inference is to be drawn against any defendant who has exercised his or her constitutional privilege against testifying as to any matters which may tend to incriminate him or her.

The defendant Ethel Rosenberg was cross-examined concerning her refusal to answer certain questions when she appeared before the Grand Jury on the ground that the answers might tend to incriminate her. Her failure to answer such questions is not to be taken as establishing the answers to any questions she was asked before the Grand Jury, but may be considered by you in determining the credibility of her answers to those same questions at this trial...

Kaufman thus exploited Ethel Rosenberg's use of her fifth amendment right, twisting it to imply her lack of credibility. He turned the Fifth Amendment into an offensive weapon instead of a means of guarding civil rights.

His telling the jury that no inference be drawn by them as to the guilt of innocence of the defendants for their having invoked the Fifth Amendment was stated by him in such a manner as to leave the jurors with the message that what he said was merely ritually necessary, a technical requirement, but that he expected them to penalize the Rosenbergs for invoking the Fifth Amendment. Judge Kaufman completed his instructions to the jury, and the jurors retired. Later in the evening Kaufman announced:

One of the members of the jury would like to hear Mrs. Ruth Greenglass' testimony, starting with first approach that Rosenberg made to her regarding securing of information for Russia...

Mr. A. Bloch: I think that covers quite a bit. It goes to conversation before she went out West; conversation she had with her husband out West, and also cross-examination on that point...

Mr. Saypol: I don't think they have asked for any cross.

Judge Kaufman: They haven't asked for the cross...I am not going to read the cross to them unless they request it.

Mr. A. Bloch: Well, I think when they ask for testimony, it means all the testimony on the subject...

Judge Kaufman: The jury is intelligent. If that is what they want, they will ask for it.

Mr. A. Bloch: They might not think there is any other testimony on the subject.

Judge Kaufman: I am going to handle it that way.

Mr. Phillips: Two testimonies go together. They didn't ask for the pages; they asked for the testimony...

Judge Kaufman: Very well, the jury may retire.

Mr. E. H. Bloch: If the Court please, I make the request that the stenographer also read the cross-examination of Ruth Greenglass on this specific point—

Judge Kaufman: Your request is denied. That has not been requested by the jury. The jury will retire. We will give the jury exactly what they request...

Kaufman more than stated to the jurors that they did not ask to read the cross-examination testimony of Ruth Greenglass; he instructed the jurors by the obvious tone of his directions that he did not want them to read it and expected a verdict of guilty from them.

VERDICT AND SENTENCE

At 11:01 A.M. on March 29, 1951, the jury brought in their verdict—guilty. Then Kaufman addressed them:

My own opinion is that your verdict is a correct verdict, and what I was particularly pleased about was the time which you took to deliberate in this case. I must say that as an individual I cannot be happy because it is a sad day for America. The thought that citizens of our country would lend themselves to the destruction of their own country by the most destructive weapon known to man is so shocking that I can't find words to describe this loathsome offense.

I want to say to defense counsel that I appreciate the courtesy that they extended to the Court during the course of this trial. I think they demeaned themselves as attorneys should.

To you, Mr. Saypol, Mr. Lane, Mr. Cohn, Mr. Kilsheimer, Mr. Branigan who isn't here, I want to congratulate you all upon your capable and fair presentation of this case, that your preparation was painstaking. And to the FBI, to Mr. Norton and to Mr. Harrington whom I never knew until this case began, I observed them in this court, in the tradition of the FBI, perfect gentlemen at all times, fair and decent.

Again, I say a great tribute is due to the FBI and Mr. Hoover for the splendid job that they have done in this case...

The jury's verdict is a ringing answer of our democratic society to those who would destroy it. First, because a full, fair, open and complete trial—in sound American tradition—was given to a group of people who represented perhaps the sharpest secret

eyes of our enemies. They were given every opportuni-
ty, as you the jury know, to present every defense
and, as I said for myself and my colleagues in my
summation, I would fight at all times for their right
to defend themselves freely and vigorously.

Secondly, your verdict is a warning that our demo-
cratic society, while maintaining its freedom, can
nevertheless fight back against treasonable activities...

Next Saypol made his statement:

I want to pay tribute to my staff and the men
who prepared this case and presented it, for the cred-
it is due entirely to them: to Mr. Lane, my chief as-
sistant; to Mr. Cohn, my confidential assistant; to Mr.
Kilsheimer and to Mr. Branigan.

I have had many occasions, like the Judge has, to
express my admiration for the work of the men and
women of the Federal Bureau of Investigation. It can
only be expressed in superlatives. It is not a police
force; it is an investigative agency. Its vigilance is
all-pervading, untiring, ceaseless—what is more, com-
pletely willing...

Privately the FBI did not feel the same about Irving Saypol or his assistant Roy Cohn. In particular,
FBI agents fretted about leaks of information that
were reaching the press, as in the case of William
Perl. One interoffice memo dated July 20, 1950, reported Agent Edward Scheidt as saying he "does not
know who is giving the information but he strongly
suspects that it came from Saypol's office." On March
13, 1951, August Belmont, a high-ranking agent, wrote
to Hoover's assistant, Milton Ladd: "In view of the
possibly questionable ethical tactics employed by Cohn

in endeavoring to secure a confession from Perl, it is believed undesirable for the Bureau to become a party to this act by participating in the arrest of Perl." The reply from Hoover's office was that while there was sympathy for Belmont's position, the case must move forward.

The day's proceeding ended with Bloch nervously addressing Judge Kaufman.

Mr. E. H. Bloch: If the Court please, I was going to refrain from making any comment. I am going to be very brief. I would like to restate what I said when I opened to the jury. I want to extend my appreciation to the Court for its courtesies, and again I repeat I want to extend my appreciation for the courtesies extended to me by Mr. Saypol and the members of his staff, as well as the members of the FBI, and I would like to say to the jury that a lawyer does not always win a case; all that a lawyer expects is a jury to decide a case on the evidence with mature deliberation...

On April 5, 1951, the day of sentencing for Julius and Ethel Rosenberg and Morton Sobell, Harold Phillips addressed the court.

Mr. Phillips: In the thing that I am about to reveal, if your Honor please, there is much that is not beautiful, much that is not creditable to the law enforcement agencies of the United States of America, and I loving my country more than anything else feel that in revealing those circumstances I might injure my country in the eyes of the world, but I am powerless to stop and not to say what I must say...

Now, your Honor please, if I am able to show that

those words "Deported from Mexico" are a downright falsehood, I need not show that the law enforcement agencies, the Federal Bureau of Investigation knew about that because they must have known about that.

Judge Kaufman: Well, you had your opportunity at the trial to show it, didn't you?...He had an opportunity at the trial to take the stand, did he not?

While Sobell had an opportunity to take the stand, he also had a right not to. Sobell should not have been forced to take the stand simply because false testimony was presented against him, especially when he was given no notice of the false documents he was to be faced with.

Mr. Phillips: I say again—

Judge Kaufman: Isn't this a roundabout way to deny allegations?...

Mr. Phillips: I assure you. I might say, however, before I reach that point, that what we did not do or what we overlooked to do will not excuse our Government in the brutal assault on a man and kidnaping a man and abducting an American citizen, born in this country, contrary to the statute and contrary to the laws...

Judge Kaufman: But you did not see fit, nor did your client see fit, at the trial to make an issue of it.

Mr. Phillips: I did not expect that the Government would introduce a card which is a falsehood on its face. I did not expect that they would introduce a false statement in order to bolster up a theory of flight...

Mr. Saypol: I feel that there is something I should say to complete the record. I submit to your Honor that the verity of what counsel has argued is as feigned as Sobell's defense...

Judge Kaufman: I think I have enough...

Judge Kaufman then addressed the defendants Julius and Ethel Rosenberg.

I consider your crime worse than murder. Plain deliberate contemplated murder is dwarfed in magnitude by comparison with the crime you have committed. In committing the act of murder, the criminal kills only his victim. The immediate family is brought to grief and when justice is meted out, the chapter is closed. But in your case, I believe your conduct in putting into the hands of the Russians the A-bomb years before our best scientists predicted Russia would perfect the bomb has already caused, in my opinion, the Communist aggression in Korea, with the resultant casualties exceeding 50,000, and who knows but that millions more of innocent people may pay the price of your treason...

What I am about to say is not easy for me. I have deliberated for hours, days and nights. I have carefully weighed the evidence. Every nerve, every fiber of my body has been taxed. I am just as human as are the people who have given me the power to impose sentence. I am convinced beyond any doubt of your guilt. I have searched the records—I have searched my conscience—to find some reason for mercy—for it is only human to be merciful and it is natural to try to spare lives. I am convinced, however, that I would violate the solemn and sacred trust that the people of this land have placed in my hands were I to show leniency to the defendants Rosenberg.

It is not in my power, Julius and Ethel Rosenberg,

to forgive you. Only the Lord can find mercy for what you have done.

The sentence of the Court upon Julius and Ethel Rosenberg is, for the crime for which you have been convicted, you are hereby sentenced to the punishment of death, and it is ordered upon some day within the week beginning with Monday, May 21st, you shall be executed according to law...

Directing his comments to Morton Sobell, Judge Kaufman then said:

While I have not the slightest sympathy for you or any of your associates, as a judge, I must be objective in the examination of the evidence in this case. I do not for a moment doubt that you were engaged in espionage activities; however, the evidence in the case did not point to any activity on your part in connection with the atom bomb project. I cannot be moved by hysteria or motivated by a desire to do the popular thing. I must do justice according to the evidence in this case. There isn't any doubt about your guilt, but I must recognize the lesser degree of your implication in this offense.

I, therefore, sentence you to the maximum prison term provided by statute, to wit, thirty years.

While it may be gratuitous on my part, I at this point note my recommendation against parole.

The Court will stand adjourned.

CREDIT FOR THE SENTENCING

It seemed as if Judge Irving Kaufman would get full and exclusive credit for the execution of the Rosenbergs. The FBI reports, however, reveal that there were others who also recommended the executions, including Irving Saypol, Roy Cohn, and Judge Edward Weinfeld. An FBI report of April 3, 1951, noted that before the sentencing Kaufman had consulted Judge Weinfeld, seeking his advice.

> *Judge Weinfeld was of the opinion that the Rosenbergs and Sobell should be given the death penalty.*

Some sixteen years later Judge Weinfeld would agree to hear, and would then deny a petition for release from prison brought by Morton Sobell. At no time did Weinfeld reveal to Sobell or his attorneys that he held strong preconceived opinions on the case. The April 3 FBI report also stated:

> *Mr. Cohn told Judge Kaufman that he would recommend the death penalty for all three, but he also thought it might be a good idea if Julius Rosenberg and Sobell were given the death penalty while Mrs. Rosenberg was given a sentence of, say, 30 years, with the thought in mind that she might decide to inform the government authorities concerning espionage activities so that other individuals involved in such activities may also be prosecuted.*

On March 13, 1975, twenty-two years after the Rosenbergs were executed, Irving Saypol vigorously claimed credit for their sentencing. He was disturbed by an article written by Alan Weinstein, entitled

430

"Opening the FBI Files"—so disturbed that he wrote to the FBI director, Clarence M. Kelly, protesting Weinstein's comment "that prosecutors in the Rosenberg case originally opposed asking for the death penalty but were overruled by Truman Administration officials in Washington." Saypol wrote:

I was never overruled by anybody. No one in Justice or out ever directed me, let alone overruled me on the matter of recommendation of sentence...

On the matter of the Rosenberg sentences, I had decided to make the recommendations which later were imposed. I made no recommendation at sentence at the direction of the sentencing judge...The day before sentence he asked for my views. I gave them and he inquired regarding the views of the Department of Justice. I had not solicited any. He asked me to seek these. I flew to Washington, met with the late Deputy Attorney General Peyton Ford and the late Assistant Attorney General in charge of the Criminal Division, James McInerney. They conveyed the views of your predecessor J. Edgar Hoover. There were differences all around among them, but capital punishment for one or both was in not out...I was then asked by the judge to refrain from making any recommendation for punishment...

O. John Rogge, while not seeking credit for the execution, wanted credit for the conviction. According to an FBI report, Rogge claimed that "he had been responsible for breaking the Rosenberg case in that he had succeeded in getting Greenglass to disclose to the Federal Bureau of Investigation his participation in the Rosenberg case...and he felt that he had contributed largely to the conviction of the Rosenbergs and Sobell."

The person most responsible, however, for the

sentencing and execution of the Rosenbergs may well have been William Denton, counsel for the Atomic Energy Commission. It appears that Denton and the AEC had a great deal of control over the prosecution of the case. Indeed, as reported by the FBI on March 1, 1951, Denton theatened that if the prosecution of the Rosenbergs was not conducted in a manner satisfactory to the AEC, "they might go so far as to take this entire matter up with the President in an effort to force the Department to send a Special Adviser from the Department of Justice to participate in this trial and see that the interests of the AEC are adequately and completely protected." The fact that the AEC and William Denton insisted on the death penalty as a prerequisite to their cooperation and could in fact enforce their wishes placed them in the position of greatest control. The March 1 FBI memo stated that the Atomic Energy Commission's decision

> to declassify this material was based on assurances given to them both by [Myles] Lane and the Department in Washington that the death penalty would be requested at the completion of the trial.

On April 6, 1951, the sentencing of David Greenglass was before Judge Kaufman. Having kept his promise to make no recommendation on the day the Rosenberg's were sentenced, since it was now the next day, Saypol felt released from his restraint, and wanted his participation in the sentencing recorded for history. Saypol addressed the court.

> Mr. Saypol: I say with all humility that the sentences imposed yesterday are substantially in accord with my views as I would have expressed them if the

Court had accepted my offer to do so at the conclusion of my presentation...

There now is presented the question of punishment as to David Greenglass...I recommend that the defendant be imprisoned for a term of 15 years.

Saypol's comments and recommendations were followed by Greenglass's attorney O. John Rogge's plea for leniency in behalf of his client.

Mr. Rogge: May it please the Court...I want to call your Honor's attention to the fact that David's fuzzy thinking occurred at a time when Russia was a war-time ally, and many other people among us were engaged in fuzzy thinking about the Soviet Union at that time. As a matter of fact, it continued for most of us until 1948. The thinking was different at that time...

Judge Kaufman: I want to make sure that I understand you. You are not condoning, are you, you are not condoning...

Mr. Rogge: I am saying that there was an atmosphere at that time. General MacArthur, in one of those years, he sent a telegram, and it was a warm telegram, it was an expansive telegram, of congratulations to the Red Army.

Judge Learned Hand was a member of the National Council of American-Soviet Friendship.

President Roosevelt made many speeches, praising the Russians.

Borough President Lyons, up in the Bronx, believe it or not, declared a "Red Army Day."...

Judge Kaufman: Well, let's get one thing clear. Russia didn't come to our aid in this war. We came to Russia's aid.

Mr. Rogge: That is quite true, Judge, but the point I am making is this: That many people far wiser than David Greenglass spoke in terms of aid and admiration for the Russians...

Now, with this background, what I do want to emphasize is that David did cooperate with the Government and almost from the outset. It took courage on David's part to confess his mistake, but he did and he did it fully. He even elaborated on it. I don't have to emphasize the point of David's courage, because your Honor observed him here in the courtroom and I think your Honor is aware of it...

You have here an individual who is wholly without malice, if your Honor please. I mean, you have someone——I know that he not only gave blood during the second World War, but I see he has an emblem on his coat today that he gave blood recently. I mean, this is the kind of man you have, a well-intentioned person, without malice, who didn't think too clearly, who came up under rather rough circumstances...

Judge Kaufman then addressed David Greenglass, saying to him:

You, like so many other foolish men and women, believed that Soviet Russia was Utopia. You learned that when you enlisted in what you believed was a cause for the liberation of men, you were in effect enlisting in the Russian Foreign Legion.

However, David Greenglass, you found your way back before the curtain fell on your life. You repented and you brought to justice those who enlisted you in this cause.

Justice does not seek vengeance. Justice seeks justice, but you deserve punishment, punishment which balances the gravity of your offense as against your aid.

I want you to know that I have given deep consideration to your case, with full recognition of the aid which you have given the Government, fully cognizant of the gravity of this offense.

It is the judgment of this Court that I shall follow the recommendation of the Government, and sentence you to 15 years in prison...

APPEALS

The sentences meted out by Judge Irving Kaufman were followed by numerous appeals. Much verbiage has been produced by students of the law concerning the worthiness of the arguments before the higher courts and the wisdom of their decisions. Deep thought has been given to interpretations of this or that judge's decision and the meaning of this or that statute. It was a waste. A climate of hysteria affects judges of the higher courts no less than anyone else. The decisions were for the most part thoughtless and unworthy of extended analysis.

It is not pleasant to review Judge Jerome Frank and the Federal appellate courts' reasoning concerning the sixteen points the Rosenbergs' attorneys brought before them. It seems obvious that politics came first, the well-being of Judge Kaufman second, and the justice of the case last.

On presenting the decision of the Circuit Court of Appeals February 25, 1952, Judge Frank's remarks were prefaced by the usual preamble of expiation:

> *Since two of the defendants must be put to death if the judgments stand, it goes without saying that we have scrutinized the record with extraordinary care to see whether it contains any of the errors asserted on this appeal.*

Frank then went on to discuss the issues raised. Here are some points as they were analyzed by him.

> *Defendants...tell us that the trial judge behaved himself so improperly as to deprive them of a fair trial.*

Frank and the Court of Appeals found nothing wrong with Judge Kaufman's behavior. Frank concluded, "We think the judge stayed well inside the discretion allowed him." Citing the Rosenbergs' lawyers to justify the court's decision, Frank pointed out that Bloch himself

> *said that the judge's alleged fault had been "inadvertent,"...that the judge had "been extremely courteous to us and afforded us lawyers every privilege that a lawyer should expect in a criminal case [and] that the trial has been conducted with that dignity and that decorum that befits an American trial."*

Judge Frank's reliance on Bloch's summary remarks, rather than on a fair reading of the trial transcript, was as senseless as it would have been to base the court's decision on Bloch's statements that his clients were innocent. Frank also reviewed instances of Judge Kaufman's bad conduct and simply concluded that they were not bad enough, as he said:

> *The judge is the only disinterested lawyer connected with the proceeding. He has no interest except to see that justice is done, and he has no more important duty than to see that the facts are properly developed and that their bearing upon the question at issue are clearly understood by the jury. If some of his questions and comments indicated his opinion of the merits of counsel's attack or of the witnesses' testimony, it cannot be said that he committed reversible error, since unlike judges in many of our state courts, a federal judge may comment outright on any portion of the evidence, telling the jury how it struck him, whom he believed,...and the like, provided only that he advises the jury that they are in no way bound by his expressions of such views...*

Judge Frank would never have conducted himself as Kaufman did. Few judges would. To think that Frank believed, or any court could believe, that a judge could go through a trial the way Kaufman did and then cure everything by advising the jury that "they are in no way bound by his expressions," is unrealistic.

Moving to another point, the question of whether Communist Party membership was improperly utilized by the prosecution during the trial, Frank wrote:

> *The government had to prove that the Communist Party was tied to Soviet causes in order to make membership in it meaningful as evidence of motive or intent to aid Russia...To that end, the government put Elizabeth Bentley on the stand. She testified that the American Communist Party was part of, and subject to, the Communist International; that the Party received orders from Russia to propagandize, spy and sabotage; and that Party members were bound to go along with those orders under threat of expulsion. If the jury believed her, she supplied the missing link connecting the Communist Party with the Soviet Union, and making Communist Party membership probative of motive or intent to aid Russia...*
>
> *Whether and how much of that kind of evidence should come into a trial like this is a matter for carefully-exercised judicial discretion. We think the trial judge here did not abuse that discretion. Each time Party membership was alluded to, and again in his final charge, the judge cautioned the jurors "not to determine the guilt or innocence of a defendant on whether or not he is a Communist."*

Thus, according to Frank, Kaufman's statement to the jurors "not to determine the guilt or innocence of a defendant on whether or not he is a Communist" was sufficient to cure weeks of pounding on the theme of the Communist menace.

Referring to the question of whether it was proper for the jury to hear evidence about the proximity fuse when Rosenberg was never charged with its possession, Judge Frank stated:

> *David Greenglass testified that Julius admitted "stealing" a proximity fuse from the Emerson Radio Company where he worked, and gave the fuse to Russia...Defendants complain of the denial of their motions to strike all this testimony. They urge it was irrelevant since it was not shown that the proximity fuse was either secret or connected with national defense. The proximity fuse, be it noted, was an important World War II development which vastly increased the potential damage range of exploding shells. The nature of the device itself strongly suggests that it was secret, and unequivocally shows that it was connected with the national defense...*

Frank again bent over backward to justify the unjustifiable. Frank made a legally impermissible determination when he ruled that the proximity fuse was connected with national defense and that the nature of the device strongly suggested that it was secret. His conclusions were outside his province. Frank could only rule on law, not facts, and there were no facts presented at the trial for Frank to reach any conclusions about the proximity fuse.

Discussing the argument that it was improper for a witness to first hear Greenglass's testimony describing the atom bomb before he was asked to provide his own knowledge on the subject, Judge Frank said:

> *The Rosenbergs contend that four Government exhibits (2, 6, 7, and 8) consisting of statements made by David Greenglass of lens*

> *molds and an atom bomb were improperly ad-
> mitted in evidence...Greenglass explained all
> four exhibits to the jury...*
>
> *Defendants...object because David's superi-
> ors at Los Alamos were allowed to examine
> these sketches and to testify that they were
> reasonably accurate portrayals of the lens mold
> and atomic mechanisms used in the experimen-
> tal stations. We see no error here.*

Judge Frank simply ignored the main point of the
argument, which was that Kaufman improperly permitted Greenglass's superiors to listen to his testimony
before giving theirs. This enabled them to conform
their testimony to his without defense counsel having
any opportunity to question their prior knowledge on
the subject.

In short, Frank ignored valid arguments, drew
sweeping conclusions which did not address the issues,
formed conclusions contrary to the facts, disregarded
the main issues and concentrated on minor ones, dis-
torted facts, and in general utilized the array of judicial ruses in the court's arsenal.

Concerning the question of whether Sobell took
part in the greater conspiracy involving the passage of
the atom bomb secrets, it was the only instance where
Judge Frank clearly gave a dissenting opinion. He
explained:

> *Sobell raises several questions affecting his
> conviction. The most important of these is
> whether or not he was proved to be a member
> of the Rosenberg-Greenglass-Gold conspiracy to
> ship information to Russia. Even accepting all
> of Elitcher's testimony as true, says Sobell...no
> evidence connected him in any way with the
> Greenglass-Gold-Rosenberg plan to ship atomic
> information from Los Alamos to the Soviet
> Union...*
>
> *If, in fact, Sobell is right that two con-*

spiracies were proved, then prejudicial error has been committed, for Sobell was jointly tried with major atomic energy spies whose acts and declarations were held binding upon him...

The writer of this opinion...thinks that there was error, in this respect, which requires that Sobell be given a new trial...If Sobell, on Elitcher's testimony, could reasonably be held as a member of the Rosenberg-Gold-Greenglass conspiracy, the question of his membership should have been submitted to the jury...The jury should have had the opportunity to choose between the inferences and to decide whether he actually joined the larger conspiracy...

While indeed Judge Frank was one of the few judges on the Court of Appeals who had some vestige of judicial courage he did not do enough—his dissenting opinion was meaningless and afforded the Rosenbergs and Sobell nothing.

Concerning the question of whether there was anything wrong in the government's introduction of a "card made by an Immigration inspector, stating that Sobell had been 'deported from Mexico,'" though the card's contents contained hearsay, and as later revealed untrue information, Frank reasoned:

When the Government introduced evidence to show that Sobell had been legally deported from Mexico...he made no move to bring to light the facts of his alleged illegal abduction. He preferred to take his chances on the verdict, withholding his trump card until the trial was over. The Federal Rules of Criminal Procedure allow no such tactic...

But it was the Federal government that had used dishonest tactics, not Sobell. Sobell chose not to take the stand, which was his right. Could the government force an accused person to testify denying him the constitutional right to defend himself in the way he sought, simply by presenting false evidence at the last moment? The fact that the government did not investigate, pursue, or indict those who took part in Sobell's kidnapping was evidence of its own bad faith.

Concerning the final point, the claim that the sentence was excessive, Judge Frank explained:

> *The trial judge sentenced Julius and Ethel Rosenberg to death...*
> *Unless we are to overrule sixty years of undeviating federal precedents, we must hold that an appellate court has no power to modify a sentence...If there is one rule in the federal criminal practice which is firmly established, it is that the appellate court has no control over a sentence which is within the limits allowed by a statute...*

While recognizing the need for a "hanging judge" and while at the same time being aware that the overturning of sentences characterized as harsh, accompanied by criticism of a judge could lead to personal retaliatory attacks upon the court, Judge Frank noted the means by which the laws enacted to safeguard judges could be circumvented to overturn harsh sentences. Frank explained how it was done:

> *This Court has said that where it considers a sentence unduly harsh, it will be more inclined to regard as harmful an error otherwise probably harmless...*

Judge Frank recited the realities. The harshness of sentences always has been subject to review; never because of the judge's sadism or cruelty— but for other reasons: minor errors, legal technicalities, and the like. Errors can always be found no matter how careful a trial is conducted. It depends on whether the court wants to find them. Judge Frank said, "We have, however, found no errors affecting the Rosenbergs," harmless or otherwise. Frank made this finding in a case that was filled with errors of major magnitude.

In the months that followed, numerous further petitions and appeals were brought, reaching the highest court of our land. They were all denied.

JUDGE IRVING KAUFMAN

HOOVER'S SPECTACULAR FRAUDS

Just when it appeared that all hope for the Rosenbergs was lost, amazingly, and ever so spitefully, on April 18, 1953, a French newspaper, *Le Combat* published Greenglass's statements given to his lawyer, O. John Rogge, shortly after his arrest. Included was a statement by David Greenglass and several memos by his attorney summarizing what Greenglass had told the FBI when he was first taken into custody. This material seemed to discredit his testimony. In particular there was a June 1950 memo that contained Greenglass's handwritten admissions of uncertainty as to who had sent Harry Gold to him and what secret documents he was supposed to have given Gold. Among other things, *Le Combat* reported Greenglass as having written:

Saturday, June 1950:

> They stated that I met Gold in NM. at 209
> High Street, my place. They told me that I
> had told him to come back later because I
> didn't have it ready. I didn't remember this
> but I allowed it in the statement.
> I told them that on a visit to me in Nov.
> 1944 my wife asked me if I could give
> information. I made sure to tell the FBI that
> she was transmitting this info from my
> brother-in-law, Julius, and was not her own
> idea...
> Also I didn't know who sent Gold to me.
> I also made a pencil sketch of the HE.
> mold set-up for an experiment. But this I'll
> tell you I can honestly say the information I
> gave Gold may be not at all what I said in
> the statement.

What occurred was a spectacular fraud. It began
this way: a confidential informer notified the FBI on
March 18, 1953, that a high-ranking member of the
National Committee to Secure Justice for the Rosenbergs advised that a professional investigator had
procured the original statements given to the FBI by
David and Ruth Greenglass. The FBI subsequently
reported this event in a memo dated March 26, 1953;
it read:

> Rosenberg defense claims to have secured
> through professional investigator at cost of
> $25,000 original statements given by David and
> Ruth Greenglass to FBI...for another $25,000
> they will receive statement of a perjured
> witness...

The FBI's response to this information was odd; no
investigation was ordered. One would have expected
that the FBI would have been most interested in
knowing about a witness whose testimony was being

bought for $25,000. But the FBI was not in the least concerned.

There were reasons for the FBI's odd response. Of prime concern to Hoover was the possibility that a reversal and new trial could establish that Greenglass never met Gold. Hoover needed help. The Greenglass statements that surfaced in France, worded as they were, would give him that help. Hoover could now show that the FBI did not manufacture the evidence since Greenglass made these statements on his own volition to his lawyers.

With the National Committee to Secure Justice for the Rosenbergs championing Hoover's version of the facts, Hoover had the most important ally he could find to establish false evidence. A fraud of this intricacy had to at least appear in part to be against the government's interest. The ruse worked. What the NCSJR thought was valuable to them was of much greater value to Hoover.

The exposures in Greenglass's statement that he was not entirely truthful when he testified about his meeting with Gold, since according to the released statements he said, "I don't know who sent Gold to me" but said at trial that Julius Rosenberg sent Gold to him, gave Hoover what he needed—that at least Greenglass said that Gold visited him. All that was important to establish was that Greenglass met Gold.

But there was one statement that the government was not anxious to release and admit to its truth; it was Ruth Greenglass's statement. It was not one of the statements released to the French Press. It was a legitimate statement and it embarrassed the FBI.

Ruth's statement said that she never met Harry Gold. Her statement also had no mention of the FBI's visit to her home to discuss David's having possibly been involved in stealing uranium.

On June 1, 1953 Ruth Greenglass made available the handwritten statement she had prepared for her attorneys. She had kept this statement in her house for three years. The statement was prepared so that her attorney would know what she had told the FBI when she was interviewed on June 16, 1950. The statement read in part as follows: "They asked if Gold had visited me. I said no...They said that Gold claimed that in June or July of forty-five, he came to the house and my husband gave something to him, and that he returned and gave something to my husband...I said this was not so, I did not know the man and such a thing never happened."

Ruth's statement was kept away from the Rosenbergs. It was a very important statement, not only because it was not part of the material released to the French press, but because of the apparent sincerity in which it was written. It was Ruth Greenglass's confession. It was her statement of the Rosenberg's innocence. Whatever she would say or do later would be the result of pressure exerted upon her, her husband, and her children; her incipient hatred of the Rosenbergs would further justify her testimony against them.

With the Rosenbergs attorneys now preparing to present appeal papers, J. Edgar Hoover's FBI, with the acquiescence of the Greenglass's attorney O. J. Rogge, engaged in what can only be described as officially sanctioned fraudulent conduct. Confident that Ruth Greenglass and David Greenglass would agree to sign anything that was asked of them, the lawyers added what they called memos to whatever the Greenglasses had already told them.

The content of these memos which the lawyers said

were told to them by the Greenglasses early on were then submitted to the Greenglasses in the form of affidavits which they were asked to sign. The added contents were then established as if they were part of the original interviews. Numerous non-occurrences were presented in this way. The Jell-O box incident, "One more thing, I identified Gold by a torn or cut piece of card"; and numerous other events in this manner were included in Greenglass's original interviews.

An FBI memo dated June 5, 1953, showed to what length this process was carried. In this instance the government insisted that the affidavit that Greenglass's lawyers sought to obtain from him say what the FBI wanted said or the indications were that the FBI would not permit them to visit or talk to him in prison. The June 5 FBI memo contained astonishing material. The government wanted Rogge and Fabricant to prepare an affidavit that said that "several days before David made his longhand, written statement, he made to them a detailed oral statement telling of the Rosenbergs' connections..."

The Rosenbergs and Bloch were also misled into believing that they could help themselves by showing that Greenglass lied when he failed to mention during trial that he was questioned about having stolen uranium from Los Alamos when he was visited by the FBI in January of 1950. The Rosenbergs never dreamed that it could have been advantageous for them to insist that Greenglass was telling the truth when he denied that he had been investigated for uranium possession.

Actually, the government prosecutors wanted to admit that the uranium issue was the reason the FBI questioned Greenglass in January of 1950, rather than letting it be known what he was questioned about on that date.

The pretended issue was whether Greenglass lied when he denied stealing uranium from Los Alamos, when questioned by an FBI agent in January of 1950. The real issue was whether Greenglass was under investigation well before that time and cooperating with the FBI, notwithstanding whether there was or was not a theft of uranium or whether he was or was not questioned about it.

One fact was clear: David Greenglass denied under oath during the trial that he was questioned about thefts of uranium from Los Alamos. But why was the government so insistent that Greenglass retract this denial? Why was what Greenglass said considered so important that Saypol and even Kaufman contradicted him about it during trial? Indeed, the need to establish that David Greenglass was questioned by the FBI about the uranium thefts in January of 1950, six months before his arrest, was almost an obsession. Even Ruth Greenglass was set upon to provide an affidavit, attesting to its truth in contradiction to her husband's denials.

While Greenglass's testimony was disconcerting and the Rosenberg defense team knew that something was amiss; the importance of the uranium theft issue was not brought home to them. To Hoover, however, it was of paramount importance. It could open up his most guarded secret—the covert operation he established. At the time Hoover could not risk revealing his undercover unit. The American public had not yet heard of such a thing. Precedence of the Watergate and Iranscam operations had not yet been established. Hoover was not sure how the public would react to learning about the roles of Elizabeth Bentley, Jacob

Golos, Morell Dougherty, Thomas Black, and now David Greenglass; and how they were recruited.

Bloch's pending appeal enabled Hoover to cover himself and his department and everyone else involved in the fraudulent prosecution of the Rosenbergs by getting as many statements as possible from witnesses. On March 24, 1953, Hoover wrote:

> *In connection with their efforts to obtain new trial, subjects are attempting to secure any information which would prove David Greenglass unworthy of belief. In 1949, Bureau instituted investigation...which involved theft of uranium hemispheres from AEC installation at Los Alamos...According to recent information received from Ruth Greenglass, David had taken a small piece of uranium from Los Alamos as a souvenir while employed there...Immediately interview David Greenglass concerning this matter and secure signed statement which should include his reasons for withholding this information from Bureau at time of original interview in January, 1950, and at later interviews. Advise immediately Bureau and New York results thereof.*

Hoover did not ask his agents to find out whether David lied and withheld information when he was first questioned. Hoover instructed that his agents "immediately interview David Greenglass concerning this matter and secure signed statement which should include his reasons for withholding this information from Bureau at the time of original interview in January, 1950." Hoover instructed his agents of what he expected to receive from them in the form of an affidavit. David Greenglass was to be told what he would say, not asked what he would say. Greenglass furnished a signed statement the next day, March 25, 1953.

Most important in this matter is that Greenglass was actually not questioned about uranium when he was interviewed on January 27, 1950 by Special Agent Lawrence Spillane who, coincidentally, was the same special agent who questioned Elizabeth Bentley in September of 1948 about her espionage rendezvous with Bernice Levin, Max Elitcher's long-time girlfriend.

Hoover not only had to protect himself from the Rosenbergs and the countless enemies he had acquired over the years, he had to protect himself from David Greenglass as well. The more signed statements he received from him, the better.

Greenglass was displaying pangs of conscience. Hoover and his agency's plans could be upset if Greenglass made a public recantation of his charges against the Rosenbergs and admitted his own guilt. Who knows what Greenglass could say. Keeping him incommunicado in jail was one solution, but it worked only in part. There were leaks. Raymond Paradis, Greenglass's cellmate at Lewisburg Penitentiary had offered to tell the FBI that Greenglass had made statements to him contrary to what he said at trial. This was only months before the date of execution was scheduled. Hoover managed to suppress that incident. Early on, Jerome Tartakow informed the FBI that during the trial itself an unidentified cellmate of David Greenglass offered information that would show that the FBI forced Greenglass to give false testimony. Of course that information was stopped from going anywhere. But Greenglass's cries kept coming.

On June 2, 1953, the New Haven Office of the FBI received information from an active Communist Party sympathizer, whose name they withheld, that

David Greenglass claimed he had been beaten over the head while in prison because of his desire to make a statement that would clear his sister Ethel Rosenberg.

On June 14 an FBI teletype reported that "rumors in Washington indicated that David Greenglass is collapsing mentally and is screaming from his cell that the Rosenbergs are innocent and that Greenglass is being held incommunicado..." Associate Warden Richmond, when contacted about the rumors, said that they were false, but nonetheless thought it best that Greenglass not be spoken to at the time, saying,

> *it would be inadvisable for Greenglass to be contacted during this period.*

David Greenglass was being held incommunicado. The execution of his sister and brother-in-law was to proceed as scheduled on June 19, 1953. Nothing as trite as a confession from Greenglass or a recantation of his testimony would be allowed to interfere with the Rosenbergs' swift deaths.

THE ROSENBERGS DIE

Before the Rosenbergs were executed, there were feverish legal attempts to save them, especially in the last weeks. Less than two weeks before the scheduled execution, Bloch presented what he termed "new evidence" that Greenglass had lied on critical matters leading to the conviction of the Rosenbergs. Bloch asked Judge Kaufman to set aside the convictions and grant the Rosenbergs a new trial. His new evidence consisted of Greenglass's statements released to the French newspapers as well as proofs that Greenglass lied when he was asked during the trial if he had ever been questioned about stealing uranium from Los Alamos. Bloch's motion for a new trial accomplished for Hoover what he needed and wanted most—proofs that events which never happened had occurred. The last section of the "new evidence" motion dealt with the console table which was shown to be purchased from Macy's for $21 just as Rosenberg testified, rather than received as a gift from the Russians. It was the only issue that was not part of Hoover's manipulations.

Only two days after receiving Bloch's petition, Judge Kaufman ruled:

> It is worthy of re-emphasis that no one Government witness has recanted after all these years. I have said before and I repeat, the guilt of the defendants was established overwhelmingly, and the present alleged new evidence does not in any way diminish the strength of the Government's case. The motions in behalf of the defendants Rosenberg are denied.

The Rosenbergs had only ten days left to live, and Kaufman did not want to give them extra time to present proofs of their innocence.

Harold Urey, a world-renowned scientist and former head of the Manhattan Project at Los Alamos, who was in attendance at many of the court proceedings, after watching Kaufman's demeanor in rejecting evidence, wrote:

> *Now that I see what goes on in Judge Kaufman's courtroom, I believe that the Rosenberg's are innocent...What appalls me most is the role the press is playing. The Judge's bias is so obvious. I keep looking over at the newspaperman and there's not a flicker of indignation or concern....*

Albert Einstein wrote to President Truman:

> *My conscience compels me to urge you to commute the death sentence of Julius and Ethel Rosenberg...this appeal to you is prompted by the same reasons which were set forth so convincingly by my colleague Harold C. Urey in his letter...*

A lawyer named Fyke Farmer, without being asked, volunteered his services and argued that the Rosenbergs were tried under the wrong law. The espionage act of 1917 was no longer applicable, having been superseded by the Atomic Energy Act of 1946, which provided that the death penalty could be imposed only during wartime and only if the jury recommended it.

It was now only a week before the scheduled execution. To save time, Farmer brought a copy of the motion to Kaufman's house. Kaufman turned the motion down as frivolous and also rejected Farmer's petition for a stay of execution. On June 17, 1953,

Justice William O. Douglas of the U.S. Supreme Court stayed the execution, but on June 19, 1953, the question was argued before the full Court and it was decided that there would be no further delays.

The FBI had installed direct phone lines to the death house in preparation for interrogating Julius and Ethel if they decided to confess. If they did, an FBI memo said, the Bureau could stop the execution and question the Rosenbergs for as long as necessary. The atmosphere of the days and hours leading up to the executions of Julius and Ethel Rosenberg were best described by Maximilian Scheer in his book *Ethel and Julius Rosenberg* (1954):

> In each cell there was a telephone and at the other end of the wires there were FBI Agents with a direct wire to the Department of Justice. All they would have to do is to take the receiver off the hook...so they had been told; one word would have been sufficient. The telephone—here, the electric chair—there. You may talk up to the last minute, until the executioner will claim you. Grab the receiver and talk, say that you are willing to say the things the government wants you to say—or else die. Telephone or electric chair, the choice is yours.

Julius Rosenberg was electrocuted on June 19, 1953. At six minutes after eight, he was pronounced dead. Ethel Rosenberg was then electrocuted. At sixteen minutes after eight she was pronounced dead. Extra voltage was needed to kill her.

KAUFMAN'S GUILT

Less than a week after the Rosenbergs were executed, Hoover had his agents visit Judge Kaufman. The Director could not risk, no matter how unlikely it was, the possibility of a guilt-ridden Judge Kaufman falling apart. The FBI agents reported the results of their visit with Kaufman, saying they

> *had visited Judge Irving R. Kaufman's Chambers and, in accordance with the Director's instructions, had furnished him certain information. We told the Judge in general terms that Julius Rosenberg was an important Espionage Agent; that we had information in our possession not disclosed at the trial which indicated that he was a high-ranking official in the Soviet Espionage apparatus in this area.*

The document indicated that Judge Kaufman, who was so instrumental in convicting and executing the Rosenbergs did so, relying on the say-so of higher-ups in government, without evidence, and was now showing signs of self-doubt. Hence it was necessary for agents to visit him and reassure him that though there was really no evidence of the Rosenbergs' guilt shown during the trial, his faith in the Bureau was not misplaced. The document also noted how appreciative Kaufman was to receive this information from Hoover, who "had thought so much of him as to make this information available to him at this time."

It had to be by mistake that a document so humiliating to Kaufman was ever released by the FBI.

In succeeding years, Kaufman was forever calling

the FBI to report this or that unfavorable comment about him, attributing anything unfavorable to a Communist plot. In October 1954 an FBI memo reported:

> *Judge Irving R. Kaufman has made available to this office a copy of a book written in German, entitled "Ethel and Julius Rosenberg" by Maximilian Scheer.*
>
> *Judge Kaufman received this book from Congressman Thomas Dodd, who purchased it in the East Zone of Berlin on July 4, 1954.*
>
> *This book has been reviewed by an agent of this office and his comments are being set forth hereinafter...*
>
> *Throughout the book the Rosenbergs are depicted as the innocent victims of a colossal "frame-up" and "legal lynch court" trial. The main participants in this conspiracy are the US Attorney, the FBI and O. John Rogge. The government, according to the book, was motivated by its desire to foster anti-Communist war-hysteria, Rogge's motivation is seen in his efforts to save his client David Greenglass by having him implicate the Rosenbergs in a com- pletely false and fabricated spy story.*
>
> *The FBI is mentioned on numerous pages throughout the book and generally depicted as an unscrupulous, ruthless, cruel secret police organization which will stop at nothing it its efforts to achieve its aims.*

In March 1955 Kaufman wrote to Hoover:

Dear Edgar:
Thank you so much for your letter of February 18th with which you enclosed a copy of Dr. Urey's address in Chicago on February 12th.
I find it very difficult to understand Dr. Urey, for as a Nobel prize winning scientist one may draw the inference that he possesses intelligence. Yet, here is a man who is willing

*to draw whatever conclusions he seeks to draw
from the most faulty reasoning...
How unscientific these scientistist [sic] get
when it suits their purpose!!
It was good to see you at the White House
Correspondents Dinner on Saturday. It made
me happy to see you looking so well.*

In April 1956 Judge Kaufman wrote to Assistant
FBI Director Lew Nichols:

*Dear Lew:
I enclose a copy of a Memorandum...in
connection with Bertrand Russell's letter to
The Manchester Guardian attacking the FBI
and his irresponsible assertion that the
Rosenbergs and Sobell were innocent.*

A portion of Bertrand Russell's comments read:

*I am certain that the majority of the
American people are unaware of the atrocities
committed by the FBI. Americans are in the
dark about the techniques used by these
defenders of what, with crass effrontery, is
called the free world.*

Like Kaufman, the FBI was very sensitive to criticism of their handling of the Rosenberg case. An
October 1965 FBI report was greatly concerned with
the publicity that Walter and Miriam Schneir's *Invitation to an Inquest* was receiving. After analyzing the
book, the Bureau discussed its strategy of response:

*Just recently a book was written called
"Invitation to an Inquest." This book has been
reviewed by this Division and its inaccuracies
accented...
The first thing we should do in this matter
is to take careful steps to secure the
cooperation of friendly television stations and
prevent this subversive effort from being*

successful. It should be kept off television programs and smothered and forced out of the public eye...

Steps have already been taken in New York and by various "contacts" of ours to refute the book written by the Schneirs. Judge Irving Kaufman has been furnished certain public source information and is having a lengthy letter written to the Editor of the "New York Times."

Invitation to an Inquest had an enormous effect and was a substantial factor in the bringing of a motion before the District Court that sought Morton Sobell's release from jail some sixteen years after he was convicted. The motion was based on new evidence: information that the Albuquerque Hotel Hilton guest card was forged; newly heard pre-trial testimony given by Harry Gold to his lawyers which contradicted his trial testimony; and affidavits from three scientists that disputed the validity and value of the atom bomb secrets transferred by David Greenglass.

The pre-trial testimony was in the form of recordings, which the Schneirs had had the opportunity to hear. Included was an interview between Gold and his attorney on June 14, 1950 that contained numerous contradictions to his trial testimony. This information, along with the other new evidence, was presented to Judge Edward Weinfeld.

The lawyers who brought the motion were filled with optimism, especially because the judge, Edward Weinfeld, had a good reputation and was said to be the best in the U.S. District Court. But in fact Weinfeld was the worst choice possible. Unknown to Sobell's lawyers, he had not only been in favor of executing the Rosenbergs, but advocated the execution of Sobell too. Weinfeld should have excused himself from the case, since Sobell's lawyers certainly would have moved to have him disqualified if they had known of his bias.

Judge Weinfeld dismissed the motion in its entirety on February 14, 1967. After first denigrating Sobell's attorneys' arguments that the scientific information supposedly given to the Russians was neither secret nor valuable and the claim that the Hilton registration card was forged, Judge Weinfeld belittled the assertion that Harry Gold committed perjury and the government suborned perjury, stating:

> Petitioner next claims that Gold committed and the government suborned perjury and suppressed evidence which allegedly establishes Gold's perjury...Petitioner relies in the main upon recorded discs of interviews between Gold and his court-assigned counsel...
> A careful reading of the transcripts of the recordings and all other material, rather than supporting petitioner's charges strongly corroborates Gold's trial testimony. The substance of Gold's statement to his lawyer on June 14...is essentially the substance of his trial testimony; the major events, times, places and persons correspond...
> The motion is denied in all respects.

Those who so actively contributed to the execution of the Rosenbergs were relieved once again. Judge Kaufman was back to watching television and plays to see that none were critical of his handling of the Rosenberg-Sobell case and writing letters and meeting with the FBI at every unusual sign as he does to this day, haunted only by the cries of the Rosenbergs who, after being sentenced, said through their lawyer.

> We were told that if we cooperated with the government our lives would be spared...

461

JUDGE IRVING KAUFMAN

We solemnly declare now and forever more that we will not be coerced, even under pain of death, to bear false witness and to yield up to tyranny our right as free Americans.

Our respect for truth, conscience, and human dignity is not for sale...

If we are executed it will be the murder of innocent people, and the shame will be on the government of the United States...

We are innocent...this is the whole truth. To foresake this truth is to pay too high a price, even for the priceless gift of life. For life thus purchased we could not live in dignity and self respect.

AUTHOR'S NOTE

Copies of this book may be ordered by writing directly to the author, Stanley Yalkowsky, 25 Central Park West, New York City, 10023. Also obtainable is *The Corrupt New York City Judges* (1988, 247pp), an autobiographical portrayal of the author's life and experiences as a lawyer in the New York courts.